SPRING FLOWER

BOOK 3: 1970 – 2014

TORN BETWEEN SHIFTING WORLDS

A China Dawn

An American Dream

Jean Tren-Hwa Perkins, MD

Compiled and Edited by
Richard Perkins Hsung, PhD

Spring Flower: Torn Between Shifting Worlds

Jean Tren-Hwa Perkins, MD

ISBN-13: 978-988-8769-71-1

© 2023 Richard Perkins Hsung

BIOGRAPHY / AUTOBIOGRAPHY

EB169

All rights reserved. No part of this book may be reproduced in material form, by any means, whether graphic, electronic, mechanical or other, including photocopying or information storage, in whole or in part. May not be used to prepare other publications without written permission from the publisher except in the case of brief quotations embodied in critical articles or reviews. For information contact info@earnshawbooks.com

Published by Earnshaw Books Ltd. (Hong Kong)

To my parents, Dr. and Mrs. Edward Carter Perkins
To my daughter, Jane (Gina–捷儿)
And to my beloved Wang-Sao (王嫂)

—Jean Tren-Hwa Perkins (裴瓊華醫生)

To Dr. Jean Tren-Hwa Perkins (裴瓊華醫生):
I finally fulfilled my promise to complete your memoir.
You can now rest in peace and savor the loving
freedom you deserve.

— Your son, Richard

To my beloved Katie Louise Ploeg: your motherly love
made all the difference for me transitioning
to this new world.

—Your kid, Richard

Dedication

We dedicate this book to all missionary workers of every race and nation who have helped China in the fields of education and health.

And to all those souls, in every era and place, who manage to preserve the most basic human kindness and decency regardless of their allegiances, beliefs, and convictions, and in spite of their own need, who survive despite struggling against oppression. These brave men and women are exemplars of a basic wish, to paraphrase Aleksandr Solzhenitsyn: *Even when brutality reigns supreme — let it not be through me.*

— Jean Tren-Hwa Perkins and Richard P. Hsung

Contents

Dedication	viii
Part VII	
Whispers from America: My Hope	1
Part VIII	
The Road to Salvation: My Deliverance	169
Afterword	
My Parents' Lives After 1950	265
Mother's Only Letter to Me from Taipei (1955)	285
1955 Letter from Dr. Edward C. Perkins from Taipei	286
Epilogue	295
Appendix One: Style Sheet	332
Appendix Two: Glossary of Names	346
Photo Credits	353
Acknowledgments	356
About the Author	363
About the Editor	365

Part VII

Whispers from America:
My Hope

75

THE YEAR of the Pig, 1971, rushed in, and I was about to turn forty; it had been twenty years since Mother and Day-Day were forced to leave the land they loved and had given their lives to. And for the first time, I looked forward to celebrating the Chinese New Year, because Paul was finally home. At the same time, the country was sinking further into the abyss economically, but strangely, no one felt poor because we were *all* poor. We all depended on rice stamps, meat stamps, cotton stamps, and oil stamps to ration these limited resources. I can't recall; there may have been other stamps, too, like egg stamps or even water stamps. The humor within this dire situation was that these stamps triggered illegal trading. On street corners, stairways, and even waiting in line for the restroom, those who had extra rice stamps at the end of the month, which was rare, would trade with those who had extra cotton or oil stamps. I guess some with bigger families had more, some simply by wearing the same clothes over and over, sewing patches on top of patches, for as long they could still wash them. That was the case with Qiu-Shuang's family, and even ours. I would pass Gina's clothes on to Eddy, and if it was too pinkish, I'd dye it black or dark blue. Eventually, everything became so worn with so many patches that they'd be beyond further repair.

    I became quite skillful at sewing, and Qiu-Shuang was, of course, even better. She was a professional, and she'd come over at night to help me after she'd finished hers, all through her one good eye that was also deteriorating. At times, I would help mend her clothes, with instructions.

Two days after the New Year, Paul and I took the kids out "window shopping." By then, stores only had things for display, not for sale, because that was all they had in stock. It was futile to save cotton or cloth stamps, because there was nothing to buy. When a store announced the arrival of a new product, there was a line around the block before you could sneeze, and it was all gone in less than an hour. When I say *new*, I only mean "newly made," not new styles. All clothes had the same style—Mao's Style (中山裝)—in gray or grayish blue. In the early 1970s, everyone on the streets looked like Mao Tse-Tung.

Our kids' clothes were really just quilts of peeling patches, and I said to Paul, "I don't care what it takes. I'll save up all our cloth stamps and make new jackets and pants for Gina and Eddy for New Year's Day." Paul seemed to cheer me on.

A week later, Paul left for the rural area to fulfill his duty to help the farmers with spring planting. We managed to get Eddy enrolled in first grade at the same elementary school as Gina, even though he was not yet six. Chang *Lao-Shih* convinced the principal that Eddy was developed beyond an average five-year-old. Our idea was for Eddy to help take care of his older sister. By the time the school agreed to accept him, the semester had already begun.

On Eddy's first day, I went with them to school. As we left the compound, Old Man Ni shouted, "Dr. Pei, do you need me to take them to school? They're big kids now. Do you think you can handle the weight on your bike?" I said I could, and I did. We bought a new school bag for Gina and gave hers to Eddy. Kids' school bags in China were also all one style: military green shoulder bags. He was so cute carrying the oversized bag over his shoulder. I was so proud of my sonny boy, who would be a first grader and a protector and defender of his sister, as he'd always wanted.

JEAN TREN-HWA PERKINS

Wu *Lao-Shih* (吴老師), a very nice man in his forties, was Eddy's homeroom teacher. He asked Eddy to sit in the last row, and I saw how much smaller Eddy was than the rest of the kids. I smiled and waved goodbye and made it clear to both Eddy and Gina they were to look after one another in all circumstances. I showed them how to walk home after school, and told them that once they were home, Auntie Luo would keep an eye on them. They were to do their homework. I felt so proud of them both as I hopped back onto my bike to pedal back to the clinic.

That night, I couldn't wait to get home to hear everything from Eddy. I wanted a full report. When I opened the door, Eddy just sat there quietly by his sister, sharing the one small desk and nightlight we had. I reached over patted his head, and was shocked to see scratches and cuts on his face and a purple bruise on his right cheekbone.

"What happened?" I asked. Gina was about to explain, but Qiu-Shuang walked in and said, "Dr. Pei, don't be mad at Eddy. He was trying to protect his sister."

Eddy stood up, and I saw that both pockets of his jacket were torn, including the patch I'd worked so hard to sew on so it would look nice on the first school day.

I was enraged and I slapped him across the face. "Is this how I've been teaching you, to be a gangster on the street? Is there anything in this world that can't be resolved in a civilized manner? I told you to protect your sister, not to become a thug!" Eddy said nothing.

Qiu-Shuang took my arm and said, "Dr. Pei, I have some food for you. Please eat some dinner. You're tired and hungry from a long day. Little Eddy is a fine kid. He didn't provoke anyone." I didn't say another word, and when the kids went to bed, I sewed his jacket back up.

After that first day, I'd bike the two kids to the clinic, then

SPRING FLOWER: TORN BETWEEN SHIFTING WORLDS

Eddy would hold onto his sister, and they'd walk together from there. As we arrived at the clinic, Sister Liu came out and said with a big smile, "Dr. Pei's prince and princess going to school together! How wonderful!"

Before they headed off, I made clear the importance of helping each other behave in a civilized manner under all circumstances. To my great relief, the next three days were peaceful and uneventful; nothing was torn, and no new scratches were on anyone's face. However, on the fourth night, it was clear that things had turned south again. Eddy's jacket was torn practically to shreds. The sleeves were torn off and stained with blood. I was so mad at him but, looking at his face, which had been cleaned up by Qiu-Shuang, I couldn't add more trauma to what he must have already gone through.

Gina finally spoke up. "Mommy, maybe we should ask Eddy to stop going to school. He's so much smaller than his classmates. I know this is for me, but maybe we could ask Chang *Lao-Shih* to take me. Or I can try going to school on my own."

"Gina, stopping school is not an option after we worked so hard to get Eddy in. How can we ask Chang *Lao-Shih* to take you to school again after all these years? We have to be more independent and less of a burden to others. Remember Mommy teaching you when you were little? We try not to rely on others for things we can do ourselves. You're now eleven, not a little kid, and you're not light anymore. I'm sure Chang *Lao-Shih* is relieved she no longer has to take you to school. So am I! Papa is now at home much of the time, and Mommy is still here. Both of you are big kids now. I have such high expectations that you will help Mommy run this household independently. We can't behave as if things are worse than they were a few years ago?"

Gina went back to her studies in silence.

I turned to Eddy. "Hey, kiddo, Mommy isn't mad, but I'm

worried that you're becoming a hooligan, fighting all day. You should be excelling in school and appreciating this opportunity that we worked hard to get for you. Remember, you were the one who said that if you could go to school, you could study and protect Gina at the same time. Remember how Mommy was proud of her boy for being so grownup at the age of four! Now you're regressing."

Eddy finally spoke up: "What do you want me to do when the other kids make a circle around Gina and push her to the ground? How do you want me to protect her?"

I didn't know how to answer, so I said, "I don't care what they do; you've got to resolve the situation without violence. Do you know the meaning of 'turning the other cheek'?" When someone hits the side of your face, you turn your head to let them hit the other side. Violence begets violence, and the cycle never ends. Resolving differences by peaceful means is always more effective and long-lasting."

Eddy just looked puzzled. "What's your point? What would *you* do?"

"I would drag Gina out of the circle and run away from those thugs as fast as I could."

Eddy went back to his schoolbook without acknowledging what I'd said. I thought about explaining how Gandhi used nonviolence to achieve independence in India, but I figured enough was probably enough, and besides, I had to finish repairing his jacket.

A few days later, it happened again, and each time was worse than the time before. So I went to the school and found Chang *Lao-Shih* and Wu *Lao-Shih*, and we reported it to the school principal. The principal (not the one we'd begged to admit Gina, but a new principal) shook his head and treated it as kids being kids, but finally acknowledged that the children shouldn't treat Gina that way. He promised the authorities would keep an eye on them when they left the schoolyard but made it clear they would not follow them all the way back to my clinic. The school's doorman could watch them for a block or two, but it was seven blocks away from the back entrance of my clinic—long enough for fights out of any adult's watchful eyes. And interestingly, Shih-Ch'ing-Fang (世青坊), where we had our tiny secret apartment, was within these seven blocks.

One afternoon, I slipped away from the clinic without telling anyone why, and I went to the halfway point between the school and the hospital's back gate. I waited there on the sidewalk but didn't see Eddy or Gina, even after the time they should have been there. Then I heard noises coming a block away and ran to see Eddy being whacked on the sidewalk with Gina sitting on the ground not far away screaming for help. Two other kids were pushing her down and not letting her stand or rescue Eddy.

I screamed at the top of my lungs, "Stop this nonsense right now!" and six or seven kids ran away. I walked toward Eddy as he was helping Gina up. I was about to strike my son, but Gina lunged forward and used her body to protect him. I had never seen her move that quickly in my life, and my hand landed right on her head.

Gina turned around and said, "How *could* you? Eddy was only trying to help me. Can't you see that he's hurt, that they were beating him? Why are you not on our side? I'm so mad at you!" I stood there speechless before picking up their bags. I dusted Eddy off and asked, "Do you not know how to run, Eddy?"

After a long silence, Eddy replied, "Mommy, of course I know how to run and hide, but you don't expect Gina to run as fast as I can, do you? If she was left behind, how would she defend herself?"

I couldn't respond. I held onto Gina's hand and walked

toward the clinic. I wasn't sure what to do. Even during the Japanese invasion, I had never seen such cruelty. But kids bully other kids they see as weaker, smaller, or physically challenged. And since it took place away from the schoolyard, it was not a job for the teachers to resolve. Just as I was deep in thought, Eddy spoke up.

"Mommy, what does it mean to be an *Anti-Revolutionist*'s son (反革命的兒子)? Where is Papa when he isn't home? Are you anti-revolutionary?" I didn't know how to answer. I just held his hand and gave him a gentle squeeze. For a moment, I'd forgotten where we lived.

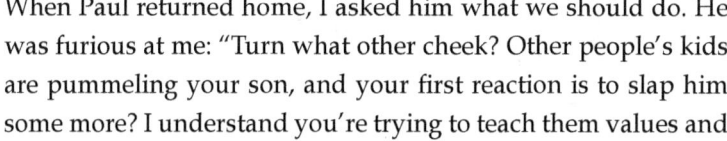

When Paul returned home, I asked him what we should do. He was furious at me: "Turn what other cheek? Other people's kids are pummeling your son, and your first reaction is to slap him some more? I understand you're trying to teach them values and the benefit of nonviolent conflict resolution, but we have a real problem that needs more than sermonizing."

He called Eddy over and said, "Son, you have to learn how to protect yourself and watch your back. Your papa was learning how to box in college. I even won a Golden Gloves award! I'll show you how. Okay?

"Stand up and mimic me," he instructed. "Turn your body sideways and spread your legs to support your stance, and — most important — maintain your balance. If you turn sideways, it gives your opponents a smaller target to land their punches." Paul pounded on his chest. "And it helps you see what's around you, even behind you," and he turned his head over his right shoulder. "If you stand flatfooted, you'll fall when you're hit, and if you face people, the punches can land on your face or your chest. See my stance. With your legs apart, rock back and forth,

SPRING FLOWER: TORN BETWEEN SHIFTING WORLDS

Eddy and Gina becoming best friends, ca. 1971

move around, bounce on both your feet, and look behind your shoulder frequently so you can defend yourself, even against three or four people. On offense, pivot on your left leg. By putting your weight on that leg, you can punch harder because your body can follow through with your punches. Watch me...."

Then he turned to me and asked, "Why are you still standing here, 'Dr. Gandhi-Pei'? We need some soy sauce, we're out! Please go try to find some at the market, to give Eddy and me some space." He literally pushed me out the apartment door and locked it. When I got back, both kids were kicking, jumping, and ready for war.

Of course, that did not solve the problem; it only exacerbated it. So on a later afternoon I pleaded for another twenty-minute break from work and went out to intervene. Before I was even out of the clinic building, I saw Sister Liu's son. He was all smiles and said, "Auntie Pei, here are Gina and Eddy. I was heading to the hospital and saw some kids ganging up on Eddy, so I scattered them."

Sister Liu's and Captain Shao's son, An-Zhong (安中), was a few grades ahead of Eddy. He was probably less than ten, but he looked older and was big for his age. I was grateful, but I also knew the timing was lucky and the problem wasn't going away. A few weeks later, I again took a break to intercept the two kids, and as I exited the hospital gate, I saw Gina limping toward me.

I ran past her in the direction she was pointing and told her to slow down so she wouldn't fall. The direction she pointed to was toward Hsüeh-Shih Road (學士路) or Hsiao-Nü Road (孝女路), near Shih-Ch'ing-Fang (世青坊). Shih-Ch'ing-Fang had dozens of three-story apartment buildings that all looked alike and were laid out in crisscrossing alleys with a few dead ends. This French-built neighborhood was a veritable maze for those not familiar with it.

I ran toward the screams and found Eddy. There were eight or nine other kids, and one of them yelled to me, "*Auntie*, help! Eddy has gone mad!" Then I saw Eddy with two kids he'd cornered at the far corner of one of the dead-ends, swinging wildly with a lead pipe screaming, "Call me an *Anti-Revolutionist*'s son (反革命的兒子) again and I'll kill you! Insult or try to hurt my sister again, and I'll kill you all!"

One kid was bleeding on the side of his face, and Eddy was bleeding too. He had gone rogue with the pent-up rage of a six-year-old on full display. I screamed, "Eddy, put that down! Please listen to Mommy!"

Eddy was surprised to see me, and, expressionless, he dropped the metal pipe. The two kids he'd cornered dashed past toward me. I grabbed the kid who was bleeding and checked him carefully. He only had a scratch; the blood was Eddy's. So, I told them all to go home. By then, Gina had come back to the scene. I didn't say a word but went over and hugged Eddy, holding him in my arms, and I took them both with me to the clinic.

With just that one time we'd taken him to Shih-Ch'ing-Fang (世青坊), Eddy had remembered the intricate details of the complex and planned the whole thing. He lured the other kids there and planned to beat them with a lead pipe he'd hidden near one of the dead-ends. My first thought was that this might finally teach those kids a lesson, but then I worried there might be a backlash and next time somebody could be seriously hurt. Wisely, I said, "This has to end now. I don't want to see anyone injured. And Eddy, you could be in jail if you end up killing or hurting another kid." I thought perhaps I could pay An-Zhong, Sister Liu's son, to escort them, but I didn't want to add more burdens to a ten-year-old.

That night, Eddy and Gina sat quietly, sharing the desk and the dim lamp. I huddled nearby, trying to sew up his jacket yet again. At this rate, Eddy's jacket wasn't going to last till the Chinese New Year's, when I'd promised to make new ones. "Maybe I'll just make a new one now," I thought, "as the fabric on this one is already shredded." But we didn't have enough cloth stamps to do that.

Just then, Qiu-Shuang came in with her second oldest son, He-Peng (河澎). After beating around the bush, she offered He-Ping's services to escort my kids to and from school, beginning immediately. He-Peng had just finished his first year of high school and hadn't been able to find work. After a brief pause, she asked if we could pay him. "Dr. Pei, I hesitate to ask you this. While it may be a good plan—and He-Peng is a very responsible young man—it could sound like we're trying to take money from you. We're a family of eight and need some help with me having to stop working altogether soon."

JEAN TREN-HWA PERKINS

"You taking from us? Do you realize how much help you've given us all these years, and how much trouble we've caused you? The only reason I hadn't already asked was that I didn't want to burden you." Qiu-Shuang smiled sheepishly and told He-Peng to give me a bow and thank me for the job.

We were tight financially, with Paul still having no salary, but this was worth more than gold. So, for five RMB (*Yüan*, 元) a month, He-Peng faithfully took our kids to school on his bicycle—Gina rode while Eddy walked alongside—and at the end of the day he'd wait at the front gate to walk them back to the clinic. Even when Gina graduated from elementary school six months later, he continued to do this for Eddy until he was in the third grade. After that, He-Peng got a job in our hospital's laundry working alongside his father, although he could have gone to college if higher education had existed at that time.

76

By the summer of 1971, the entire staff at the hospital was concerned about the next *Rustication-Reeducation* program and when it might come. We'd been understaffed for months, with no help on the horizon. The government had suspended all higher education and professional training five years earlier, so China had produced no new physicians or nurses in all this time. We had as many clinic patients, procedures, and operations as ever, and yet the brilliant WDT (工宣隊) still planned to ship us in groups to different places in the countryside. They said it was so that farmers wouldn't have to travel to see us, which might have been true except these rural places didn't have decent facilities for us to practice in and we were also put to work in the fields as soon as we got there. The entire country seemed to be on a suicide mission, consciously intending to implode.

At home, by contrast, I was so much happier with Paul coming home regularly. Our home was becoming a real home, and I had to rely on the kindness of neighbors less. At the same time, I could sense Paul sinking into depression. When I came home late from work, he'd often be sitting in the narrow hallway with Old Man Ni yapping loudly and drinking cheap liquor. They were having a good time, but the hallway smelled like turpentine.

"It's late to be still drinking, no, Paul?" I'd ask. "Don't you have to get ready to travel for the harvest season?"

"You're treating me like your third kid. I don't have any

homework tonight, 'Mommy,'" Paul would say, and then the two of them would laugh loudly. Old Man Ni would add, "Dr. Pei, please have a drink with us."

"It's getting late, and I'm turning in, thanks," I'd politely decline and leave them alone. The day before Paul was to leave for the rural area to join the harvest, when I came home, he had been drinking by himself all day long.

"They asked me to reshelve all those books in the Institute library. I suggested they stack them above a fire pit. That's what this Revolution is all about," Paul said, laughing eerily.

"Paul, please don't get into any more trouble."

"What trouble could I possibly get into that I haven't already?" he asked, and took another gulp of cheap whiskey. When he burped, it smelled like rubbing alcohol.

"Please, Paul, don't behave this way, especially in front of the kids."

"What 'way'? I just want to show you something," he answered, and pulled out a notebook that was filled with notes, drawings, and numbers. "When I was at the labor camp, they'd line us up in the field or along the roadside to shovel shit, and I began to notice the wild plants and flowers growing nearby. I would gauge their growth and height, the amount of sunshine they received, and the shade they'd endure. I tried to figure out how they could survive in a toxic manure dump like the one we were working in, determined to someday publish the results."

His drawings were beautiful and the data was meticulously organized. I was taken by his determination to keep thinking scientifically and keep his mind active. I also knew for certain that he was depressed—one of the thousands, if not millions, of highly talented individuals wasting away in Revolutionary China.

"Now I'm stacking books in an empty library that no one

uses," he continued. "They intentionally mess the piles up when I'm not there. The other day, I found a book that describes some of the wildlife I found, so I read it while no one was watching. If I didn't, Jeanie, I'd go crazy just keeping on planting, harvesting, and stacking books endlessly. I'm not even allowed to make suggestions! Even book stacking is a science." Paul was becoming even more agitated. I tried to soothe him, but that wasn't working. I knew how much he loved research and teaching, but there was nothing we could do. I suggested that we maybe could feel grateful we were still alive.

"Physically alive, yes, but empty inside—mentally and emotionally. I'm not sure that's better than being dead." Then he began to sob, and I stopped my sewing and walked over to comfort him. "Paul, please tell me what they did to you all those years. Please tell me, instead of keeping it all inside."

"The wall, that damn wall!" Paul said, and glared straight ahead.

"What wall—the Great Wall?" I tried to cheer him up.

"They asked us to build a wall, a few hundred yards long and twelve feet tall. We built it, they'd topple it, and we'd rebuild it again and again...."

I held him tight. My darling was shaking, and he stopped crying. "That damn wall maimed and killed a lot of people."

"How, Paul?"

"We were not engineers or construction workers. The bricks and cinderblocks were heavy. I was lucky because I'd worked in rice fields for years and was strong enough."

He felt into a deep silence.

The next day, I came home and saw Gina sitting by herself and reading. Then I spotted a note on the table.

JEAN TREN-HWA PERKINS

Dear Jeanie, thank you for listening to my incoherent, drunken rambling last night. I feel so much better today and realized that I haven't been completely fair to you. I understand how hard it has been these past few years for you, too—even though you were outside and I was inside. Anyway, I cooked enough food to last you two for days. I decided to take Eddy with me for a couple of months. I'm sorry for not discussing this with you ahead of time, but I think this may help lessen your burden, or at least that of our angels next door.

Eddy should be fine. I have a tiny room among all the regular farmers, and it's close to the library, so he can study there. I think it will be good for him to see the countryside; there are other kids he can play with, and it will be an eye-opener to see how even poorer people live. Did I mention, the library has a broken-down piano? I have no clue who it belongs to or where it came from, but I'm sure Eddy will find it fascinating.

Lovingly, your Paul,

P.S. See you in a month. The kid will be back before school starts.

I didn't know what to think, but it turned out to be a stroke of genius. A few weeks later, Qiu-Shuang told me she would be away for a month. All the factory workers were ordered to participate in a new movement called *La-Lien* (拉鍊, meaning "brutal long-distance backpacking"). People were forced to march hundreds—in some cases, thousands—of miles on foot carrying heavy backpacks in the hot summer sun.

This mother of all revolutions was continuing to peel the onion. First, they persecuted dissenters. Then they went after

SPRING FLOWER: TORN BETWEEN SHIFTING WORLDS

the educated. Then they sent away the Red Guards, effectively destroying a generation. And then they went after doctors and professionals. And now, the Great Revolution's very own *Proletariat Class* (無產階級). It was workers' turn to stand in front of a firing squad.

I wrote Qiu-Shuang a physician's note that she was nearly blind and should be excused from this exercise. A long trek like this would be a nightmare for her. They claimed they were already accommodating her by allowing her and Old Man Ni to undertake this trek at different times. I wasn't sure how else I could help her. I found a wooden stick and asked Old Man Ni to paint one end bright orange, and I trained her to follow the orange color on the stick as she probed road conditions and uneven depths ahead of her feet.

A month later, everyone returned. I ran into Qiu-Shuang in the kitchen, and she looked well and seemed to have gained a lot of weight. I was baffled and asked, "How did the long march go?"

"Well, Dr. Pei, it was terrible at the beginning and hard on everyone's feet and backs. But thanks to my walking stick, I got used to walking and was able to see the road with it. Then a funny thing happened. I started to feel better while everyone else was getting worse. They were suffering from massive blisters and a lack of appetite, so I had to eat their dry food, which wasn't much, but it was still food. I realized I was getting stronger and enjoying the fresh outdoor air and the scenery. It felt like a vacation from my kids and my dumb Old Man! I felt carefree."

We looked at each other and burst out laughing. "You do look relaxed and wonderful. I'm sorry you had to come back."

"If I stayed away any longer, my household would soon be on fire. And I missed you and your kids!"

Once inside, I saw that my sonny boy and Paul had returned

too—both well-tanned. I was still mad at Paul for taking him away. As much as I thought Eddy might have enjoyed playing the piano, even under godforsaken conditions, after he returned from Shanghai, I'd vowed never to let him out of my sight again. Unlike after Shanghai, though, Eddy couldn't stop talking about what a great time he'd had at the farm, especially while the adults were at work in the rice field. He got more and more excited telling me that he became ringleader among the kids in a matter of days because he'd been attending the grade school and they were unable to go to any school, and how they followed his orders and they were chased by two German shepherds at a nearby military base because he was curious what the dogs ate.

As I was getting a headache from his buzz and tried to tune out, Eddy shouted, "Each morning and afternoon, everyone would line up at the cafeteria and wait for 'the harvest seasonal treats!' They dished out food for the hardworking farmers. Morning meals included red bean paste dumplings, and in the afternoons, everyone was served artificially sweetened, carbonated water."

Paul added, 'Yes, the kid is thoughtful. He saved half of everything every day for me to have when I got back from the field."

I became a little jealous of their bonding.

Then Eddy began to use his finger to "play the piano" on our small desk as he told me how much he enjoyed the quietness in that big dusty, empty room. He remembered what his Auntie Jane had taught him, and he practiced the piano every day.

"What did you play, Eddy?"

"One song was a hymn, maybe 'Be Thou My Vision,'" Paul said.

"What?"

"Auntie Jane taught me that. She said it's a song with a range of simple notes, good for learning to play the piano."

"Did you know Mommy also played the piano?" I asked Eddy, my mind floating miles and decades away, thinking about playing for church gatherings with Chum.

"Can you teach me?" he asked.

"We don't have a piano, kiddo. But I will teach you some day," I promised.

"Let's teach him to swim first!" Paul chimed in.

"If it's that much fun, next summer I want to go to the farm too," Gina joined in.

"Great idea. I want to go back now," Eddy said, still super-excited.

For him, it had been like going to Silver Bay or Lake George; it was summer camp.

Early one morning a few weeks later, before Paul had to return to the labor camp, I told him I might be pregnant again. He looked shocked.

"How?" he asked.

"What do you mean 'how'? Anyway, I'll go check, and if it's true, what do you want to do?"

"I understand you love kids, but we can't handle this." He pointed to the two sleeping kids. "First, childbirth is dangerous for a forty-year-old woman. And second, why bring more children into this horrid world? We're not in America!"

His comments saddened me. Two days later, after my condition was confirmed, I had a hasty abortion and fell into a deep depression, feeling tired and dizzy every morning. At first, I thought the physician had done a careless job. I was bleeding for days. As the months went by, it got even worse, and I felt lethargic and anemic, having lost so much blood. But I kept working my regular hours, thinking "this too shall pass."

JEAN TREN-HWA PERKINS

By late fall 1971, we began to hear street fighting between workers of different manufacturing plants. With the economy increasingly depressed and more and more downtime at the factories, the workers needed something to do. Wearing hardhats and facing each other with long, painted rebar in hand, different colors representing different factions, they'd read passages from Mao's quotations, then whack each other (工人武鬥) with their metal poles. It was just horrible, and our hospital began to receive more and more of the wounded from these street fights. In a short time, we were overwhelmed with fractured eye sockets and punctured and even displaced eyes.

These fights took place near our children's schools. Old Man Ni was so worried that he started taking Eddy and Gina to school himself. He didn't want He-Peng to be anywhere near this insanity. At the hospital, we were not only buried under with fight-afflicted traumas, we were also overwhelmed by anxiety. Only when schools were canceled could we exhale, continuing to wonder when the authorities would stop this horror show.

Finally, the People's Liberation Army (PLA) moved in with guns to prevent fights, but then the workers joined together to fight the PLA, just as it had been with the Red Guards five years earlier.

One cold December afternoon, someone knocked on the operating room door and shouted, "Is Dr. Pei in here?"

I responded through my surgical mask: "Here I am. What is it?"

"Old Man Ni is looking for you!"

I wasn't sure who was asking, but I rushed out fifteen minutes later.

"What took you so long?" Old Man Ni looked worried.

"What's happened?"

"Are your kids not with you?" he asked.

SPRING FLOWER: TORN BETWEEN SHIFTING WORLDS

"No, I thought they were home. I thought school was canceled today." I began to worry.

"He-Peng went with them this morning, and I was going to pick them up after school, but classes let out early and by the time I got there, two fights had broken out. The PLA is everywhere near the school, and I can't find them, Dr. Pei. I've been shouting their names along the streets." Old Man Ni had tears in his eyes.

"I have to finish this procedure. Please wait for me, and we'll go together. They might not recognize your voice." I dutifully stitched up a factory worker whose eye socket had been bashed in. Once outside the hospital, I could hear *"pop-pop-pop"* like firecrackers coming from several directions. With my heart racing, I jumped on the back of Old Man Ni's tricycle, and he began to pedal furiously.

"Slow down please, you're going too fast!" I called out. He was nervous, and so was I. I also knew he had to evade a small group of workers who were in an intense tangle a block away from the hospital. "Eddy! Gina!" we both began to shout, and my mind went back to 1938 when the Japanese soldiers moved into Kiukiang.

"Gina! Eddy!" we shouted again in unison.

"There, who's that?" I said loudly and stood up on the back of his tricycle.

"Where? What?" Old Man Ni asked. He stretched his neck and tried to see what I was pointing to.

Then we both heard an explosive sound coming from that direction. Old Man Ni ducked his head.

"Sit down, Dr. Pei. It's safer sitting behind me," he said in no uncertain terms, and began to pedal even faster.

"Oh, there, yes," he said. "I see a few heads peeking out from behind that big iron gate. Let's take a look. Even if it's not Eddy and Gina, they may know what happened to them."

Sure enough, Eddy and his sister had been hiding behind the small slab of concrete that anchored the iron fence by the school gate, and three other kids were with them. One was the kid Eddy had been about to hit with a lead pipe months earlier.

"Ni *Shu-Shu* (倪叔叔)!" Eddy shouted.

"Come on, kids, let's go!" he cried, grabbing Gina by her collar and dropping her right next to me, all in one swift motion. The other three kids stood paralyzed with fear.

"Don't just stand there! Hop on, we'll take you all home!" I shouted.

They suddenly awoke from their fear and hopped on. Old Man Ni was once again pedaling furiously with five kids and me sitting in the back, watching the shadows of adults swinging at one another. With firecrackers booming in the distance, I put my arms around the terrified children and drifted in my mind's eye to the era of the Japanese invasion and thought about Mother and how much I missed her.

A month later, the fighting was finally suppressed, but debris on the streets and the wounded people at the hospital served as a reminder that we'd gone through yet another tragedy. I was grateful we had been able to escape from the jaws of death yet again.

In mid-February 1972, a few days before the New Year, Paul had to return to the labor camp, cutting short his stay in Hangchow. Neither of us knew why. It was a reminder that he still wasn't a free man. I was becoming progressively more lethargic. One night after arriving home around 9:00, I could hardly breathe as I walked up the stairs. I told the kids Mommy was very tired and would be going to sleep early, that they should wash their faces with the hot water still in the thermos and get themselves to bed soon. Then I fell on the bed with my clothes on. It was so cold — we still had no indoor heat — that sleeping with my winter coat on was not uncommon.

At 2 a.m., I woke up with a sharp pain in my chest, struggling to breathe. I didn't want to wake the kids up, so I got up and tried stretching my arms and taking a deep breath to relieve the pain. Instead, I fell to the floor. I got back up, but I felt extremely dizzy, and my breath was quickening.

"What's happening?" I asked myself.

I managed to stagger across the hall and feebly knocked on Qiu-Shuang's door. Within seconds she and Old Man Ni were at the door. They looked blurry to me; I couldn't focus. I blinked my eyes hard, then squinted, but I could only manage to say, softly, "I think I'm having a heart attack...."

Then I passed out. I thought I was dreaming — a nightmare — but I was awake. My vision still blurry, I could see Qiu-Shuang sitting on the tricycle guardrail and our upstairs neighbor, Dr. Zhou, sitting next to me. Old Man Ni was pedaling hard in the deep winter night.

"Are you awake, Dr. Pei? Can you see me?" Dr. Zhou, who was an internist, asked while waving his fingers and hand.

I nodded and tried to decipher how many fingers he was waving, still feeling intense pain and congestion in my chest. Old Man Ni pedaled even harder, and I could hear every cold breath he took. Things became increasingly blurry, and I began to pass out again, except I could still hear the pedaling and see a few dozen stars in the dark-black sky.

"I can't just die like this," I thought. "What about the kids? They're so young. And what about Paul? But we all have a date with destiny, and this could be mine."

I hoped the cold winter air would keep me alert, and I knew these saintly neighbors were doing their best to save me.

77

Spring 1980...
Recalling my first heart attack was interrupted by the screeching of Shan's (善) brakes. We were heading north; Shan was driving us from Hangchow to the Shanghai airport for our trip to Japan and then to America.

"We're making good time, so let's stop and give the brakes a rest," Shan explained. "This is the 'company jeep,' not supposed to be for personal use. If the police stop us and ask where we're headed and who authorized this trip, we could be in trouble."

"What should we do if that happens?" Paul asked.

"Sit quietly, and I'll tell them your mother in Shanghai is ill and we're going to see her."

"Worth a try, and not entirely a lie," Paul said with a nod.

Shan added, "I'll do everything I can to get you to Shanghai on time, but if we run into trouble, you'll have to find another way."

I understood what he was saying was important, but I couldn't focus. What if we were left on the roadside? And what if he and Paul were charged with unauthorized use of the Institute's jeep? For Shan, having a driver's license in China was a rare privilege in the 1970s and '80s. And being a driver was a highly revered position. I looked out to the fields of farmland, and my mind focused on that cold evening when I almost lost my life.

―――∽∽∽―――

SPRING FLOWER: TORN BETWEEN SHIFTING WORLDS

I was uncertain how many days or perhaps weeks had gone by; I felt like I'd been dreaming for a long time. I was sure I'd seen my parents, but I couldn't recall what we said to each other. Suddenly, I felt the sensation of a warm hand; I opened my eyes and the first face I saw was Paul's. He wiped away his tears and said, "Nurse, she's awake."

Two nurses came over. I'd been *gone* for a day or two. For some reason, they had me sedated. To this day, that's all I remember.

I struggled to sit up. One nurse held me back and said, gently, "Dr. Pei, no." It didn't take much convincing, as I felt extremely weak. But I did notice Gina and Eddy standing at the far corner of the room. Slowly, they came toward me. Gina's face was covered with tears, and Eddy, expressionless, was holding onto her.

I stayed in the hospital for three weeks. On the day of my discharge, Paul lifted me onto the back of his bicycle and threw my duffel bag over his shoulder. He draped a blanket over me, and off we went. Between occasional shouts—"Are you okay? Hang on to my waist!"—I could hear firecrackers nearby: *"Pi-la-pa – pi-la-pa."* It was Chinese New Year, 1972, the Year of the Rat.

I slumped my head onto Paul's frigidly cold back, wondering what this year would bring and what I might be able to celebrate. By the time we reached our compound, I painstakingly got off the bike to walk to the stairs, but Paul insisted on carrying me. I was already embarrassed for being away for three weeks and refused. I was determined to get up the steps on my own. The stairs had no handrail, so I clawed the wall with both my hands as so many had before me. The second floor felt like Mount Everest, and I kept thinking about Eddy tumbling all the way down a few years earlier.

It took me fifteen minutes to get up one flight—what would normally take a minute. Between breaths, I'd rest. My mind went to Dr. Zhou, who had been laboring with these steps too. These

JEAN TREN-HWA PERKINS

memories felt like another lifetime. "This is no way to live," I thought. "I'm just forty." When I entered our room, Eddy and Gina shouted in unison, "Mommy!"

"Hey, dearies, Mommy's home," I said in the strongest voice I could muster and went straight to bed. Eddy brought me a glass of warm water. I smiled and reached out my hand to stroke his face. He sat down alongside me and leaned his head on my arm. A few minutes later, he said, "Mommy, I am so sorry. You don't have to worry about me anymore. I will never fight again."

"Oh, Sonny Boy, Mommy's going to be okay. This is not your fault." I put my arm around him, but barely had the strength to squeeze him.

"Let Mommy rest now," Paul said as he tried to tidy the bed. I obligingly lay down, my mind in a tangle. After just five minutes, I sat up and said, "Paul, please get the scissors and the cloth I measured and cut up. They're on that table, I believe."

Paul looked surprised.

"I won't do anything taxing. I just want to finish making the clothes I promised the kids for New Year's. Lying in bed doing nothing only makes me feel anxious. Sewing new clothes will calm my mind."

"Absolutely not!" Paul said and put the things I'd requested on a higher shelf so the kids and I wouldn't be able to reach for them.

A few days past the New Year, I became even antsier. I needed to do something. When Paul left the room to buy hot water for the kids and me, I pleaded with Eddy to climb up on the desk and bring down the scissors, the sewing kit, and the cloth. When Paul got back, he was furious at Eddy for being selfish and not caring. But I told him my rationale again, and finally he agreed. He said I could work on these new clothes for two hours a day — maximum. I felt so much better having something to do instead

SPRING FLOWER: TORN BETWEEN SHIFTING WORLDS

of just lying there depressed. On the last day of the official Chinese New Year (年十五), I finished new winter coats for Gina and Eddy. They were fifteen days late, but at least my poor kids would have something new to wear for the coming year.

Chinese New Year has fifteen days of celebration. The last day is called *Yüan-Hsiao* (元宵). We could still hear firecrackers, and since we had some food stamps left, we sat around our tiny dinner table and enjoyed dumplings stuffed with sweet sesame (汤团). The kids loved their new clothes, and Paul commended me on how well-made they were and how efficient I'd become as a seamstress. I never told him I'd used Qiu-Shuang's sewing machine while he was away. We ate the dumplings and I sang "White Christmas," celebrating being alive.

Two weeks later, I felt ready to go back to work, but Paul would have nothing of it. As we tangled, he suddenly changed the subject, "I have some news. I've been keeping it from you because I didn't know how you'd react. I'm telling you now to try to impress upon you how important your health will be for all of us. Maybe if you listen to me, you'll rest a little longer."

"Please tell me," I said, anxiously.

"Jeanie, take a look at this newspaper clipping. I've been saving it for you." Paul took a small handkerchief out of his pocket and it had a few pieces of paper neatly wrapped inside. He handed the papers to me. I was trembling, uncertain what the news would be. I saw photos of an American couple shaking hands with Chairman Mao and with Premier Chou (周恩來). A chill went up my spine. President Nixon and his wife, Pat, had just made a historic visit to China.

"Where did you get this?" I asked.

"I found a newspaper at the Institute library. You know I've been cleaning the building and maintaining what's left of the books. I didn't know who left it there, so I stole it and cut out these pictures. The paper says they came to Hangchow a few weeks ago, which is as close to a live American as we've been for twenty-two years. It's mind-boggling!" Paul exclaimed.

"Paul, only certain people are permitted to see this newspaper." It was called *Reference News,* meaning *Ts'an-K'ao-Hsiao-Hsi* (參考消息), and had restricted access. We had to take anything it said with a grain of salt, but even if it had been altered, it would still be based on some truth.

It turned out that Nixon's Security Adviser, Henry Kissinger, had made a series of secret visits in 1971 and met with Premier Chou in anticipation of a historic trip by the American president. And in 1971, the US had sent a team of ping-pong players to China to play against Chinese players. The event was dubbed "Ping-Pong Diplomacy," and we learned many of these things well after the fact. The Nixons' visit in February 1972 was monumental, as it symbolized an end to the diplomatic silence between the two countries that had lasted almost a quarter of a century.

"At the very least, the visit means the two countries would cease to be enemies and end the mutual hostility since the Korean War," I said and became visibly excited.

"My dear Jeanie, there's hope! Now you see why you have to rest and get well." Paul grew animated.

"Keep your voice down, Paul! I'll rest a little longer," and

President Nixon and his wife's visiting China in 1972: Neither my son nor I was in this staged documentary photo. But their presence opened the door of a forbidden world and brought hope to people like me.

SPRING FLOWER: TORN BETWEEN SHIFTING WORLDS

I kissed him on the forehead.

I leaned back on the pillow. I hadn't been as happy as this for years. But my happiness was short-lived. As I turned the clipping over, I read: "Americans and their Anti-Communist allies have been actively engaged in helping South Vietnam fight Hu Chi-Minh's Communist North Vietnam, which is backed by China, Russia, and other Communist-bloc countries." Even though the US had been engaged in Vietnam for over a decade by then, it was news to me. Ordinary citizens in China at the time didn't know much about this or other international or even domestic news, and what we *did* hear understated the scale, extent, and progression of the Vietnam War and other world events until well into the 1970s. China was sealed airtight, and whatever information got through was filtered, censored, and rescripted. Most Chinese were too caught up in the Great Cultural Revolution as persecutors or victims. The majority of the people didn't know that Nixon and Mao shook hands in 1972, or even that 20-plus million people had disappeared within thirty-six months in the late 1950s.

Oh, dear—here was Korean War II, with Americans fighting Chinese on another people's soil! How will we ever normalize the relationship between the US and China? How will I ever go home to America? I felt sad again.

Paul was much more hopeful. He believed the two countries would ultimately renew diplomatic relations. He tried to explain why, using *Romance of the Three Kingdoms* as an analogy—Russia, China, and the US. For two weaker countries to survive, they must always try to find a way to be in an alliance against the one perceived to be the strongest. On the opposite side, to annihilate the weaker ones, the strongest should always try to break that alliance by pretending to be aligned with one of the two or by creating conflicts between the two. And when all three are at an impasse, the fear is always that the other two are stealthily building an alliance. In any event, Paul thought the Vietnam War wasn't the same as the Korean War in terms of direct engagement between America and China and that it'd be a short-lived distraction. He even thought that Americans' visiting China could help end the war.

For me, it was a restless night. Day-Day would be ninety-five now if he were still alive, which I doubted. Mother would be eighty-seven. Oh, how I wished I could go home and see her one more time! If that could happen, I would name Eddy after President Nixon. Well, he would still be "Edward," to honor Day-Day, but he could be Edward Richard Perkins Hsiung. "A long name," I said with a smile, as I drifted off to sleep.

A month later, Gina's elementary school announced there'd be no more sixth grade. She had thus officially graduated from elementary school after five-and-a-half years. I didn't care how the decision was made. I was proud of my little girl finishing elementary school without falling behind. Of course, we began to worry about her going to junior high. We knew it'd be a big ordeal trying to find a school that would take her. We'd been fortunate that Chang *Lao-Shih* had both persuaded her elementary school to enroll her and been instrumental in getting Gina through these difficult years. We didn't know who would help us going forward.

But first things first. One Sunday night that spring, Paul made a simple dinner, and

Gina soon to graduate from elementary school, ca. 1972

SPRING FLOWER: TORN BETWEEN SHIFTING WORLDS

we invited Dr. Zhou's family from upstairs, along with Chang *Lao-Shih* and her husband, Dr. Chang and their little daughter Fang-Fang, as well as Qiu-Shuang and Old Man Ni, for a little gathering. While the kids sat around our tiny table, we grownups hovered over a makeshift dining table we'd pieced together. We all felt deep gratitude for having survived the horrors of the past decade and were clinking our glasses filled with cheap liquor. Dr. Zhou toasted, saying, "Hope can be a very powerful medicine!" The room was filled with camaraderie and genuine laughter.

In the summer of 1972, Sue's husband, Conductor Hsie, took Gina back to Shanghai, Paul's mother homeschooled her until we could find a junior high school that would take her. Paul got busy again with spring planting, which left Eddy and me—mother and son—alone. Qiu-Shuang's son, He-Peng, was still walking Eddy to school, and Qiu-Shuang was minding him after school, since she had completely stopped working. However, to lighten their workload and give Eddy and me time together, I would walk him to my clinic, which was halfway to his school, and he'd go on from there by himself. At first, I put him on the back of my bicycle, and I'd either push the bike or pedal, depending on the weather. I was still afraid of riding my bike with someone else sitting on it. Eddy took this separation from Gina much better than the last time, and he enjoyed riding on my bike.

"Mommy!" he shouted from the back.

"Yes, Sonny?" I peered back.

"Your biking skills are getting better."

"What do you mean? Was I bad before?" I teased.

"No, you seem to bike faster than before," Eddy explained.

"Thank you, dear. I guess with just you, it's easier. Or perhaps you're right. Maybe I have improved after practicing all these years. I'm also trying to get some exercise by biking more quickly," I answered.

A few seconds later, he asked, "Mommy, what does 'girlfriend' (女朋友) mean?"

I chuckled. "Girlfriend means a friend who is a girl."

"How many girlfriends can a boy have?"

"As many as you wish, kiddo. Why?"

"I was told if I have more than one, I need to rank them."

"What?" I found the conversation both amusing and disturbing. I turned around, and Eddy looked serious.

"Kids from school and the compound have told me I have too many girlfriends and that I have to rank them, like the way a king had a queen and many concubines."

"No, Eddy. If you have a friend who is a girl and is very special to you, you should have only one at a time."

"Why?" he asked.

I tried to catch my breath, literally and mentally, thinking how to explain this to a seven-year-old! "Who *are* these girls? Is one girl very special in your heart, like Mommy is to Papa?"

"Well, there's Fang-Fang [Chang *Lao-Shih*'s daughter], Hong-Hong [Dr. Lei's older daughter upstairs from us], Yao-Yao [the Zhu family's daughter in the middle tier], and Mei-Mei. And there's also a girl from school named Yu Qing, who was assigned to be my desk-mate."

I nearly fell off my bike. "First, you should treat these girls all equally and respect all of them equally."

"And...?" Eddy nudged my waist.

"That's it. There is no 'and'." I wanted to end the conversation here, but after a long pause, Eddy said, "Okay, I guess as long as I treat them with equal respect, I can eventually marry all of them."

On the way home that evening, we stopped to get a bite at the cafeteria. It was part of my plan to lessen the burden on Qiu-Shuang and become more independent.

"Up we go, Sonny Boy," I shouted as I parked my bike and as we reached our stairway. Eddy had grown up quite a bit. Lickety split he was up the stairs. After I took just two steps, I felt a rapid tightening in my chest. I stopped and took a deep breath, thinking, "Oh no, not again. It's been less than six months since my heart attack and I'm still that weak." Seconds later, I regained composure and felt better, or at least I wasn't panicking.

"Mommy, look! I'm already at the top, way ahead of you." Then he saw me and came running back down. "Mommy, are you okay? I can carry you up," he said.

"Mommy's okay, Eddy. Just give me a second and I'll walk up with you." I was trying to catch my breath.

"I guess bike riding is easier than climbing steps," I said to myself, but aloud.

"What?" Eddy asked, not catching the meaning.

"Oh, don't worry, Sonny Boy. I'm okay. See, I'm catching up with you. You'd better hurry!" I slapped his bottom and he giggled and continued up the stairs.

That night I lay sleepless, wondering if I'd be okay and if more Americans would be visiting China. Was it legal to phone America now? I missed Day-Day and Mother so much. I tossed and turned and wondered if Paul could get more news from the library or if he was too busy in the field. I wanted to know more about Vietnam, and whether that dreaded war had ended.

Right then, I recalled Paul's words: "Get healthy, stay alive, and wait for a chance to go home." But I couldn't even get up the stairs without stopping and sighing. "Something has to change," I thought, and I tossed and turned some more.

The next morning, I woke Eddy up half an hour earlier than our usual time. I could tell it disturbed him, but he asked politely, "Mommy, why am I getting up early today?"

"From now on," I said, "you and I are going to run to my

clinic, and when we get there, I'll get you something simple for breakfast and then you go on your way to school. How about that?" I was excited about the new plan. He wasn't.

"Why?" he asked. "Because I made fun of your biking yesterday? I'm sorry. You're a really good biker, Mommy." He was trying to appease me.

"Oh, no, Eddy. It has nothing to do with that. Mommy wants to get healthier."

"Oh, but can we eat first and then run?" He really didn't want to get up.

"It's bad for your belly to run after eating. Please help me out, kiddo." I was practically begging him.

So he got up. I helped him put his jacket and a dry shirt in his backpack, which I offered to carry for him. "Let's go, soldier, hut-hut!" I gave him a salute, which he found amusing.

And off we went. We began to run, and two blocks later, we both were out of breath, panting heavily while leaning forward with our hands on our knees. Eddy looked at me and said, "Are you okay, Mommy? Let me carry my own bag."

"It's too heavy for you," I said.

"Okay, Mommy, let's run another block." He jumped up and grabbed my hand. And just like that, hand-in-hand we ran another block, then rested for a few more minutes before running yet another block. Finally, we reached the hospital gate. The doorman found it amusing: "Dr. Pei, running to get to the daily Mao's quotations study? Good for you, your spirit moves me."

I changed Eddy's shirt, told him not to get a cold, and hoped we'd do this every day.

Amazingly we did, and a month later we could both make it to the clinic without stopping. It was less than two miles, but we were proud. Soon I would be jogging with him to his school and then run back to the clinic by myself. Paul was impressed.

SPRING FLOWER: TORN BETWEEN SHIFTING WORLDS

One morning, while we were out on our jog, I asked Eddy, "How would you like to learn English? I can teach you."

"What's English, Mommy?" he asked.

"English is another language, dear, like Chinese. Some people in the world speak English and not Chinese," I explained.

Eddy was in deep thought, then asked, "Okay, Mommy, but who taught you English?"

I knew this day would come, and I was better prepared than when Gina asked the same question.

"Eddy, you know Mommy also has a papa and a mama. They taught Mommy how to speak English."

"Oh, where are they? I'd like to meet your papa and mama. I know Papa's mother."

"Maybe someday in the future. For now, I will teach you while we run, but you mustn't tell anyone in school that Mommy is teaching you English."

"Okay, Mommy, but only if you promise to tell me what your mama and papa are like," Eddy bargained.

"Okay, kiddo, I promise, Scout's Honor." I put my hand over my heart.

"What's Scout's Honor?" he asked

"That's why you have to learn English," I said.

"Okay," he said, and he sounded excited.

After a couple of minutes, I began the first lesson. I could hardly wait. "I'll teach you the twenty-six letters of the English alphabet. A, B, C, D, E, and F." I spoke slowly while we were still jogging to school.

He was a quick learner, and he was able to get each letter right the first time.

"Here are five important vowels: A, E, I, O, U. Please repeat them."

He did, but quickly asked, "Mommy, I thought it was A, I, U,

E, O."

"Where did you learn that?" I asked, startled.

"I heard you chanting those sounds some nights. Was that English?" Eddy sounded confused.

"No, that was another language." I tried to change the subject.

"You know another language, too? Who taught you that one? Your papa and mama too?" Eddy was excited.

"How about you keep learning English, and I'll tell you everything later."

"Scout's Honor?" Eddy asked again.

With that, spring sped into summer, and by the time Eddy was about to complete second grade, he knew some basic English.

"What's your name?" I asked in English.

"My name is Edward Perkins Hsiung. That's a long name, Mommy, isn't it? And why 'Edward'?'"

"Keep learning, and I'll tell you everything as promised. What grade are you in school?"

"I am in elementary school, in second grade."

"Nice job, kiddo. Mommy is proud of you. If we keep this up, you'll soon know a new language." I patted him on the head as we both swung our arms while jogging.

"So, after I learn the new language, you will tell me about your mama and papa?" Eddy was persistent on this.

"Yes, Sonny Boy, Mommy will tell you about them. Okay, from the top, what's your name?".

"My name is Edward Perkins, and also Hsiung," Eddy shouted back and gave me a salute as well.

I took a deep breath and looked up at the sky. "I hope you can meet your grandchildren. You'll be so proud of them, and someday I hope to bring them back to America!"

78

For the first time in 1973, the Year of the Ox, Gina and I were not together during the Chinese New Year. I suspected that she enjoyed Shanghai a lot, though, and liked being with her grandmother and Auntie Grace. Our Hangchow slum compound was subdued, aside from a few firecrackers bursting inside and out. The country was sinking further into the abyss and experiencing the full consequence of Mao's senseless and meaningless Revolution, now in its seventh year. All anyone had to do was look around and see we were *all* very poor, with increasingly fewer products in the shops. Most items were labeled "For Display Only," and so our rice stamps, meat stamps, oil stamps, and cotton-cloth stamps were essentially useless.

My best memory for that Chinese New Year was a small pork strip that Paul bought on the black market. He removed the fat and fried it to set aside some lard and then marinated the rest of the meat in salt and soy sauce, since we had no refrigeration. Then he hung the pork on a string attached to a hook near the apartment door for nearly two months. The fermented stench was tempting but unreachable for the family of three rats that had been living with us symbiotically for years. Paul took slices from it ever so slowly, so we'd have a little salty meat stir-fried with Chinese cabbage, along with turnips, as the staple of our daily diet. Qiu-Shuang and Old Man Ni came over a few times to borrow a couple of slices. The stench made it hard to swallow, but it helped us enjoy otherwise bland rice. We soon learned to marinate or ferment a variety of vegetables in salt and soy sauce to flavor the rice. We were grateful to have any rice at all; we had to ration it carefully, so it'd last till the end of the month.

China was impoverished when Chairman Mao proclaimed our long-awaited independence from the world, and now we were even poorer. Beggars proliferated; some had traveled hundreds of miles from the countryside to beg in cities. They would knock on Sister Liu and Captain Shao's door, because they lived on the ground floor by the compound's front entrance. I lost count of how many times the kind couple gave whatever they had to these beggars, some of whom were dragging along their children. We and other neighbors did the same. Eddy joined me a few times, although I cautioned him to stay a few yards back as some of the beggars might have had contagious diseases. Leprosy had returned to China. The simplest gestures of human kindness were on full display in our tenement as well as from neighbors up and down the street. However grim the reality, the human heart refused to be buried or swept away during this incomprehensible time.

With Chinese New Year mercifully over, the weather unexpectedly turned warm, and as Hangchow's renowned plum blossoms faded, cherry and peach flowers began blooming prematurely. By planting season, Paul was gone to assist farmers and fulfill the duties, mandated by his labor camp. He still received no pay for his labor, including stacking books at the library during the off-season. He was reminded that his status as an *Extreme Rightist* (極右派) and an *Anti-Revolutionist* (反革命分子) had not changed. I sensed that he liked being in the rice fields more than restacking books that someone had intentionally scattered so he'd have to do it again.

It had been more than a year since the unthinkable news of President Nixon's visit to China, and there was no further news about America, as though it had all been a dream. Eddy and I were left behind on our own, with Gina wanting to stay in Shanghai through the spring. It was almost a year since I'd seen her, and I knew we had to find a way to enroll her in high school. But with the weather getting warmer, Eddy and I resumed our running and our English lessons.

———∞———

That same spring, Jade became the de facto Chief of our Division of Ophthalmology, and Sue became the head nurse in our division, although there was no real change to their official status. I couldn't have been happier for both, although I wasn't sure why the hospital suddenly decided we needed heads. We hadn't had any leadership besides the *Shu-Chi's* and then the WDT (共宣隊) for seven years. I was also a little saddened I'd never gotten the promotion to the rank of Full Attending Physician (正主治醫生) that was promised in 1965, eight years earlier.

As a result, I saw Sue much less, and two junior residents and I shared a nurse, who had the same family name as my biological parents, "Hu (胡)," so I called her "*Hsiao* Hu (小, Little Hu)." Little Hu was in her early twenties. The two new residents were Dr. He (河) and Dr. Chen (陳), both female and also in their early twenties. Jade asked me to train them and gave me complete autonomy in doing so.

Having such young women taking significant responsibilities was yet another result of Mao's Great Revolution. Because there was a generation that had fallen through the cracks, Jade and I were now the oldest physicians, while those we were training were more than twenty years our juniors. Those who were older than Jade and me had been persecuted as too bourgeois and were gone. And the few younger residents who were at the hospital when I first arrived had been reassigned to other parts of the country. When I was still in medical school in the early 1950s, the country was already short of physicians, and especially ophthalmologists, and the shortage was now more acute. And there was still no sign of reopening the nation's colleges.

Finally, those hiding behind the Forbidden City Wall noticed the shortage of physicians, so in the years leading up to 1973, a few *select* individuals were rushed through high school, shuffled into the medical professions with about two years of training, and assigned to hospitals. By *select*, I don't mean qualified, but those who had "excellent" family backgrounds—relatives of Communist officials or descendants of poor farmers, factory workers, or soldiers (the *Five Red Categories*) who had pledged their loyalty to the Party and were eternally grateful to Chairman Mao for lifting them from the edge of fire and brimstone, levitating their lives from hell. They named the so-called school the *Workers-Farmers-Soldiers College* (工農兵大學). But despite these hasty efforts, the shortage of personnel in our healthcare system, not to mention the quality of these newcomers, left room for improvement.

So there I was, mentoring these "instant doctors," and I quickly grew to like them. They worked hard and were humble and eager to learn—hungry for knowledge and experience. Most of all, despite their alleged outstanding family background, they never spoke to me of politics. I just assumed they were descendants of workers, farmers, or soldiers, but I never asked. I did learn later that Dr. Chen's parents were elementary school teachers in the countryside. I loved that they called me *Lao-Shih* (老師, teacher), which marked a new phase of my career. I was proud to once again follow in the footsteps of Day-Day and the Auntie Ploegs, who had trained so many young Chinese physicians and nurses. I came to believe that when done properly, a lot of clinical work could be learned more effectively *outside* a classroom, since it is

SPRING FLOWER: TORN BETWEEN SHIFTING WORLDS

experiential. I also recognized and appreciated that teaching is also learning.

One morning, Li *Shu-Chi* and Jade came over to my desk as I was finishing up with a patient, and Li *Shu-Chi* said in a low voice, "I think Peng *Shu-Chi* is here, but I'm not sure."

"Oh, where?" I looked up and asked.

"I think she is standing in line waiting," Jade said.

So, I took a quick trip to the bathroom and as I walked back to my desk, I scanned the line and saw Peng *Shu-Chi* waiting in line like everyone else. I hadn't seen her for several years, and she looked the same. It didn't feel right to greet her then, but I thought, "What an interesting woman, standing in line like everyone else!"

I quietly asked Jade who had been assigned to see Peng *Shu-Chi*. She said, "I think one of your residents, but I'll place her file in your basket."

"Good," I replied. And an hour later, *Hsiao* Hu (小胡) brought Peng *Shu-Chi* to my desk.

I smiled and asked, "What brings you here today, Mrs. Peng?"

"Dr. Pei, I have been seeing floating dots in both eyes. I'm concerned because that was the first symptom my husband had."

"Have you seen flashes of light or cloudiness, or had headaches or blurry vision?" I asked.

"Maybe a little."

After going through a few simple visual acuity tests, approximating her visual fields with my finger, I decided to dilate her pupils. I took her into the dark room and asked her to give me about twenty minutes.

After completing work with another patient, I returned to the dark room and carefully examined her visual range, eye pressure, and the condition of her retina. At first I thought it was a simple case of posterior vitreous detachment (PVD), when the gel that fills the eyeball separates from the retina, which is a natural part of aging. While that may have been true, I observed her left lens becoming cloudy.

"Peng *Shu-Chi*," I said, lowering my voice.

"Yes, Dr. Pei?" she sounded concerned.

"I think the good news is that these are just garden-variety floaters. Your retina looks good. Your pressures are good, so I don't believe you have what your husband had."

"What's the bad news?" she asked anxiously.

"Your left lens is beginning to become opaque, which explains the cloudiness you occasionally experience. I think it's a matter of time before you'll have to have cataract surgery to remove and replace that lens," I calmly explained.

"Oh." She looked disappointed.

Seeing her face, I tried to assure her. "Actually, Peng *Shu-Chi*, this is common when we get older. I know this may not make you feel much better. While you look very young, how old are you?"

"Sixty-three," she replied.

"Still young," I said, "but cataracts can begin to cloud our vision as we enter our sixties."

She sighed.

"We can wait for a while. It'd probably be a good idea if you come back in three to six months, and I can examine you again. If you trust me to, I can operate on you in the future."

"Of course, Dr. Pei, it would be my good fortune if you could do it. I'd prefer to wait as long as I can, though. I'm afraid of coming to the hospital, let alone surgery—seeing the needles and knives," Peng *Shu-Chi* quietly shared.

"Oh?" I was surprised to hear that.

"I know what you're thinking," she said, and chuckled wholeheartedly while pointing her finger at me—"that a warrior woman who nearly died on the Long March (萬里長征) and went through battlefields with bullets raining down and bombs going off would not be afraid of a scalpel. Governor Peng is even more scared of needles and knives than I am! The difference is that I'm more honest about my fears."

I began to laugh, then suddenly stood up and said, "I'm so sorry, Peng *Shu-Chi*. You must think I have no manners."

She was startled to hear me say that. "Not at all, Dr. Pei. I'm just joking with you. Please feel at ease."

"Oh, Peng *Shu-Chi*, I'm having such a good time listening to you that I nearly forgot that I wanted to ask you something."

"Yes?"

"I believe you and your husband had something to do with Paul's being able to come home from the labor camp. Thank you. And not only for that. I put together what you said that day in your jeep. You risked your life to alert my husband that Red Guards were coming to search our home for copies or the letter you had confiscated. I always wondered what those Red Guards were looking for, although I knew my husband was trying to get rid all of my things from home to protect me. I read the letter he wrote to the Central Government. Although I did not comprehend all of it, it was a great warning to our country. I realized that you and Governor Peng have saved his life many times. And it was also you who helped remove him from the execution list. Thank you so much!" I blurted everything out all at once, and in the dim light of the darkroom, I knelt down in front of her.

She looked even more startled, and she nearly screamed, "Weren't you brought up by Americans and in America? Do they bow and kneel there? I don't think so. Where did you learn this, Dr. Pei?" She grabbed my arm to pull me up. "Please, Dr. Pei, get up this instant! Someone is going to walk in and wonder what we are doing."

She laughed and made me laugh too. Then I heard a loud sigh. "The truth," she continued, "is that *Lao* Peng (老彭 – meaning Old Peng, her affectionate way of speaking about Governor Peng) and I *both* wish we could have done so much more to save people from their tragic demises. I wish we could relive the last decade and do better this time. Fighting to have an independent China was one thing; that was our job. But building a nation and making our nation strong again, we needed talented people like you and your husband. *Lao* Peng and I both know he has the potential to be a transformative figure in agriculture. What a waste!" and she sighed again.

I sat in silence, trying to absorb this highly unusual moment shared by two women from completely different backgrounds. Then again, we might not have been that different.

"Well, Dr. Pei," Peng *Shu-Chi* said, holding my hand, "please forgive us. Again, this is not to mitigate our responsibilities for the atrocities in the making that have no end in sight. But we are simpleminded soldiers who only take orders from our superiors with a tunnel vision, or we die on the battlefields, even when the chain of command is deadly wrong. But we are not oblivious to how these terrible mistakes have been destroying our country for years and may be disastrous for generations to come."

These were words of wisdom from a remarkable woman, regardless of her belief and allegiance.

In early summer 1973, I received a letter from Taka. My heart was racing and my hands were trembling as I opened it. In those days, it was still difficult to receive letters, especially uncensored ones. Taka had become a ghost of my past.

He wrote that he'd been living like a king for the past seven

SPRING FLOWER: TORN BETWEEN SHIFTING WORLDS

years. His aunt and uncle passed away shortly after he was sent to rural Northern Kansu Province, one of a heart attack and the other from a fractured skull. After Japan and China renewed diplomatic relations in 1972, he was repatriated. He wrote that if that could happen, anything could! He said he took one last walk along the Huang-P'u River before writing to me after visiting the Japanese Embassy in Shanghai. They located his father and grandmother in Japan; both were alive. He ended by describing his last five years in China:

> Who would have guessed in that tiny Northern village, people would treat me with unexpected kindness, leaving me at a loss because I couldn't find reasons to end my life. Instead, when I came out of my doldrums, I realized the extent to which these impoverished people needed medical care, with ailments the result of malnutrition and starvation. The village elder (村長) eventually asked me to establish a clinic, and I ended up teaching a group of former Red Guards (紅衛兵) who wanted to learn medicine and become barefoot physicians. Irony aside, those welcoming distractions, along with unforgettably happy images sitting with you and Gina along the Huang-P'u River, kept me alive.

He gave me his addresses in Chitose, Hokkaido, the northernmost of Japan's main islands. Although I was excited to receive a letter from him, after reading it I felt empty, as if Taka had now officially disappeared from my life. Yes, I was happy that he was miraculously alive and going to a place where he would be free and have hope again, but I also felt moody and depressed for the next few weeks. Then, suddenly, I realized why. In 1964, when he left, we all still lived with hope. Now that seemed like another lifetime. With everything burned to the ground by this senseless Revolution, the only instinct I had left was the will to survive. And now, with Taka walking toward real hope and freedom, I felt profoundly alone.

From that summer on, I began two new habits, both of which I'd learned from Taka. The first was to take two hot baths a week, year-round. Old Man Ni found two discarded wooden buckets in the hospital laundry. Eddy and Gina shared the smaller one, while the larger bucket about four feet in diameter and three feet deep was for Paul and me. We'd boil water or buy hot water down the street. I even gave Eddy the chore of buying hot water with an allowance of a penny per trip.

At first, Paul wasn't into it, but it turned out to be a great idea. We no longer had to wait in line for the cold showers on the first floor in summer or carry hot water thermoses down those dangerously steep steps in winter. We also used the warm bath water to do laundry and other washing. I'd yearned for our own bath ever since coming back to Hangchow from Shanghai, where I had my own bathroom. Not just our compound, the entire country suffered from personal hygiene issues because hot showers were a luxury most people didn't have.

The second habit was to clean and wax our floor and then walk barefoot indoors. So by May of each year, I would scrub every corner of the cement floor and use some industrial-grade wax to polish it until the cement shined. After that, we'd take our shoes or slippers off when we entered the room. We could even sleep on the cool floor on hot summer days. The neighborhood kids loved to come over to play with Eddy and Gina. Eventually, some other families in our compound began walking barefoot on clean floors, too.

In May 1973, Eddy and I celebrated his eighth birthday

with a picnic alongside West Lake. During our time together, I suggested a new routine, and Eddy agreed. He would come to my clinic after school and do his homework there. Then he'd go to the cafeteria and pick up our dinner, which we'd eat at the clinic. This would reduce the burden on Qiu-Shuang. Then we'd go home together.

It worked well until one day he didn't show up until after dinnertime. I didn't say much. I'd picked up dinner myself before the cafeteria closed. He told me he had some sort of after-school activities. I was curious what activities had left him with dirt on his back, but I let it slide. My precious sonny boy had never lied to me.

A few days later, it happened again, and as the weeks passed by it became more and more frequent. I was becoming concerned, and on days I was too busy to pick up dinner, we just didn't eat. So, late one afternoon I went to Eddy's school and his homeroom teacher told me there were no after-school activities.

When Eddy showed up late that evening, I asked in my most stern voice, "Where were you? You lied to me. Your teacher said there are no after-school activities. It's all okay as long as you tell me the truth now. Where have you been after school these past weeks?"

He seemed shaken. He stared at me for about a minute with no tears. Then slowly, he said, "I've been going to the railroad yard."

I exhaled and probed again, "Fighting or doing bad things with friends, like smoking or stealing?"

"No, Mommy. I haven't fought since Gina graduated. No one has come after me. And I'm not stealing or smoking, I just go to the railroad yards."

"By yourself or with a friend?"

"I don't really have any friends."

"I thought the kids from our compound were your friends, like Dr. Zhou's eldest son and teacher Chang *Lao-Shih*'s daughter Fang-Fang. You said she was your girlfriend."

"She's not. I don't have any friends from school, and the kids from the compound go to different schools."

"How do you get in the railroad yard? You know it's illegal."

"I squeezed through the broken fence until they fixed it. Now I climb over it."

"Is that why you have dirt all over your jacket?"

"Yes. The fence is high, and a couple of times I fell."

"No one sees you?"

"I don't go to the train *station*. I go to a stretch of tracks kind of far from the station. I like watching the trains going by...."

"Eddy! That's dangerous!"

"I stay far from the trains."

"It's still dangerous. You are to do no such thing again. The fence is to keep people out." After a long pause, I asked him, "Why do you like to watch the trains?"

"I wonder where all the people are coming from and where they're going."

"You find that fascinating?

"I do. And sometimes I wonder if I could hop on a train and get out of this place."

I was startled by what he said and didn't reply. Instead, in a gentle tone, I suggested, "Hey, kiddo, let's eat. The food's getting cold."

I couldn't sleep that night. All I could think about was Eddy's wanting to get out of this place. He was only eight.

The next day, I forbade Eddy from going near the railroad again. Then, a few weeks later, he was missing again, and I jumped on my bike and headed to the Hangchow Train Station. I looked in every direction but didn't see him. So I arbitrarily headed north and saw him sitting outside the fence watching a train passing by, crowded with people. I wanted to shout but decided not to. I was just happy to find him, and he was perfectly safe outside the fence. I got off the bike and walked over to him. I stood about ten yards behind and watched him.

Then I said, softly, "Eddy, there you are, watching trains again."

He jumped up, turned toward me, and said, "Mommy, please don't be mad."

"I'm not mad, honey. Can I join you?"

"Yes, Mommy, if you want to." So there we were, mother and son sitting on the dirt waiting for the next train to pass.

"If you could get on one of these trains, where would you go, Eddy?" I asked, ruffling his hair.

"I don't know. As far away as possible, I guess."

"You hate this place that much?" I asked. "Papa, Gina, and Mommy are here. And we have Auntie Luo and Uncle Ni next door, and their kids have been so nice to you. And all your friends at the compound, right? You want to leave us all?" I laughed a little and ruffled his hair again.

"That's not what I meant, Mommy." Eddy stared at me.

"What do you mean then?"

"I don't want to leave anyone. The train is big enough to take all of us."

Just then, a train roar sounded in the distance, and soon it was headed toward us before it roared again and sped by. As I watched the train, which was saddled with people, some even sitting on the top of the railway cars, some with half their bodies hanging out the doors and windows, my thoughts drifted far away. I thought of Grand Central Station in New York in 1941, saying goodbye to Chum and the Aunties. I thought about sitting in Nanking Train Station shaking in fear before Paul stopped

JEAN TREN-HWA PERKINS

me from going to Canton. I thought about the long train ride to Harbin. I thought about standing on the platform of Shanghai Station, watching Taka disappear. And I thought about getting Gina off the train in Hangchow and Eddy getting onto it.

"Mommy," Eddy asked, "do you believe there's someone in the sky who looks down upon us and sees all that's going on?"

I was shocked by his question, not only because he was only eight years old, but also because I wondered where he would have heard such a thing in Communist China.

"What made you think of that? Did someone suggest something to you?"

"No, I just wondered. Sometimes when I get tired of waiting for the train, I look up to the sky and ask if anyone's listening. And if they are, would they take us away from here."

I didn't know what to say. I certainly didn't want to tell him about God, fearing that my truth would bring more unwanted wrath upon us. Nor did I want to lie and say that no one is up there listening. I realized that while he was growing up way too fast, I wasn't sure how much he could understand. And, more unnerving, this might have been our only real heart-to-heart chat.

79

GINA FINALLY returned to Hangchow in the late summer of 1973. I couldn't believe how much she had grown. My little girl had just turned thirteen! Her grandmother, Eve, taught her high school math, Chinese history, and even English. I had to hand it to her. Eve was a veteran teacher from Rulison Girls' High in our Kiukiang days. She did a great job of imparting knowledge to Gina. Gina's Auntie Grace taught her both geography and Chinese writing. And her Uncle Bart taught her chemistry and physics.

Welcoming Gina home to face the next battle: to attend a junior high

JEAN TREN-HWA PERKINS

Bart had not fared much better than Paul. Although he wasn't jailed or sent to a labor camp, he had been barred from working at the pharmaceutical company in 1966 and was forced to write endless self-criticisms and attend meetings to renounce his past, including that of his (and Paul's) father, who had been the principal of William Nast Academy in Kiukiang. Teaching Gina turned out to be the highlight of his day, and he fell in love with his niece and her speed-of-light learning ability.

Gina returned a different person—a real grownup. Paul and I wanted her to attend a junior high, and we found one in our district, Public High School No. 8. So we applied, showing them Gina's elementary school academic record, a recommendation letter from Chang *Lao-Shih*, and her diploma, and we noted her cerebral palsy. The school's principal, named Guan (關), invited Gina and me to meet with him on the first day of school.

On a bright and sunny early autumn day, I put Gina on the back of my bike and off we went to Public High School No. 8, which was about a mile away. She was big now, and I didn't dare pedal her, so I walked the bike.

"Mommy's little girl has grown up and is going to be in junior high! Aren't you happy?"

"Very happy!" Gina shouted and began to hum a joyful tune.

"Wow, my girl can sing too!"

Gina chuckled. When we got to the school, the gateman looked at us warily, but was pleasant enough and didn't ask any questions. I locked my bike, and Gina and I walked up to the fourth floor. A woman walked out of the Principal's Office and asked, pointedly, "Who are you and what are you doing here?"

"We're here to see Principal Guan (關校长) to enroll my daughter in your school."

"Principal Guan is not here today. But Vice Principal Wang (王) is, and you can see her." She took a long hard look at Gina and exhaled a sneering sound through her nose. Gina and I walked into the office, sat down, and waited. Half an hour later, a tall, striking woman walked in, and I asked, "Are you Principal Wang."

"Oh no," she answered. "I'm a teacher here, looking for Principal Guan. Principal Wang is at a meeting. She should be back soon." Then she walked out.

It was already midday. I was glad I'd asked Jade and Li *Shu-Chi* for a rare day off. "Are you hungry, Gina?"

"No, Mommy. I just want to go to school."

"Okay. I'm pretty hungry, but we'll tough it out. And as long as we can get you into school, we can endure anything, right, kiddo?"

Finally, a woman in her fifties walked in. "Hi, are you Vice Principal Wang?" I asked.

"Yes, and you are...?" She looked at us while dusting chalk stains from her blouse.

"My name is Pei Tren-Hwa. I'm a physician at the municipal hospital. This is my daughter, Gina. We registered Gina to enroll in Public High School No. 8, and Principal Guan told us to meet with him on the first day of school."

"Oh, Principal Guan isn't in today. And I don't know anything about this. Maybe you can come back tomorrow; he should be here then."

"Could you register Gina so she can begin classes? I rarely leave work, and so I wouldn't be able to accompany her tomorrow."

She looked at Gina, and said, "I don't have that power. You have to come back tomorrow. But I must warn you. There's no way your daughter will be allowed to attend this school."

"She suffers from *cerebral palsy*," I protested, "but she's highly intelligent. I submitted her stellar academic records from elementary school to Principal Guan. The files must be here."

"From where I'm standing," Vice Principal Wang said, "she's no different from any other mentally retarded imbecile. Come back tomorrow and ask Principal Guan." She then went to an inner room, presumably her office, and locked the door behind her.

I was infuriated by her choice of words but managed to hold back my anger. I calmly walked out and took Gina home. "Mommy will go with you tomorrow, and we'll get this sorted out."

Gina did not reply, but I knew she was disappointed. The next day, I was more prepared, as I had thought all night about what to say. Off we went, and the gateman greeted us, "Ah, you're back."

I smiled and nodded at him. We marched straight up the stairs to the principal's office, and there was Principal Guan standing and chatting away with Vice Principal Wang. He didn't say a word or smile, but he did nod his head to acknowledge us and told us to follow him. We entered an inner room, and Vice Principal Wang came in too.

"Dr. Pei, to save us all valuable time, I'll be straightforward. There's no way we can accept a child like that. We don't know if it's deaf, dumb, or blind, and don't care to hear the details. You can say whatever you want, but my answer is no. There is no way this child will be able to make it here."

"Why? She completed elementary school with flying colors. And her grandmother, who is a retired high school teacher, homeschooled her this past year. I believe she has eighth-grade standing. She may be disabled, but she is very intelligent. Ask her any questions you wish! Ask her math, chemistry, or Chinese history." Gina was getting visibly angry and anxious, and the more anxious she became, the more she displayed uncontrollable facial and bodily expressions.

Principal Guan said, "Dr. Pei, I can appreciate a mother's love for her child, but take a realistic look at your daughter's situation. Please be objective. You're a doctor!" Then he turned to Vice Principal Wang and asked, "Do you agree with me?" adding, "We're running a school here, not a circus."

By now I was boiling over, and I stood up and banged on his desk. "You're an educator, and this is the way you treat a child? You call her 'it' and think I should send her to a circus!"

Vice Principal Wang stood up and said, "Please don't be angry, Dr. Pei. We are just trying to state the obvious. She may be a fine girl, but she's not going to make it in high school. She looks pathetic. The best thing would be for her to stay at home, have enough food and water, and have a good life." I felt like slapping her, but Gina had become so angry and rocked her chair so hard she fell to the ground. I reached over to pull her up and gave them both a death stare before slamming the door behind me. As Gina and I went down the steps, hordes of kids were racing by, some stopping to stare at her. Rage and a profound sadness radiated from Gina's eyes.

We went home in silence. Then, just as I was getting ready to leave for work, Gina spoke up: "Mommy, I hate you! And I hate this world! Why did you let me live? You should have let me die when you had the chance? I don't want to go to school anymore, so you can stop worrying about me." I looked at her with tears swirling in my eyes. I tried to say something to comfort her, argue, or plead for myself, but nothing came out. She turned away and didn't say another word for the next two weeks.

When Paul came home after the harvest season, he was equally angry at the school officials, and also at me for my inability to convey Gina's gifts to them and argue her case. "In moments like this," he sighed, "I wish you were a real Chinese and not an American."

I conceded I could have done better, but I wasn't happy that he didn't give me a shred of credit. I shouted back and said, "Okay, Professor Hsiung. If you think you can think faster on your feet and are more skilled at making sound arguments, you try!"

A few days later, the three of us headed back to the school. The gateman shouted, "You're back with your old man, eh?" I just glared at him.

Paul advised me, "He's not our problem. Save your energy."

This time, only Principal Guan was around. With Paul there, the bastard was much more polite.

"Principal Guan, please accept my apologies for my wife's behavior last time. She is not very skilled at speaking, and she didn't mean any harm." I thought, "Okay, Genius, let's see if you can do better."

"That's okay," Principal Guan said. "Who doesn't appreciate a mother's heart?" He was being much more diplomatic this time. Paul took out two brand-new packs of cigarettes and gave them to him.

Principal Guan pulled out a cigarette, lit it, and took a puff. "All differences aside," he said, "my position hasn't changed. Your daughter is unfit for our school. She's not going to make it, so that's that."

"But how do you know that without testing her? To be in your esteemed position, you are obviously a highly accomplished educator, so you would at least test her intelligence before reaching such a conclusion," Paul said.

I was impressed he could stay so calm. His voice didn't have a trace of anger.

Principal Guan leaned forward, rested his elbows on his desk, and said, "Thank you for saying that. I presume you're also in education." Paul grinned and nodded his head humbly. "And what would you suggest I ask her in a test?" he asked.

"Whatever you'd ask any seventh-grader. Or you could ask her to write something. That would test her intelligence," Paul replied.

Principal Guan was becoming engaged. "Okay, let's. Well, Gina, is your name Gina?" Gina smiled and nodded her head.

"Can you say your name?"

Gina proudly shouted out her name. Principal Guan couldn't quite make out the sound and looked at Paul with a frown.

"Gina, say it slowly and clearly," I nudged her, even though we were still not on speaking terms.

Gina waved me off and proceeded to pronounce her name clearly.

"Okay, Gina. Can you write it for me?" Principal Guan asked and handed her a pen.

Gina grabbed the pen from his hand while accidentally cutting his finger with her nails, and then struggled mightily to hold onto it before starting to scribble away.

"Stop," Principal Guan raised his voice. "This proves that she won't succeed. It's well over thirty seconds and she hasn't even finished a single character of her name. How do you expect her to be sitting in a classroom, taking notes, doing her homework, and taking exams? It can't possibly work." He threw up his hands and, after another inhale of his cigarette, looked at the blood on his finger.

"Please, wait, Principal Guan. She's disabled and has difficulty holding onto a pen. But she can do it once she has gripped it," Paul pleaded. "Let's be fair and give her a chance to finish what you asked her to do."

Principal Guan looked at the two packs of cigarettes Paul had just given him and said, "Okay, go ahead, finish writing your name, Gina."

Gina finally completed writing her name and proudly but respectfully handed it to Principal Guan. The headmaster examined Gina's writing of "My name is Gina Hsiung." He then pointed out that Gina's strokes were so heavy that the pen had pierced the paper and some of the words were missing. "This is not going to work," he said. "*You* know it, *I* know it, and all the gods, nymphs, and devils know it. What do you want me to do?"

"Why not? She understood and completed a task given by an esteemed educator — however trivial the task might be," Paul said.

"Okay, I've got to attend a meeting. Let me think about it." He seemed pushed to his limit.

"Thank you. We've taken up enough of your time, Principal Guan. We will wait patiently for your decision." And we left.

After a week with no news, Paul and Chang *Lao-Shih* took Gina back to the school, as I had to work. Paul thought Chang *Lao-Shih* might be persuasive and could attest to Gina's abilities. When I got home late that evening, Chang *Lao-Shih* was in our room working with Gina, while Paul was in the kitchen cooking for us all. They had made a little progress. Principal Guan agreed to a series of qualifying exams, and Gina would be able to take as much time as she needed.

By now, a month had gone by, and even if Gina were allowed to enroll, she'd be far behind her classmates. "Dr. Pei, have some faith," Chang *Lao-Shih* said. "Your daughter is extremely smart. I like your son a lot, and someday he will be a perfect son-in-law for me or any other mother. And he's a handsome boy, like an 'Albanian' kid. But, intellectually, he's no Gina. She is ten times smarter and will be a gem for any teacher who gets to teach her. She will pass these exams and have no problems catching up, once she's allowed to enroll. Trust me. I was her

SPRING FLOWER: TORN BETWEEN SHIFTING WORLDS

homeroom teacher for five years!" I nodded my head and didn't know whether to laugh or cry.

It was October 1, 1973. With red flags flying on every corner and the awful scent of fresh glue and black ink permeating the air from every newly pasted wall poster (大字報), the country was celebrating its twenty-fourth National Day. Shouts of worn-out slogans and screams of love for the greatest leader on earth were peppered through bullhorns on moving vehicles, coming from all directions at all hours. As always, the *Little Red Book* was read aloud, followed by the pumping of fists in the air at each key juncture of the book by devotees standing in the back of the vehicles. During the week of National Day, no one worked. Even the hospital asked us to take time off, with only a few of us on call.

So, there we were—cooped up in our tiny apartment, bored out of our minds. We didn't dare go anywhere, fearing the crowds and the chaos. So I leaned out the window, as our room began to feel very small, and saw a parade marching behind the slow-moving vehicles, winding their way through the streets. Suddenly, members of the marching band broke into joyful and intricately coordinated dances, spiraling a long red ribbon in each hand, trumpets blaring and snare drums rolling loudly. They must have practiced for hours and hours, and the more I stared at them, the more pleasing it actually became. It was like the summer of 1966, except there were only a few curious or bored onlookers; no one else cared. I could even hear my neighbors closing their windows.

I realized one of us had always been missing, for one reason or another, all these years. Now we were all in one place and crammed into this tiny room for the first time after a very long haul. Perhaps I, too, should break out in dance or join those wreaking havoc below us to express my thanks that we were all together at last.

"What are you staring at, Jeanie? Get away from the window before we get in trouble again," Paul growled.

"I'm watching the celebration, Paul. We aren't burning anything!" and I stuck my tongue out at him. Paul sighed, Gina laughed, and Eddy inquired, "What were we burning, Mommy?"

"You were too small to remember, Eddy," Gina answered on my behalf.

"You mean the time all those people in green uniforms were trashing our room?" Eddy replied.

"How did you know?" I asked. "You weren't even two."

"Please lower your voice, and let's change the subject," Paul growled again and then changed the subject: "Schools will reopen next week, and we'll get Gina's test results. What strategies do you recommend, Dr. Pei?"

"Strategies?" I asked. "Gina will do so well, as Chang *Lao-Shih* predicted, that they'll simply have to let her in."

"Please, Dr. Pei, I'm serious," Paul said.

"I am too, Professor Hsiung. What strategies do we need?"

Gina shook her head and said, "Mommy, you're so naive." Paul nodded in agreement and asked Eddy to go down the street to get soy sauce so he could make lunch.

A week later, Chang *Lao-Shih*, Paul, Gina, and I went together to Principal Guan's office. To make sure he would feel pressure coming from all directions and make the right decision (Chinese idiom: 四面楚歌), we brought two bags of sugar plus a pound of meat we'd traded for on the black market. As in betting, we put all our chips on the table. Vice Principal Wang was in the room too.

As we'd hoped and anticipated, Gina passed the exams with flying colors and had an eighth grade standing. While kudos were due to our very smart daughter, her grandmother, aunt,

SPRING FLOWER: TORN BETWEEN SHIFTING WORLDS

uncle, and Chang *Lao-Shih* all deserved credit too.

"I know you are all happy with her exam results, and you deserve to be," Principal Guan said. "You should be proud of her. I concede that she is very smart, and please accept my sincere apologies for some of the comments I made earlier. Nevertheless, my position remains the same. She cannot enroll here."

Chang *Lao-Shih* and Paul responded in unison, "Sir, why not?"

"If we could give her ten times longer than the other kids to complete class assignments, take notes, do homework, and complete exams, she could do very well. That's clear. But she won't be able to keep up with the other students at normal speed. And she writes so big and clumsily that the paper is torn to shreds before she's done writing, and the space provided for answers is never enough. Practical details are important."

After a brief silence, Paul spoke up. "These important details are all critical, and there are other challenges you haven't mentioned. Still, I believe an intelligent child like Gina deserves an education, regardless of her physical challenges. Since you are an esteemed educator, won't you at least agree with me about this on principle?"

After another brief pause, Principal Guan lit up a cigarette and said, "No, Professor Hsiung. Actually, I disagree. Not all children are born equal. I don't expect every child to become a math genius or a long-distance runner. A school like ours is not set up to educate your daughter, and your daughter is not fit for this school."

"I appreciate your perspective, but I think you could not be more wrong, Principal Guan," Paul began his rebuttal. "You accept all these kids into your school because you don't know who among them will develop into a long-distance runner, a great singer, or a math genius. You accept them all, because it gives them an equal opportunity to develop into what they eventually may excel at. You know my daughter is intellectually sound and equally deserving of this opportunity so that she too can discover what she may be good at. As an educator, you're depriving her of this invaluable opportunity because you're prejudging that she will become good at nothing." Principal Guan listened respectfully, and Paul continued, "If we disagree on fundamental values underlying education, where do you think we should send our daughter? Is there a school that would be suitable for children like her? If there is, we'll leave immediately. And if there isn't, we will stay here until you change your mind, because it would be your mandated responsibility to accept her and educate her."

Principal Guan sat in silence for perhaps a minute, then said, "Don't threaten me by saying you'll sit in my office day in and day out, because that would be interfering with our work, and I'll call the police. However, I will give your daughter one last chance. I will ask two of my best teachers if they will agree to take her on as homeroom teachers."

"Thank you. Please do," I finally spoke up, but it was more like letting out a muffled scream.

Principal Guan looked at me and said, "Okay, but I want *both of them* to agree, not just one."

Vice Principal Wang went outside and called in the two teachers: One was a math teacher, Ma *Lao-Shih* (馬老師: Teacher Ma). He had a cigarette dangling from his mouth and a stained tea mug in his right hand. Ma *Lao-Shih* pulled up a chair, squeezed in between Paul and me, and had his cigarette pointing directly at my face. I began to choke a bit. The other was a Chinese language teacher, Yuan *Lao-Shih* (袁老師), the tall, striking woman we'd met a month earlier when Gina and I first came looking for Principal Guan. Yuan *Lao-Shih* sat next to Chang *Lao-Shih*.

SPRING FLOWER: TORN BETWEEN SHIFTING WORLDS

Ma *Lao-Shih* invited Yuan *Lao-Shih* to speak first. "My answer," she said, "is no. I cannot assume such a huge responsibility, and I'm unqualified medically."

"Medically?" Paul asked her to clarify.

Principal Guan interrupted before she could reply and asked Teacher Ma what he thought. After Yuan *Lao-Shih*'s response, I had already lost hope, and I didn't want to sit there listening to this walking ashtray yap away. I moved my chair a few inches toward Gina and leaned my head away from his smoke. Perhaps sensing my disgust, Ma *Lao-Shih* quickly put out his cigarette in his teacup and began to talk.

I tried to tune out, but he got my attention when he said, "This girl is a math whiz! Look at her scores in the math exam. She could enter my eighth-grade geometry class today and do better than most of the kids I've taught in my entire career. Yes, it'd be impressive if kids could answer multiplication or division problems (加减乘除) within milliseconds, but math is a cerebral discipline that involves time-consuming problem solving based on logic, and the harder or more advanced the problem, the more time is needed. Gina is perfectly suited for that. Why don't we try before reaching any conclusions?" I tried to smile at Ma *Lao-Shih* and give him an appreciative nod, but his smoke-stained breath came straight at me, enough to make me choke.

"Still, I cannot," Yuan *Lao-Shih* said. "I met this kid two months ago, and I still can't shake her image from my mind, awake or asleep. I know life can be cruel, and this is cruel. But I honestly can't say if this is even a human being." My anger level shot up, and I was about to give her my "two cents" when Principal Guan interjected, "That's another matter, Yuan *Lao-Shih*. In any event, I told Professor Hsiung and Dr. Pei that I need you both to agree to take her on."

"Why two?" I practically screamed. "Ma *Lao-Shih* agreed to

take her!"

"Dr. Pei, your daughter will be a huge responsibility. Two homeroom teachers may not be enough," Principal Guan replied, practically growling at this point. He stood up and said, "Thank you. That's all I need, Yuan *Lao-Shih* and Ma *Lao-Shih*. Professor Hsiung and Dr. Pei, I believe the issue has been resolved most reasonably."

"We have bothered you enough today," Paul replied. "But the issue has *not* been resolved. We'll be back tomorrow." I was so angry I nearly kicked the gateman when he cordially said, "Come again," as we walked away.

Chang *Lao-Shih* hopped on her bike and said, "Don't worry, Dr. Pei. We'll keep fighting. When there's a will, then there's a way (堅持到底就是勝利)."

"Yes, you're right. And thank you so much for your help. We are eternally indebted to you, Chang *Lao-Shih*," Paul said.

I was so busy being angry I didn't even think of thanking her for her time and help. It seems my emotions had just two settings — happiness and anguish — with nothing between. Well, maybe sadness too. On the way home, neither Paul nor I said a word. I knew he was at his wit's end too.

"Papa and Mommy, can I go back to Shanghai now?" Gina asked while sitting on the back of Paul's bike.

"No, because we're going back tomorrow," Paul answered in a stern voice.

"Please, Paul, let's not get in trouble again. Principal Guan has made it clear he might call the police." After so many years apart from Paul, I didn't want more trouble.

"For what crime, pleading with a school principal to accept our intelligent daughter to a junior high?" Paul was visibly angry. "And what if he calls the police? Another four years in a labor camp? Thanks to those years, I'm now tough as nails.

SPRING FLOWER: TORN BETWEEN SHIFTING WORLDS

I really don't care!"

"Please lower your voice, Paul. We're on a city street in broad daylight."

"I'm not afraid, Jeanie," Paul said, his voice getting louder.

"Can we go home first?" I pleaded, seeing a few people staring at us and others glaring at Gina.

The next day, Eddy and I headed to the clinic and Paul began a new routine. He put Gina on the back of his bike and pedaled to Public High School No. 8. At night when we'd see each other, Paul would shake his head and say, "Not today." A few days later, he added, "The police showed up today, but they left, saying there was no crime as long as I stayed out of their way. The school is owned by the State, not Principal Guan."

On hearing that, I sighed deeply and said, "Maybe this is enough, Paul. We've made our point. Let's quit while we're still ahead and figure out other solutions."

And each time he'd say no, and the next day he would put Gina on his bike and off they'd go to Public High School No. 8. One night when I came home really late, Paul was still waiting for me. He looked up and grinned and said, "Still no, but we'll go back tomorrow." I went over and sat next to him, put my head on his shoulder, and held him tightly in my arms.

"When the police came to Principal Guan's office today, the gateman was with them, and he said we could sit in his hut by the gate to protest. I need to get some cigarettes for him! How many meat stamps do we have left? Even on the black market, good cigarettes require meat *and* clothing stamps now."

"The police came again?" I asked, more concerned about the police than the gateman.

"Yes, but they left with the same answer, even though Guan tried to fabricate some kind of schoolyard violation."

"I'm coming with you tomorrow, Paul. I don't feel it's safe for you and Gina."

"Right. I'll feel safer with an *American* sitting next to me," he said, smiling and stroking my hair.

"Laugh all you want, but you can't keep doing this."

"Jeanie Perkins, I'll do it until they admit that Gina deserves an education." Paul was determined. I foresaw a disaster.

Three weeks went by. I managed to go with them a few times, and Chang *Lao-Shih* came on a few occasions too. One day, Ma *Lao-Shih* even joined us for a while in Principal Guan's office. On the days I was there, Principal Guan was polite to us. I could even feel a sense of admiration from him for our determination. But he didn't budge, and we simply sat and stared at his bookshelves. I memorized the titles of his books; of course, they were all about Mao and his revolution. We watched students and teachers come in and out, some with aluminum lunch boxes. Some would smile and nod their heads at us, as we became fixtures in Principal Guan's office, as if we worked there. One time, the gateman came up with a box of hot soup to thank Paul for the cigarettes and liquor. Later, he began coming up more often, saying that his "Old Lady" — his wife — had made some red bean paste-filled buns for us.

Days became weeks, and weeks became months, and I'd completely lost hope. On the days I sat there, I wondered what it might be like in America for physically challenged kids, whether they would receive an education. Day-Day and Mother had opened a school for disabled children in Kiukiang decades earlier. I began to contemplate sending Gina back to Shanghai to study with Eve. Then one evening when I arrived home, Paul looked at me with his thumbs up. Before I could say a word, Gina raced over and grabbed my legs and said, "Mommy, your little Gina is going to school next week!"

"What! How?" Tears of joy began to pour out of my eyes.

SPRING FLOWER: TORN BETWEEN SHIFTING WORLDS

"I honestly don't know," Paul admitted, "except today Principal Guan stood up and said, 'Mr. Hsiung, you win! Let's give it a try and see if it can work. Let me check with Yuan *Lao-Shih* to see if she will change her mind.' And moments later, he came back with both Ma *Lao-Shih* and Yuan *Lao-Shih*. Yuan *Lao-Shih* shook my hand and took hold of Gina's hands and said to Gina, 'Welcome to my seventh-grade homeroom. I'll be your Chinese-language teacher, and Ma *Lao-Shih* will be your math teacher and academic advisor.' Just like that, they registered Gina — and she starts on Monday!"

I was speechless.

"Dr. Pei, hello? Is anyone there?" Paul began snapping his fingers.

"This is unbelievable. Please pinch me — it must be a dream." Gina took me literally and dug her fingers deep into my thigh. "Ouch!" I shrieked. "Are you serious? Why the sudden change of heart?"

"I don't know, Dr. Pei, but I leave you with an important task. On Monday, please take Gina to her first day of junior high. I need to get back to my all-too-important library with all those books waiting to be reshelved."

"Yippee!" Gina shouted.

Monday couldn't have come faster. Nearly eighty-five days after Gina and I first went to Public School No. 8, we were once again marching toward the front entrance. When we got there, to my surprise, the gateman offered to keep an eye on my bike. "You and your daughter just go straight ahead," he said. "They are all waiting for you inside."

I thanked him and placed Gina's faded green bag over her shoulder. I was so proud. Her homeroom was on the third floor, and to my great shock as we entered the building, the stairway was lined with students attired in their fall-winter coats. Principal

JEAN TREN-HWA PERKINS

Guan was at the second-floor landing.

As soon as he saw us, he invited us to Public High School No. 8 warmly and announced so all could hear, "These students are all here to welcome Gina, their newest classmate!" I was, to say the least, dumbfounded, and my heart began to race. Gina, as nervous as ever, began to jerk around so much that we both nearly tumbled down the stairs. Luckily, I grabbed the railing and prevented a free fall. As we walked slowly up the remaining steps, Principal Guan told the assembled students, "From this day on until you graduate or whenever you end up leaving this building, you will have a very special classmate. Her name is Gina. I want you all to know that although she is physically disabled, her heart is not. And most important, her mind is as bright as any of yours, if not brighter. Treat her with the utmost respect, as you would respect your sisters. Help her whenever help is needed. You are never, I mean *never*, to make fun of her, ridicule her, stare at her, or demean her. If you do, you will be expelled from school. Do you hear me?"

"Yes, Principal Guan," the students replied in unison.

"Thank you. Now please welcome Gina to your class." And as he said that, a round of applause broke out. By the time we reached the third floor, Yuan *Lao-Shih* was standing there. She smiled as she took Gina's hands from mine. I was still not a fan of Yuan *Lao-Shih*'s for what she had said, but I tried my best to smile—taking a page from Paul's playbook. But seeing her genuine smile, I couldn't hold back my appreciation, and I said, "Thank you all so much for accepting Gina and giving her this valuable opportunity in life."

"Don't worry, Dr. Pei. We'll take good care of her! She will be in great hands here," Ma *Lao-Shih* chimed in as he sipped tea from his mug with a slurping sound.

"Yes, Dr. Pei, we can take it from here. We have everything

arranged for Gina. I know you need to go to work now," Principal Guan said.

"Thank you so much for everything, Principal Guan," I told him, and then I heard, "*Hsiao* Xing and *Hsiao* Yin, where are you?"

Two young girls stepped up and said, "Here, Principal Guan!"

"You are now officially assigned as Gina's guardians."

"And where are *Hsiao* Yue and *Hsiao* Mei?" Two more young girls stepped up and asserted, "Yes, Principal Guan?" Guan pointed to them and said, "We met with the class last Friday, and during our meeting, we selected some of the most responsible kids in Gina's class. *Hsiao* Yue and *Hsiao* Mei live near you, and from here on, they'll escort Gina to and from school."

I was speechless. Just like that, Gina was in junior high and an instant celebrity in the process. With so many people to be thankful for, regardless of their initial attitudes, I didn't know where to begin. To this day, I have no idea what changed their minds. Was Peng *Shu-Chi* alerted because Paul was on the police registry, as a kind of parole, and did she get involved? Whether it was Paul's persistence alone or if we had invisible assistance, what he and Chang *Lao-Shih* did was a rare display of the human spirit that seemed almost Gandhian. It was hard for me to let into my head the notion that kind souls like Principal Guan, Yuan *Lao-Shih*, Ma *Lao-Shih,* and the gateman even existed.

Outside of being a chain smoker, Ma *Lao-Shih* was a great man and was a great teacher for Gina all her years at Public School No. 8. and for Eddy too, who later attended the same school for his junior high. Yuan *Lao-Shih* became instrumental in Gina's junior high education; she made countless trips to our tiny apartment to tutor Gina, helping her make up for lost time. She was such a good teacher, and Gina loved her dearly. To our great sadness, Yuan *Lao-Shih* died at a young age. Within two

JEAN TREN-HWA PERKINS

years of Gina's admission, she began to suffer from a rare form of rheumatoid arthritis, and soon after that, she was diagnosed with amyotrophic lateral sclerosis (ALS), a degenerative neurological disease known in the West as "Lou Gehrig's disease." It was a sad moment when I visited her for the last time at our hospital. As I held both her hands, she told me, "It's amazing how much inspiration I received from your little girl. Her will to go to school is what kept me fighting."

80

DURING THE EARLY winter months of 1974, the Year of the Tiger, Gina performed exceptionally well in school. Then she contracted pneumonia, and not long after that, Paul got pneumonia, too. Penicillin saved both their lives, but since antibiotics were in short supply, it was administered late and their coughing persisted for months. Amid the chaos, Eddy sustained a second-degree burn on his leg.

By then, we were taking weekly hot baths, which was great for the pneumonia patients. One day, I gave Eddy nine pennies to go down the street to buy hot water, including a penny as a tip. I had seen him carry four one-gallon thermoses at a time, so I thought it'd be safe. But when he got home, he feared four gallons wouldn't be enough, so he decided to boil some more water. Our metal kettle was heavy and our makeshift stove rather high off the ground, and the boiling water spilled, scalding Eddy's thigh. Qiu-Shuang's eldest son, He-Ying (河英), took him to the emergency room.

That year, China sank even further into recession. I remember the aunties telling me about the Great Depression in the 1930s. They lived on a farm in Michigan and unemployed city folks down on their luck would come up their dirt road daily looking for a day's work in exchange for food. In China, it was the opposite. The poor farmers would come hundreds of miles to the city looking to work for food. They had been devastated by the Revolution. I remembered some farmers telling us during our

JEAN TREN-HWA PERKINS

Rustication–Reeducation, "If we had a bowl of rice, an egg, a fish, or an ear of corn for every slogan we shouted, we wouldn't be poor." It reminded me of Jesus feeding the multitudes.

By the 1970s, China was barely able to maintain a veneer of normalcy. So Peking, Shanghai, and Tientsin were designated by the government as places no one would be allowed to starve to death. Hangchow was less significant, so all the crops and resources were shipped to Peking, Shanghai, and Tientsin, leaving little for the rest of us, including the farmers—the very people Mao's armies fought to their last drop of blood to save. Now they were starving to death for the second time in as many decades! I was never a fan of President Chiang Kai-Shek (蔣介石總統) and his corrupt Republic Nationalist KMT Party (*Kuo-Min-Tang*: 國民黨) regime, but I wondered what would have happened if....

Farmers who needed medical attention would travel hundreds of miles to ours and other hospitals with no money, so they brought what little food they had as payment. It was unworkable; hospitals needed currency, not food, to stay open, and they needed both food *and* healthcare. Nevertheless, the farmers' food was accepted as payment, yet we had no idea where it all went—certainly not to the cafeteria, where the menu remained the same: rice with lettuce or cabbage sprinkled with shreds of meat or egg and tons of salt. And that was on days we were lucky. Sometimes the rice would be floating in water (泡飯) to serve more of us with less grain; sometimes it would just be porridge (稀飯). And over time, with inflation, each meal require more food stamps than the last.

After a while, we hospital workers were given access to some of the food the farmers brought, as long as we reported it to leadership. One day, I was permitted to bring home a big bag of mung beans. I was appreciative; we'd had nothing decent to eat

SPRING FLOWER: TORN BETWEEN SHIFTING WORLDS

for weeks. And I had learned the health benefits of these beans from Paul. He knew how to mash them into a sweet paste to fill buns and dumplings, but this was the middle of the harvest season and Paul was away.

So I boiled the whole bag and dumped what seemed a month's supply of brown sugar in to sweeten them. (Our sugar stamps were good only for crude brown sugar, which came mixed with sand and tiny stones. White sugar had become white gold.) I'd seen Paul mash mung beans to make *Hei-Tou-Sha* (黑豆沙), meaning red bean paste, and I knew it took a lot of effort, straining it all with a porous cloth. But really, I had no idea what I was doing. I got impatient, especially with hungry Eddy standing next to me.

So we sat on the cool, clean, waxed cement floor, and joyfully ate the boiled beans as if there were no tomorrow. I thought Paul would be so proud of me for cooking! And the more we ate, the less there was left in the big pot, so I told the kids, "Maybe we should save some for Papa." The kids, still hungry, looked at each other, and so I said, "Well, we have no idea when Papa will be home, so let's finish it and not let any go to waste."

After another big bowl of boiled mung beans, Eddy said, "I can't eat another bite, Mommy. I'm really full," and Gina said more or less the same thing. I wasn't pleased, I didn't want it to go to waste, so I said, "Let's finish all this good food." So, the joyful event became a chore, and the more we ate, the harder it was to finish it all.

"Mommy, I really can't eat any more," Gina protested again. I paid no attention to her and nudged Eddy instead, urging "Just a little more.... Be a good boy and help Mommy." Finally, Gina said emphatically, "No more, Mommy! Are you trying to kill us?"

"What?" I asked, unable to let in her words. "We are fortunate to have this nutritious food. Don't be so ungrateful, Gina!" She wouldn't budge, so I had to lean on my good boy instead. He had been famished for days. Finally, we licked the last beans from the pot. I felt great. "See, kids, we did it. We had a great meal, no?"

The kids were quiet, and I stood up to clean up. Moments later, Gina let out a bombastic fart, and they both laughed hysterically. In no time at all we were all passing wind like it was a hurricane with thunder and lightning, and we laughed and farted hysterically for more than an hour. Then Eddy stood up and said, "Mommy, my stomach hurts," and Gina said hers did too. She immediately had diarrhea, and Eddy began rolling on the floor, wailing. He was bloated like a balloon. I rubbed his belly to release some of the pressure, but the reprieve was temporary. His stomach kept expanding, and he was in a lot of pain.

Our neighbors next door were out, so I asked their youngest daughter to stay with Gina, while I carried Eddy down the steps and propped him onto my bike. I pedaled as fast as I could, and he screamed at the top of his lungs most of the way to the emergency room. Once there, the internist on call understood what was going on. He didn't even look at me or say a word but rushed Eddy into the critical care room and closed the door behind him. Eddy was suffering from acute abdominal distension (expansion of the stomach, 胃擴張), which could have been life-threatening if I had waited any longer. They tried everything they could to release the immense pressure Eddy was experiencing. They pumped his stomach, induced vomiting, and repeatedly administered enemas. Later, they told me they were very close to opening him up.

I called Paul as I waited outside helplessly. I hadn't known that beans and legumes induce gas. I was older and my body could handle them better, and Gina had wisely stopped eating. Paul came rushing into Eddy's hospital room and lashed out at me right in front of everyone. I knew I deserved it, and I didn't say a word. I just felt like the worst mother in the world. I'd almost killed my dearest Sonny Boy! It was well past midnight when Eddy was finally stabilized, and when we walked into his room, he looked completely worn out. I stayed by his bedside for the rest of the night, and when he woke up, he said, "Mommy, I don't want to see another mung bean the rest of my life. Would that be okay?"

Not long after, the country's food and cotton inventories were becoming depleted, and we had shortages of medications, medical supplies, and other manufactured goods — while factory workers focused on Mao's *Little Red Book* and hailing the Great Revolution. The solution that our great *Workers' Declaration Team*, or WDT (工宣隊), had for this was to create more slogans and to require patients to endure pain without anesthetics.

"The country has gone mad," Jade stood up and shouted at the members of the WDT at yet another staff meeting. "Do you have any idea how elaborate the system of nerves around the human eye is? Pull out one hair of an eyebrow and see how much it hurts?"

This time it was me who gripped her hand, trying to pull her down to her seat. I was as angry as she was, listening to these numbskulls announce through a bullhorn the new surgical practices we were to follow, all done without anesthetics. The WDT had become the most powerful entity in the hospital, although none of them had a clue what we did.

A male WDT member shouted back at all of us, "What do you know of pain, you spoiled capitalistic pigs and sissy sons and daughters of bourgeois fat cats! Where were *you* during the Long March (萬里長征)? Did you fight the Republic Nationalists in their American tanks? Have you charged your enemy while bullets were raining down upon you?"

"Of course not!" someone in the back shouted. "But at least you had access to morphine on the battlefield! You don't remember? I guess it was your fathers, since you aren't old enough to have been on *any* marches, let alone the Long March!"

A female WDT member took the bullhorn from her comrade and shouted, "Shut up right now or we'll detain you! We all have to make sacrifices. We were not afraid of pain in the war zones, and neither should anyone be in today's Great Communist Society under our beloved Chairman Mao's leadership. I will now read a passage from Chairman Mao's *Little Red Book*."

But before she could open the *Little Red Book* to her bookmarked page, another voice shouted from the crowd, "I thought all those great efforts were to prevent poverty, not to live like shit!" That was brave, I thought.

"Someone doesn't want to live anymore," whispered a resident from the Ear Nose and Throat (ENT) Division sitting near me.

Another male WDT member stood up and shouted, "That statement is anti-revolutionary and not allowed. I know who you are, and you won't be going home tonight. Those soldiers who fought so bravely to secure a new world were not afraid to die, and they were certainly not afraid of a little pain. Now, raise your right hands and repeat after me: 'Long Live Chairman Mao! Long Live the Proletariat Class!'"

Amidst the bedlam, Li *Shu-Chi* gestured that Jade and I should see her after the meeting. As the raucous meeting mercifully adjourned, a WDT member told us they would make impromptu checks at operating facilities. At this point, we weren't shocked or even angry, just concerned about our patients. With no anesthetics, how would we operate, amputate, or cut open

SPRING FLOWER: TORN BETWEEN SHIFTING WORLDS

a human body or an eye? How could the hospital continue to function?

We spent the entire afternoon in Li *Shu-Chi*'s office, agonizing over how to respond to these policies. Finally, we agreed to continue using anesthetics whenever needed and to have someone on the operating team on the lookout. They would cough when they spotted a member of the *Workers' Declaration Team* coming around, and we'd put away syringes and needles, and shuffle back into their boxes our ampules of anesthetics like Benzocaine, procaine (brand name Novocain), Lidocaine, and cocaine (which was still being used as an anesthetic in China in the 1970s). For general anesthesia, it would be more complicated. We'd have to shut off regulators on the nitrous oxide lecture bottle and stow away haloforms, ether reagent bottles, and some barbiturate solutions used at the time for general anesthesia. Another member of the surgery team was assigned to stall the WDT members, but we knew they'd probably barge in and that we'd have a minute or less to accomplish all of this.

I believe we weren't the only division doing this. Once they entered our room, we would pretend to be going about our business, and we even asked patients to pretend they were in pain. Words and slogans would then come out of the mouths of these WDT members to encourage the patients to "be brave" and "think about the Long March" (萬里長征) and the soldiers who sacrificed for us during the Yangtze River Crossing.... Some would hold the hands of patients as if they were on the battlefield comforting the wounded. And some WDT members even jumped onto patients' beds and lay next to them for some time while we carried out business as usual.

Not all patients were lucky enough to have already received the needed anesthetics, so we found ways to suddenly cancel a procedure due to "an unforeseen complication" or some other excuse. One time, to our collective surprise—the lookout had dozed off—WDT members walked in suddenly before we could stash the evidence. Nurse *Hsiao* Hu (小胡), ever alert, screamed and pointed to the wall near the door. When everyone turned in that direction, she squirted and splashed a vial of Novocain out of her syringe into the patient's left eye, then stuck the empty vial in her pocket. That was quick thinking, I thought. While it was most effective when injected locally, it could also work as a topical agent.

As a consequence of all this insanity, safety was compromised and patients suffered. We had to delay or cancel procedures when we couldn't proceed safely without anesthetics. Even the surgeries we were able to perform took longer than usual with these people interrupting us, and became progressively more dangerous to the patients. Our hours and days grew longer, and the backlog of operations mounted. Between the day clinic and our afternoon-and-evening surgeries, we were becoming exhausted. We were able to do more at night, as that was the time the WDT members were having dinner at home with their families.

At the same time, Paul was becoming increasingly depressed and disillusioned. "What's the use of being out of prison if you can't use your skills to contribute?" he complained, and he began to drink more and lash out at me. At first, I tried not to respond, thinking about how difficult life must be for him. Our room was small and there was no place to turn or hide, so I absorbed his anger.

Then, he began coming home less, even after the harvest season, complaining about the distance. I thought that might be a better option, since too many times he had biked home to our compound while dangerously drunk. I began to rely on Qiu-Shuang to help with the kids again.

I continued to be, arguably, the worst mother in the world. One day in early December 1974, I came home around 9 p.m. and found Gina's teacher Yuan *Lao-Shih* tutoring her (this was before Yuan *Lao-Shih* became gravely ill). We chatted a bit, and before she left, she said, "Maybe this isn't a good time, but there's something I want you to know."

"Yes?" I asked, as we stepped out onto the landing.

"Everything is going well at school, except…" Yuan *Lao-Shih*'s voice trailed off.

"Except what?" I asked.

"All the students have been very kind to Gina, and Gina seems to have become queen of the class. She has started to pick and choose who will receive the honor of helping her. To me, that isn't good behavior. I'm sorry to tell you this, Dr. Pei."

"*She did what?*" I asked, raising my voice.

"Gina is a really good kid and very smart. Please just help her understand the impact of her actions." Yuan *Lao-Shih* put her hand on my arm and smiled before heading down the stairs.

I stormed back into the room, looked straight at Gina, and said, "You probably heard it all. *Did you do that?* You should be grateful when anyone offers you a helping hand. You should be deeply indebted to each of them for their kindness. How could this be the other way around?" By now I was screaming, and Eddy brought me a glass of hot water and the wooden stool he'd been using as a desk. "Mommy, please have some warm water and take a rest."

"I don't need a rest, Eddy. Go about your business, I'm talking to your sister, and this is a serious matter."

"Yeah, I did that," Gina said. "So what? What are you going to do about it? You're a terrible mother, anyway! You have no idea how to take care of us!" I'd met my match.

"Okay, I'm not the best mother. But who brought you up so

you can read, write, and walk, and speak? Did I teach you to behave like you're the queen of the land? How dare you talk to me this way, you ungrateful brat! Turn around and pull your pants down this second, and I'll teach you how *not* to be a queen." I was screaming even louder.

"I am not afraid of you. Go ahead and spank me! But I just want to tell you that you're unfair as a mother, and I hate you. You never, ever spanked or scolded Eddy. Why? Is he such an angel?"

I was taken aback by her comments. "Of course, he's not an angel. But who fought to protect you when you went to elementary school together? Who risked his life for you? I don't recognize you anymore. You can't possibly be the sweet and understanding girl I brought up. When did you become so ungrateful to all those who love you?" I was shouting in her face, and she was not going to back down.

"Did you know Eddy steals from stores?" Gina protested. "Did you know he skips classes to sit by the railroad until Auntie Luo goes out to look for him? Did you know he doesn't do his homework and is failing math? Did you know he *smokes?*" Gina was screaming back.

I turned around. Eddy was sitting in a corner, his face turning different shades of white. He stared at his beloved sister, his best friend, who had just thrown him under the bus.

"Is that true, Eddy? Is what Gina just said true?" I asked in a deeply disappointed tone, my lips beginning to tremble. "Please tell me the truth, Eddy. Have you been stealing, smoking, skipping school and homework, and failing math?"

Eddy stood up from his chair and nodded his head, looking terrified.

"So, what are you going to *do* about it?" Gina shouted. "I'm working so hard and succeeding in school, but nothing is ever good enough. But with Eddy, anything he does is fine by you! Why do you favor him? What's so special about him? I'm your child too!"

"First of all, stop shouting, young lady! You have no right to shout at your mother. Eddy is special and you are special. There is no difference!"

"Are you sure? You find every imaginable way to protect him. Is he your Shanghai lover's son? When are you ever going to come clean about that? Don't you think people haven't figured it out?"

That hit a nerve, and I became furious. "What 'lover'? Have you gone mad?" and I slapped her face.

"You never raise a hand to him, but you discipline me even when I get A's in my exams. You hit me when I excel as the only handicapped kid in this junior high school or maybe even in the world because you think I'm arrogant and in over my head! You don't even notice that I'm a very good kid, trying my very best all these years to be your perfect daughter!" She wouldn't let up.

"You want me to spank Eddy too? Is that it?" I was not going to back down to a kid, not that night, anyway.

"Yes! I want to see if you're capable of disciplining him as you've done with me all these years."

"You smoked and stole, Eddy," I shouted at him, "and you told me you never lied to me. Okay, you come here this instant, young man!"

Eddy walked over, and I threw the glass of water he was still holding onto the table. "Prop yourself down on that stool and take your pants down." He did just that, and I swiftly raised a hand and began to spank him hard, shouting, "This is for stealing, this is for smoking," and so on.

Gina had no expression on her face or the slightest sense of shock. She turned her head and looked out the window. I then raised my head and shouted to Gina, "Is that enough, my queen? Does that satisfy your ungrateful urge? Tell me when I should stop." No reply from Gina, and so I continued. There was no peep from Eddy, and I had to change to my left hand when my right hand began to sting. Qiu-Shuang rushed in and grabbed my arm and said, "Please, Dr. Pei, that's enough. They're just kids, and you're tired and haven't eaten. Please sit down and rest, and remember you had a heart attack just two years ago."

I looked her straight in the eye and said, "Qiu-Shuang, please get out of my apartment. This is none of your business. Please get out this very minute! I don't believe my kids care if I live or die tonight." Qiu-Shuang knew I'd gone mad, as I'd never spoken to her that way. As soon as she left, I locked the door behind her and resumed spanking Eddy.

Gina looked on and refused to say another word. And there wasn't a single cry from Eddy. Then, suddenly, there was another loud knock on the door. "Dr. Pei, I beg you to stop. Please open up!" It was Old Man Ni in the hall, crying, "Dr. Pei, I understand how you feel, but these are your kids, your flesh and blood. These are very good kids. Think about your life, about how shitty things were, and that they were the main reason you wanted to live. You can't have better kids than these two!" He was shouting and continuing to pound on the door.

"Please, no more, or I'll break the door down! Dr. Pei, I have no education, but I know that moments like this are not times to turn on each other. Please!" I stopped and looked up at the ceiling, drenched in sweat. And it was then I realized that my face was soaked with tears, dripping onto the winter jacket I made Eddy last Chinese New Year. I slumped onto the floor in complete exhaustion, physically and emotionally. Eddy pulled his pants up and quietly walked to his bed and lay down on his stomach. After that, he didn't say a word to me for a very long time. For several weeks, he could only sleep on his stomach. Gina didn't speak to me either. A month later, Paul came home completely drunk and lashed out at me. The next day, he took Eddy and left a note, telling me to explain to his teachers that Eddy would be missing school for a while. To this day, I regret what I did. It's a lifelong burden I'll carry to my grave. And from that day on, a gulf appeared between Eddy and me that would only widen.

My hours at the hospital continued to mount, combined with the insane policy of no anesthetics. Late one evening in January 1975, I came home at nearly midnight, exhausted. Gina was sitting at the desk with her back toward me, continuing to give me the silent treatment. I sat on the edge of the bed finishing a bowl of rice with fermented vegetables and half an egg that Qiu-Shuang had kept warm for me. Suddenly, the bowl slipped out of my left hand, followed by the chopsticks from my right hand, and I fell to the floor. I moaned, "Gina, please, help me!" Hearing me, she turned around and saw me clutching my chest.

I was still clear-minded and could tell she was gauging whether I was pretending. Within a few seconds, she stood up and raced toward Qiu-Shuang's apartment, only to find they were both at a friend's house, so she recruited their two oldest kids, He-Chuan (河川) and He-Ying (河英). He-Ying helped me down the stairs, and He-Chuan had already run to get his dad's tricycle ready. So, just like that, I watched Gina's teary face disappearing at the compound front entrance, with Old Man Ni and Qiu-Shang's youngest daughter, He-Xian (河仙), holding her. I wondered if this would be it—punishment for what I had done.

Here I was on yet another cold winter's night, this time with Old Man Ni's son pedaling me toward the emergency room, with He-Ying running behind. Our angelic neighbors were trying to save me again.

Luckily, it was only indigestion. Although it was a false alarm, I was forced to stay in the hospital for the night. The next morning, Paul walked in with Eddy and Gina, and none of us said a word. We just embraced. When we got home that day, Paul forced me to lie down. Gina came over, sat at the edge of the bed, and held my hands for quite some time. Finally, she spoke, "My dearest Mommy, I'm so sorry."

"It's okay, Gina. I understand. It is *I* who should be sorry. You were right. I haven't been fair to you. I haven't been much of a mother." Before I could go on, she put her hand over my mouth, and a few minutes later she said, "I know now, Mommy. You can't stay here. You want to go home to see your mother, and you *must* go home soon because you are not going to survive much longer here."

With tears streaming down my cheek, I sensed that Gina had learned about my past. Strangely, I couldn't lift my left arm over my head for the next six months, and no one could figure out why.

81

THE YEAR OF THE RABBIT, 1975, arrived, and soon I'd be turning forty-four, which, according to Chinese superstition, is an unlucky number, although not as bad as fourteen. The word *four* in Chinese is the same sound as the word *die* (死), so the number forty-four means "to die twice," or "to be dead is to die." And the word *fourteen* in Chinese sounds the same as 是死, which means "already dead."

In the final days of the prohibition on anesthetics, accidents were mounting due to improperly conducted procedures or patients squirming in pain. Unnecessary delays and backlogs were literally murdering patients and exhausting physicians. With everything taking ten times longer, some doctors and nurses even began dozing off during surgeries. After the WDT (共宣隊) took away our nitrous oxide tanks, we just splashed anesthetics—bottles, needles, or syringes—onto these patients, wasting more valuable anesthetic agents than conserving them.

Suddenly amid the chaos, we realized that the *Workers' Declaration Team* members were nowhere to be found. They were in hiding, intending to leave their mess behind for us to clean up. As angry as I felt, I had to agree with what Peng *Shu-Chi* said, that WDT was only an instrument of this senseless and destructive Revolution, soldiers carrying out their superiors' orders. Like the tens and millions of Red Guards, they, too, were victims of the circumstance created by our dear "Great Leaders" at the top!

Saddest perhaps was that most of these patients were

from poor rural areas or urban factory workers. And I repeat myself: If those brave soldiers sacrificed their lives during the incomprehensibly difficult Long March (萬里長征) and then sailed across the Yangtze River under raining bullets to defeat President Chiang's vastly superior, American-aided armies, hadn't they already sacrificed for these desolate farmers and factory workers? This so-called Greatest Revolution was in its ninth year, supposedly to better these people's lives. Day-Day would be so saddened by what I saw in 1970s China. (Day-Day would have been 100 years old in 1975, so I assumed he was dead, although I had no way of knowing.)

I learned later that there was also a grave shortage of medications and anesthetics in the early 1960s, due to the souring of the Sino-Soviet relationship at the time, and that the prohibition of anesthetics was practiced then too. We hadn't experienced it in Shanghai, suggesting again that Shanghai and Peking were spared the pain of some of these shortages. I had no interest in politics, but witnessing the regime's infuriatingly destructive policies, I felt I was being suffocated — personally — by my country of birth.

At home, the atmosphere was becoming even more strained, although the kids finally let me back into their worlds. I borrowed Qiu-Shuang's sewing machine and made them both new clothes for the Chinese New Year and a new jacket for Paul, but it lay there untouched when he left two days after the New Year to get an early start for spring planting, or so he claimed. The jacket stayed there for a month, the same way I had folded it. I thought about Old Man Ni's words. Perhaps we had indeed finally cracked under the pressure and begun to turn on each other.

Gina continued to excel in junior high, and Eddy, now ten, entered fifth grade! He was struggling in school, and I began to be concerned about where he might enroll for junior high. "It'd be great," I thought, "if he could attend Public High School No. 8." After six months of hard work reconciling with my kids after the disaster, one Sunday afternoon, I asked Eddy, "Do you still like playing the piano?"

"No, Mommy, not as much as I used to."

"Why not?" I asked, bracing for more anger, but instead he said, "Playing the piano might be for another lifetime when we can afford a piano. I accept that."

"Is there something you would like?" I persisted. "Papa has a friend who plays the violin and could give you lessons."

"I tried violin when I was in Shanghai. It sounds beautiful, but somehow, I'm drawn to the music of a piano," Eddy answered.

"Why?" I asked, curious.

"Violin melodies are sad. They push you down. Piano music can be depressing too, but a piano also makes sounds that are uplifting," Eddy said as if it were a matter of fact.

"Um..." I said, surprised by his insight.

"So I guess you wouldn't like to play the *er-hu* (二胡) then," Gina interjected with a laugh. It's a Chinese two-string fiddle whose sound is so sad it's usually associated with the image of a blind elderly man wearing dark glasses sitting on the street on a broken stool while his granddaughter holds a small bag begging for money from passersby.

"Don't be sarcastic, Gina," I said. "What would you like, then, Eddy?"

"I don't know," he shrugged.

"Come on, Eddy. Tell Mommy what you've been up to, or *I* will," Gina giggled.

"C'mon, kiddo, tell Mommy, please."

Reluctantly, Eddy brought out a folder with dozens of beautiful pencil drawings of flowers, human faces, and trains— lots of trains. I was speechless. That was Day-Day's favorite pastime.

"Those are beautiful!" I said, and refrained from asking where he got the money for drawing pencils and paper. Could he have stolen all of that? Was that why he was hiding his art from me? I held my tongue, worried this precious moment would lead to another ugly end.

Eddy sensed my tension and became withdrawn, preparing for another lashing. Just then, Gina chimed in. "Don't worry, Mommy. I gave him my allowance and borrowed money from my friends that I'll return next month." A year earlier, we began giving the kids one RMB (*Yüan*, 元) each on New Year's Day as a gift. And after Gina turned thirteen, we started giving her fifty cents a month, so she'd learn to be responsible with money.

Of course, for all the hot water runs, Eddy got a penny per trip. But what Gina said began to sound quite familiar to me. Life had come around 360 degrees. I was irresponsible with money, buying sweets while Day-Day and Mother were being driven out of China, and Mother gently scolding me for not being careful.

So how could I be mad at them for any of this? I was sitting on my bed, and I slipped down to the floor to pat Eddy on the head. "Kiddo, these are beautiful. What talent you have! Mommy's proud of you. I'll give you some money for art supplies, and Gina, I'll give you the money you had to borrow. And going forward, how about two pennies per thermos when you go and get hot water?" Eddy smiled. I tried hard to assure him I wouldn't be mad even if Gina were lying about the loan, as I knew I had to crawl back toward them inch by inch from that ugly night, even if it took a lifetime. I was happy he'd found something he enjoyed.

A month later, a patient at the clinic named *Hsiao* Wan (小万, Little Wan) told me he'd been working at an Art Institute that had recently reopened. He was also doing cartoon sketches for

SPRING FLOWER: TORN BETWEEN SHIFTING WORLDS

newspapers and magazines. He seemed duly impressed by what Eddy had drawn without any lessons, and he became Eddy's informal art teacher. Paul was delighted to hear that; it was about the only thing he approved of my doing in more than a year, and the only decent conversation we'd had in half a year.

We heard that the conflict in Vietnam was raging on, and that the Americans were retreating. I didn't know whether that was true or not. But I did know that as long as the US continued to be at war, I would never be able to return to America. So I prepared myself to live in China as a "traitor" for the rest of my life.

It turned out I was right—Gina had learned about my past from her grandmother when she was in Shanghai. And Gina was wise to say I wouldn't be able to survive much longer here in China. With no hope in sight, I couldn't help but feel saddened that my family, the only anchor I had, was beginning to fall apart and that I had played a big part in it.

So I decided to put up one last fight. I knew we needed outlets, and I thought of films and outings. There had been no movies or plays since the Revolution, except *Eight Revolutionary Exemplified Shows* (八個樣板戲). Mao's wife, Chiang Ch'ing (江青), led the effort on this front. Themes of these eight shows were always about how Mao came to power as the leader of the Communist Movement, about the Long March (萬里長征), about how they fought valiantly against the Japanese invasion (omitting any contributions from President Chiang's KMT armies, who did most of the fighting in World War II), and about their victory over President Chiang's KMT armies that ended the civil war. From 1967 until now, these eight shows were played like a broken record over and over again, even when no one showed up in the remaining unburned movie theaters.

But by 1975, things had improved a little, and some films were shown from countries that had diplomatic ties with China, mostly East and Southeast Asia countries, including Japan. It didn't matter to me whether it was an Indian movie or a movie from an Eastern Bloc country, as long as it wasn't the *Eight Revolutionary Exemplified Shows*. So my plan was to see movies and shows whenever we could. The kids loved the idea, but Paul thought it was stupid and wishful thinking. I knew it was important, and I asked him to come home on one particular Thursday night so we could all go to a movie together. It was supposed to be a love story. He barely consented, and I asked Jade to let me go home early that day because it was important for my family *and* my marriage.

I was super-excited, and once I got home the kids were buzzing with energy. The movie was at the Open Sky Theater (露天電影院), under the stars like an American drive-in, but without the cars. There were walls and a big screen in front. It was already late spring, so it'd be warm enough to sit outside, but still I dressed the kids in jackets and layers of clothes.

Six o'clock came and went, and we sat at home, waiting for Paul. The show would start when it got dark, which was around 7:30, so we still had time to get there. It was just a twenty-minute walk to the theater. Seven o'clock came, and I went downstairs by the front entrance to wait for him. It was getting dark and cloudy, and finally I saw him arriving by bike.

"Hey Paul, it's great you're home!" He stumbled off his bike, drunk, and I pretended not to notice. "Have you eaten yet? We still have time if you want a quick bite before we go."

"'Go,' for what?" He looked puzzled.

"To see the movie. The kids have eaten and are waiting upstairs."

"A movie on a weekday? Who says that's a good idea!" He looked annoyed.

"There wasn't a better time; we're both so busy. And it will only be playing for a couple of days. It's rare we're both home early. It's not a long movie. Please, Paul, can we try to have a good time? It'll be good for us."

"Good for who?" he barked as he staggered up the steps. "I'm very tired, and I've been biking for an hour. I'm hungry, and I am not going to any movie."

"Please, Paul, do eat something." I began to feel hopeful we might all go peacefully.

"No!" he declared. "And I don't think the kids should go either. They have school tomorrow."

By the time Paul got to the apartment, Eddy shouted excitedly, "Papa's home, we can go to the movie. Yay!"

But Paul went straight to bed and said, "I'm very tired. Just leave me alone. I need to rest," and he almost immediately began to snore.

I nudged him, "Please, Paul, for us, for the kids?"

"No, I said. Leave me alone! If you want to go, go. But leave me alone."

"I thought we would do this as a family. And we agreed when you left on Monday." It was becoming futile.

Eddy came over and said, "Come on, Papa, let's go." He dragged Paul's big arm to no avail, while anger was boiling inside me.

I rose and said, "Paul, please stand up like a good father, and let's go."

That touched a nerve. "You want me to be a good father? How about you? You beat the crap out of them and you call yourself a good mother?"

"Please, Paul, I don't want to fight. I just want to have a pleasant evening and be a family for a change." I went into full gear for my last-ditch effort.

He wagged his finger at me while burping his liquor breath

and shouting at the top of his lungs, "You don't know a thing about being a mother! You don't know how to cook, you don't know how to educate kids, and you don't know how to treat them humanely. You don't know *anything!* Like my mother said, I never should have married you."

I slapped him, and he was now shocked and wide awake.

"You hit me now, too?" Paul shouted.

"I'm sorry, Paul! I thought you were going to hit me, and I was scared. I've never seen you like this before. Please, no more."

"When did I ever lift a hand to you? Now you sound righteous hitting me." Paul began to shout even louder. I began to speak English because I couldn't keep up with him in Chinese. He probably didn't understand what I was saying, and I couldn't hear what he was saying. He said something about his mother and his family, about my life in Shanghai and my lack of career focus, something about my inability to live in Chinese culture, something about why he was coming home at all and about how many lovers he could have had. It got really ugly. We shouted for what felt like an eternity, but it was probably only ten minutes. Suddenly he stopped and put on his jacket.

"Where are you going, Paul?"

"I'm taking the kids to the movies. Isn't that what you want? Well, I'm going right now. Are you happy now?" He was still muttering about something as he walked toward our two very frightened kids. They had never seen us fight like this.

"It's 8:30! The movie is almost over. Just forget it."

He grabbed Gina and clamped Eddy underneath his arm, and off he went downstairs. I quickly followed, still saying, "Please don't, Paul!" He stumbled down those steep steps and miraculously managed to maintain his balance and hang onto the kids.

He put Eddie in the front of his bike and Gina on the back,

and he stumbled out the front entrance of the compound. It had begun to rain. "It's raining," I shouted at him. "The movie is either over or it's canceled. Let's go back!" He would have none of it as he zigzagged into the rain that had become a downpour.

I scurried upstairs to get the kids' raincoats and the only umbrella we had, and I ran after them. Since he was drunk and couldn't walk a straight line, I caught up with them. He was surprised to see me but pressed on even though he and the kids were already drenched. I asked him to at least stop for a second so I could put raincoats on the kids. He stepped on the brakes, lost control of the bike, and both kids flew off. Luckily, no one was hurt. Once they had their raincoats on, I pleaded with him again that we should all go home.

Paul didn't even acknowledge my words or his bicycle accident, and he threw the kids back on the bike and pedaled, this time in a straighter line. I chased behind, holding the umbrella to try to shield him from the rain and with my other hand holding Gina in fear that Paul could slip and throw the kids off again. We got there, and the four of us charged toward the theater in the pouring rain. There was a soaking-wet note on the front door saying that the show had been canceled. The only thing wetter than that note was *us*.

"Paul, let's go home now, please."

He didn't respond. He just stood there, staring at the movie theater's front door in what was by then a torrential rain. Then he stooped down and began to cry. I wanted to walk over and comfort him, but I didn't, fearing I'd trigger another shouting match. I figured he might need to cry on his own. And so, the kids and I stood about ten feet from him, watching their dad bawling and muttering some indiscernible words. Then he turned around, picked up his bike, and headed home. As soon as we got back to our room, I changed clothes for our two shell-shocked kids.

Paul had put on dry clothes and his jacket. Trembling, I asked, "Where are you going, Paul? Why are you putting on your raincoat, my dear?"

"I'm going back to the farm where all my lovers are, as you have accused," Paul replied calmly.

"I'm sorry, Paul. Those were angry words. Please stay. It's wet and dark outside. I said I'm sorry—isn't that enough? Please, Paul. Please stay home!" The tremble in my voice was increasing.

"Papa, please don't leave!" Eddy shouted.

"I'm leaving, and that's that. You take care of yourself and the kids." Paul's voice was emotionless.

I lunged toward the door and locked it, and then stood in front of it and continued to cry, "Paul, I'm begging you to stay. I'm sorry for everything. Please forgive me for all of this, for the last ten or twenty years. It's all my fault. Please don't go! Please don't leave the kids." Tears were streaming down my cheeks.

"Move away from that door, or I'll make you. I need to leave tonight. I need time and space to think. I cannot stay here."

"You can think here; the kids and I will stay out of your way. Please, Paul, it's not safe to be biking back to your farm. You can go back first thing in the morning." I stretched my arm to block the door further.

He began to pry my hand that was gripping the doorknob while he was trying to shake free of the two kids, who had clamped onto his legs. He was stronger than the three of us, and he effortlessly pried my hands loose and pushed me to the side. He grabbed both kids and threw them onto their bed. When I attempted to block him again, he swiped me away to the side with one hand and walked right out the door. I slumped to the floor. I had never imagined our marriage might end like this.

A month later—by which time I still hadn't seen Paul again—

SPRING FLOWER: TORN BETWEEN SHIFTING WORLDS

I suffered a second heart attack. Once again, Old Man Ni pedaled like a madman to get me to the emergency room, and I managed once again to sit on his tricycle's flatbed while leaning against the rail. I watched my two stunned kids disappearing at the front entry of the compound, flanked by Qiu-Shuang and a few other residents. It turned out to be a mild myocardial infarction, and I was given a stern warning that I might not be so lucky next time so I needed to find ways to calm down.

In June 1975, word came that Saigon had fallen. US troops had retreated, and Americans and an array of allies aligned with both West and East declared the end of their involvement. Ho Chi-Minh's Communist North Vietnam had overtaken the South, which was also ruled by autocratic leaders. For me, it was the Korean War revisited — people slaughtering one another because of ideological differences and America's naiveté jumping at any chance to assist anyone who claimed to be anti-Communist, even when they were equally brutal and autocratic.

Sue passed the news on to me, thinking I'd be interested, but instead I was numb. I had no illusion of ever leaving China as long as the US kept picking fights with it. I was certain I'd die and be buried here, and that 1975 might be my last year alive, as I had I just turned forty-four (44 *si-shi-si*: 死是死, "dead-is-dead"). I chatted with Sue and told her the whole story about my fight with Paul. She promised me it would blow over and that she and her husband, Conductor Hsie, fought all the time, like a daily diet, and it helped release their frustrations and anger. She was quite surprised to hear that this was our first real fight, not counting minor skirmishes, although she agreed that a fight between two highly educated and intelligent individuals could be uglier. I, on the other hand, was sure our marriage was over and that we had finally succumbed to the oppression and had turned on each other for good. What would be the point, then, of going home to America if that were to happen? I wanted to take all of them with me. I felt hollow inside, as if my soul had been sucked out of me.

On a light Saturday afternoon, I left work early. The kids were about to begin summer break, and I had wanted to clean and wax the floors so they could begin their summer fun barefoot. Eddy even offered to help. As I approached the front entry of our compound, I saw a familiar shadow. And there she was, my dearest Wang-Sao (王嫂)! I hopped off my bike and ran to her, nearly knocking her over. By then, she was in her eighties. I gave her a big squeeze and she stroked my hair. "How is my baby girl doing?" she asked gently.

"Not very well, Amah! I have failed everyone and everything—my kids, my marriage, my career, and my life," and I began to sob.

"Now, now, you're a tough girl! I've always known that. Nothing can stop you when you try your best."

I lifted my head from her shoulder and wiped my tears. "I guess the kids already told you," I said.

"It's no big deal, Jeanie girl. Without a little fight, it wouldn't even qualify as a marriage," Wang-Sao said reassuringly.

"I thought we'd be partners through thick and thin, and all of these years it's been mostly thin. But I never thought we'd turn on each other like this," I said, shaking my head in disbelief.

"Sometimes it seems that way, but everyone has a boiling point. And when that's reached, there has to be a release or Paul would go mad. Think about all those years, all that suffering and humiliation! We don't know the half of it! We only see it from the outside, and we could hardly stand getting a taste of what Paul went through for nine years and counting." As always, Wang-Sao offered words of wisdom.

"I appreciate how much he has suffered, but…" and I caught

myself pouting like a little girl. I was forty-four now, and so I nodded my head to accept what she said, then asked, "How do you know to come exactly when I needed you the most? How long will you stay with us this time? Forever, I hope."

"I don't know. I dreamed of your parents again. They asked me how I was and how you are. And I know your little one is ten now, so I thought I'd better come and see him. No one lives forever. I won't want to impose on you for too long—maybe a few weeks if that's okay?"

"Oh, my dearest Amah, what are you saying! You look so young and strong and you'll probably live forever. Please stay with us and don't leave again. My kids will love having you here. They think I'm a lousy mother anyway."

"Now, now, don't be silly," she said. "I told Qiu-Shuang I would make dinner for a few weeks." I grabbed her hand and began to skip ahead like a little girl.

The kids had a great time with Wang-Sao. Now that Eddy was older, he could understand the stories she was telling him, mostly from *Romance of the Three Kingdoms* (三國演義) at the end of the Han Dynasty (漢朝) in 220 CE, and also some stories from *The Warring State Period* (戰國) in the Eastern Chou Dynasty (東周朝), around 250 BCE. For someone who never went to school, Wang-Sao's knowledge of Chinese history was vast. She also talked about the Ch'in Dynasty and the Opium Wars, and Eddy was entranced. Some of these stories were in books that had been forbidden or rewritten in recent decades. Wang-Sao told Gina a love story from the Hangchow area, something about Liang Shan-Po (梁山伯) and Chu Ying-T'ai (祝英臺).

Paul came home once before Wang-Sao left. He acted indifferent to me but was extremely attentive to Wang-Sao, knowing that, essentially, she was my mother, the only link I had to my distant past. I was happy he was there and appreciated that he treated Wang-Sao well. When Wang-Sao's final day came, I begged her to take a bus to the train station, and Paul offered to pedal her there. She laughed heartily, pointing out how it would look when people saw a handsome young man pedaling an eighty-year-old woman holding an umbrella. "They'll think that I like beautiful, youthful-looking older women, or that I'm a filial son pedaling his mom somewhere," Paul said.

But she preferred to walk and asked me if I would accompany her to the station. As we were ready to head out, Gina grabbed Wang-Sao's legs. Tears swirled in my eyes. I saw Eddy sitting in the corner expressionless, and I waved at him, "Eddy, c'mon and give Grandma Wang a bow and thank her for all these wonderful weeks of food, games, and stories."

He didn't budge. "Please be polite, Eddy. Stand up and say goodbye to Grandma Wang." Finally Eddy rose and walked slowly to Wang-Sao, gave her a bow and a light smile, and said, "Thank you, Wang *Nai-Nai* (王奶奶: Grandma Wang)," and walked back to his stool. Wang-Sao smiled and looked at me and said, "Let's go! I'll be back again soon, and we'll have more time."

It was a forty-minute walk, and we talked about many things. Most memorably, Wang-Sao told me that she took Eddy out to buy cookies as a belated birthday gift one day (she had already given Eddy his first toy ever, a black rubber handgun that looked all-too real).

"Jeanie, your boy is unusual."

"Yes?" I asked.

"Being a country bumpkin, I was shy going into a big city store, so I asked him to lead the way and told him to pick out any cookies he wanted—anything—because Grandma Wang would pay for it all! He said he didn't want anything. Finally, he picked one because I forced him to. The clerk said that cookie was just for display, and I forced him to pick out another, and then another, and all the cookies he picked were just for display. Only then did he smile and said, 'See, Wang *Nai-Nai* (王奶奶)! Let's go home. There's nothing to buy here.' Finally, I found one that was for sale. and I asked him how many he'd like. He barely lifted one finger. You have to forgive me, Jeanie, I'm old and slow, and so I bought one for five cents. And then, I asked him how that would work, just one cookie for four or five people, including me. He gestured a cross, indicating four pieces with one each for you, Paul, Gina, and me.

"After we left the store, I asked him, 'How can you just give it all away! It's for your birthday.' He didn't say anything, just grabbed my hand and began to walk. So I began to walk back into the store to buy more so we each could have one to celebrate his tenth birthday, a great occasion. And he grabbed the door handle and began to cry. 'Wang *Nai-Nai* (王奶奶),' he said, 'one will do! Please don't waste your money on me. *Ma-Ma* told me you are also poor like us. She'll be angry at me if you waste money on me. She'll never forgive me!' I told him not to worry because even his mama has to listen to me! So, I went inside and cleaned the store out—well, at least every cookie that was not on display."

"Thank you. You are always so kind to us," I said.

"That's not the point of my story. You see, Gina is a very outward person, but Eddy is a very inward kid. He thinks deeply and holds on to his emotions."

I nodded my head and thanked her for telling me. Wang-Sao stopped walking and sighed. "When I came out of the store, Eddy was sitting on the sidewalk. So I sat down with him and tried to sweet-talk him into eating one cookie right there, so that he could have more later, and he began to cry. So, I asked if he was crying because he was worried about being scolded by you. He said no. He said he was crying because no one had been this kind and caring toward him before."

A huge lump filled my throat. I gripped Wang-Sao's hand, but she continued, saying, "We sat there for hours as he told me stories of his childhood, and what a miserable existence it has been, and how much everyone around him was suffering. He told me how he feels terrible that he couldn't help you and Gina and that he fell well below your expectations. I was so sad. I couldn't help but think about you and Chum, Jeanie. What were you *thinking* when you were ten and living in Kiukiang?" Listening to her words and looking into her eyes, all I could think was that I just beaten the crap out of my son while knowing that I had no courage to confess to her.

"Jeanie, I'm not blaming you. You're doing the best you can; we all are, given the circumstances. But please talk to him whenever you can, or he has no place to let it out. He even asked if I knew of any superpowers that could 'get us out of here' and save us all." Wang-Sao then pounded her head. "I'm getting old. I had to tell you this before I forgot it."

"Is there something else you want to tell me?" I asked with both anticipation and sadness.

"You know the dream in which I saw your parents! They spoke to me softly, saying that the end is near, and they wanted to thank me for coming to see you."

"You're not going anywhere without me, Wang-Sao," I said, my voice trembling.

"Silly kid, either my Chinese is bad or yours hasn't improved much. I'm not going anywhere. See how tough I am? I'm taking this long trek to the station, aren't I?"

I laughed as I held onto her arm and asked, "So what do you

mean? What did *they* mean? And does Mother still speak to you in Chinese?"

"Yes, dear. Mrs. Perkins still speaks Chinese to me, even in my dreams. I think they meant you should continue to be strong and live, and that you'll be going home soon. So, you have to keep on hoping; you cannot lose hope! Hope is what keeps us alive." I didn't ask any more questions, and we walked silently the rest of the way. As the train pulled away from the platform, I waved my arm till it felt like it would break.

82

AFTER WANG-SAO left, I felt bereft, and then Paul took Eddy and Gina to his farm without asking me or telling me. Being alone, it turned out, gave me a chance to do some soul-searching, to think about Wang-Sao's words of wisdom. It was the fall of 1975.

When Paul brought the kids back nearly a month later, he and I had our first real conversation in half a year. He told me that Lieutenant Governor Peng and Peng *Shu-Chi* had visited the farms near his Institute and stopped by to meet him. They told him they needed help from people like him to prevent the next famine, which was on the horizon.

It seemed that Paul's knowledge and his words, consistent and strong for many years, were now in accord with China's highest leadership. A forgotten man named Teng Hsiao-Ping (鄧小平), who himself had been persecuted during the past ten years and was fortunate to be still alive—many leaders and generals did not survive the purges—was absolved of his "crimes" and once again in Mao's inner circle.

One day at the clinic, I spotted a familiar face in the waiting line. I asked *Hsiao* Hu to put her file in my metal basket, and when she reached my desk, I asked if we had met somewhere. She said no, that she has a common face and hears that frequently. She had retina degeneration in her left eye and could go blind, so I quickly scheduled her surgery, and just then, I blurted out, "I know; it's been a long time, but some faces I don't forget. I'm terrible with names but not faces. You were in my home with those Red Guards the day they took my husband away. And you were so young, probably just entering junior high." She had grown into a tall, beautiful woman.

She covered her mouth and let out a whimper, then said the Chinese equivalent of "Oh my God (我的天哪)!"

I smiled at her with no sign of anger. "It was you, yes? And when my son fell to the ground during the chaos, you were the one who picked him up and comforted him. That's something else I will never forget."

She was shocked beyond belief. "I am so sorry, Dr. Pei. I am so sorry!" She stood up and began to kneel, and I grabbed her arm and said, "Young lady, please don't!"

"I'm so sorry. I was barely fifteen," and she kept apologizing with tears streaming down her face.

"It's okay. My husband is home now. My kids are grown up. You should meet my little one sometime. He's in fifth grade."

"Yes, I should. I still remember your son's face. He was so cute, and I felt terrible when he fell to the floor with all that mess and chaos."

"I was touched by your kind gesture. Most important now, come back on Friday and we'll get this critical procedure done. We still have a chance to save your eye."

Her name was Ying (英), and her parents were workers at a factory that made bolts, nuts, and nails. She was sent to the countryside for *Rustication–Reeducation* (for young people, it was called *Chih-Ch'ing*, 知青) shortly after the Revolution's most violent stage and had recently transferred back to Hangchow because of her deteriorating eyesight. In the fall of 1966, when Paul was taken away, she was in seventh grade and was following her older brother, whom she adored. And now Ying was a beautiful, twenty-four-year-old woman. This unexpected encounter was redemptive and brought some reconciliation that dissolved a little of of my anger and allowed me to look at things a little differently.

After her successful surgery, Ying began to spend a lot of time with Eddy and Gina, babysitting them once a week so I could focus on my work. She took them everywhere and showered them with candies and cookies. Gina's being handicapped did not deter Ying from taking them to faraway places by bus. I kept telling her not to waste her valuable money. I doubted she and her parents had much, and she also had a little brother at home. Most of the time, I had no idea where they went or how they got back, except one very cold day when they were caught in a downpour and all three of them caught terrible colds. My kids fell in love with a former Red Guard who was fourteen when they ransacked our apartment and took Paul away, the same age I was when we headed to India!

One night while we were asleep, suddenly the earth shook, and our compound rattled violently. We heard screaming from all directions. "Get out now! Earthquake!" Old Man Ni knocked on our door, "Dr. Pei, Professor Hsiung, grab the kids, fast!"

Paul wasn't at home. I got the kids dressed in as much clothing as we could grab and headed downstairs. The compound was old, and leaving the building seemed the safest thing to do. Old Man Ni carried Gina down the steps, fearing she might slip in such a hurry, and by the time we got out, the shaking had long stopped. We walked to the street, where Qiu-Shuang and her two youngest kids were already standing. We saw Sister Liu and Captain Shao, and Sister Liu said, "Hangchow almost never has earthquakes. Something huge must be happening."

"I hope it's something good for a change," Old Man Ni replied, still holding Gina. Soon we all returned to our rooms.

Eddy was tossing and turning. "What if there's another one after this, Mommy?" he asked.

SPRING FLOWER: TORN BETWEEN SHIFTING WORLDS

"We've been here ten years, and this was the first and the only earthquake we've felt. I'd guess it will be another ten years before we have another. Please try to relax, Sonny Boy. You have school tomorrow."

The next day, we discovered that the far wall near Ni and Qiu-Shuang's apartment had a huge crack from top to bottom. We went to the *Neighborhood Management Center* (居民區管理中心), which received monthly payments from us, but no one came, so we continued to live in a structurally damaged compound.

Paul came home and said it shook much harder where he was, closer to the ocean. He believed it was an earthquake in the Pacific, and since we felt it in Hangchow, it must have been shallow. Later, we learned there had been a massive earthquake in the Liaoning Province (遼寧省) near Haich'eng County (海城縣) earlier in 1975. Perhaps this was an aftershock.

A week later, Paul came home and told me he'd asked the *Shu-Chi* at the Institute if he could trade our room at the compound plus our secret hideout, Shih-Ch'ing-Fang (世青坊), for a new place. His *Shu-Chi* was, of course, surprised to hear we had a second place, but it sounded like they were considering it. I guessed they were beginning to treat him with more respect after the Pengs' visit.

I didn't argue, but I was reluctant to leave our beloved slum compound and the companionship of our Shih-Ch'ing-Fang (世青坊), not to mention so many beautiful memories. But things moved quickly, and on December 23, 1975, we were told the trade was complete and we could move. It happened much faster than I'd anticipated, especially with the pace of how things usually worked in China at that time. My mother would have been ninety-four on that day.

"Paul, I don't want to leave here. I don't want to lose our Shih-Ch'ing-Fang (世青坊)," I pouted.

He looked at me quizzically and said, "You're joking, right? I already paid some people from the farm to help us move, and the Institute found this place that's nearly twice the size of this apartment. Our kids are grown now, Jeanie. It was really hard to get approval from your hospital and my Institute to make such a swap. I'm not sure what you're thinking, but please, let's get ready. They will be here in an hour." Paul would not entertain any of this nonsense from me.

"It's too sudden," I protested, "and we're just going to leave these people after ten years?"

Seeing my sad face, Paul stopped packing and came to me. He held me close and said, "Jeanie, I thought you hated this place. From the day we moved in, you hated it and wanted to move back to Shanghai. This is our chance to move into a far better place. This room is too small for four of us, and this slum is no longer safe."

"But these people are still here." I continued to pout.

Soon the movers, people Paul had befriended at the farm, came, including the guard from his old labor camp, Shan. He smiled widely and politely called out, "Dr. Pei, happy to see you again. My mother sends her well wishes to you!" He then handed me a bag of potatoes from his mother. I nodded in appreciation.

We had so little to move—beds made of old doors, wooden planks, and benches; a few stools and chairs; and an old desk. The small wooden chest with sliding glass doors was our most precious possession, but it had broken nine years earlier and was never fixed. Qiu-Shuang had given me her sewing machine, which was the only other item of immense value, and we were taking it with us. Within an hour, they were done. Everything was packed onto their motorized tricycle. In a flash, this small square hole was emptied, and it looked much bigger. I knew I would miss every square inch of it. I rubbed my shoes against

SPRING FLOWER: TORN BETWEEN SHIFTING WORLDS

the still-shining cement floor and waved goodbye to our river-rat friends that, I believe, were sad to see us go and concerned who the next tenant might be. I grabbed Eddy's hand and we walked out together, only to run into a tearful Qiu-Shuang. We embraced tightly, both of us in tears. I nodded my head to their children and thanked them for being such good friends for Eddy and Gina.

Qiu-Shuang walked me down the steps holding my hand, with Eddy following behind. Once we reached the bottom of the stairs, many of our neighbors were lined up along the front entrance hallway to see us off. Ironically, as much as I hated this place when we moved in, I had come to know and care about many of our neighbors.

"So sorry to see you go!" Mr. Yao yelled out.

"Dr. Pei, has it been ten years?" Mr. Li, the pharmacist, asked in a low voice.

"Yes, it has, Mr. Li," I nodded. "Thank you!"

"Dr. Pei, I'm so sorry to see you go. My Yao-Yao teased Eddy a few months ago," Mrs. Wei spoke up behind me. I turned around, our eyes met, and we both broke into a hearty laugh. "Mrs. Wei," I said, "that only made Eddy more determined to become Yao-Yao's boyfriend."

Chang *Lao-Shih* nodded and said, "I guess my daughter Fang-Fang just fell out of favor!"

The three of us laughed, but Eddy wasn't amused. Humor gave me the strength to walk to the front entrance, and I just kept on nodding and smiling. Then I saw Sister Liu and said, "Thank you for your stories."

I couldn't believe they were all out here on this cold day. Once outside the entrance, I heard Old Man Ni's familiar voice saying, "Dr. Pei, I will see you aplenty at the hospital, but this may just be my last honor of being your chauffeur! Come on, Eddy boy, hop on!" Paul and Gina rode with the men from the farm, and Old Man Ni took Eddy and me.

I turned around and smiled at everyone, and just as I hopped on his tricycle, I said, "Please wait one more second, Old Man Ni."

I jumped off and said to everyone gathered, "Thank you so much for everything during these past ten years. Thank you for saving my life and the lives of my family. Maybe you already knew, but I want to tell you. My real name is Jean Perkins (我的真名是吉恩·裴敬思). I was brought up by Americans. I was Dr. and Mrs. Edward Perkins's adopted daughter (我是裴敬思醫生的養女)." I then made a full bow from my waist to this group of people I had come to respect and admire. The exuberance I felt afterward was liberating.

As Old Man Ni pedaled away on that deep winter day, I held Eddy close to shield him from the wind, while my mind was scattered in a million directions. Paul was right, I had hated this place. It was hard to realize I had become so attached to it. So much had happened. These weren't just neighbors, they were a very special group of human beings, or perhaps angels impersonating human beings. They were a true testimony of love, strength, and courage.

I understood and appreciated why our neighbors in the compound came to see us off. They were there to thank us, too. That might sound surprising after sharing only stories of how they helped us. But there are other stories too; I just had to choose — this book is already 1,300 pages. Everyone and every family in this slum had an equally sad story to share, and there were many things Paul and I did to support them and the compound. One mundane but not insignificant example: One hot summer day two years earlier, Paul single-handedly dredged a clogged sewage line with his bare hands after the bathroom hadn't been working for a month. The *Neighborhood Management Center* (居民區管理中心) was just another Revolutionary hypocrisy, and they never responded to our requests and then pleas for help. So, when the sewer line was finally cleared, the whole compound celebrated, despite the horrible stench permeating in all directions. Paul famously told the community, "I've been in so much shit all these years, I'm just a professional doing my job!"

I wrote this book in memory of all of these people, these souls of many beliefs and allegiances who managed to preserve kindness in their hearts through a period of brutal oppression. These angels protected, consoled, and uplifted us in the worst of times.

"Here we are, Dr. Pei!" Old Man Ni shouted, jolting me back to present-day reality.

"I guess we're here." As Old Man Ni lifted Eddy off the cart, I stood up in the back of his familiar old tricycle.

"Yes, I guess this is it," he said. "I won't go in and bother you further, Dr. Pei. You've got plenty to sort out." Old Man Ni smiled and nodded his head. That was the first time I noticed how much he had aged in the past ten years.

"Please do come in! Have some hot water at the least. It's cold. I'm sure Paul wouldn't mind having a shot of rice liquor with you."

"Thank you, Dr. Pei, but no. No amount of liquor would make me feel better right now! I'll see you at the hospital." He turned his tricycle around, hopped on, and disappeared into the cold night. And just like that, we moved out of our slum compound and into a new place and a new chapter of our life.

———∞———

Our new home was on the third floor of Apartment Building #13. Chinese people don't have a problem about thirteen being unlucky, but I still felt strange to be there. There were twenty buildings arranged in a village-like setting. Every floor had eight to ten apartments, and every building had three floors. And each floor looked like an indoor motel.

Our unit was at the end of a long hallway. We had two rooms, each about ten by fifteen feet. The two rooms weren't joined or connected but with doors facing one another across the same long hallway. Since each of the rooms was the size of our single room at the slum compound, we now had twice the space, which in the kids' eyes meant we now lived in a mansion. Cleaning and waxing its cement floors was harder every spring, but I insisted that we walk barefoot indoors for half the year. And one of the rooms had a balcony.

The communal kitchen was at the other end of the long (some fifty or sixty feet), narrow third-floor hallway, near the stairs, and the walk to and from the kitchen was exercise for Paul. He had to remember to take everything he might need to prepare the meal with him, or he'd have to make the walk twice. And then, when the food was ready, after the long walk back to our apartment some of the dishes were already cool before even being served. Eddy became our de facto busboy, for twenty-five cents a month.

The kitchen was spacious and had real gas stoves, so families took turns buying compressed gas cylinders. It also had three sinks. Like Paul, I also had to be vigilant about what I took with me for washing the dishes or doing laundry.

The biggest improvements were the bathroom and showers. Men and women were finally segregated, and only two to three families shared a shower stall or a toilet, not twenty as at the compound. Although the toilets were still just a foot-wide ditch, they were tiled with small white porcelain squares and had a faucet anchored directly above each station for flushing. Paul again became the building plumber, as he was fearless when

SPRING FLOWER: TORN BETWEEN SHIFTING WORLDS

The historical Grand Canal (大運河) near our new place after moving away from the compound on Sun-Yat-Sen Road (孫中山路): The poverty along the canal was visible in the 1970s. Chinese people's lives were not that different from the time Day-Day and Mother rode a barge on the Grand Canal in the early 1900s.

facing sewage, and the narrow pipes would clog every time someone "flushed" paper down the ditch.

Hot water remained a challenge, though, and Eddy still had to go down the street to buy hot water from a station, now five cents per gallon. I encouraged him to carry less and take more trips by paying him per trip, but Eddy still hustled to get it done in the fewest number of trips possible. He was reluctant to make extra trips because when he arrived at the station, the lady who managed it would shoo aside the grownups and let him go first. Still, with all the money he was making, he could buy drawing pencils and paper. But his art teacher, Hsiao Wan (小萬), had started teaching him watercolors. And Hsiao Wan even brought over leftover paint, soon-to-be-discarded brushes, and used water-absorbent paper from his Art Institute to *finance* Eddy's training.

The new apartment was closer to Paul's Institute, but farther from Gina's junior high. Gina's new homeroom teacher, Liu *Lao-Shih* (劉老師), assigned two of the best kids I've ever met to escort her to school every day, whether it was raining, snowing, or even sleeting. It was wonderful to meet these kids, who had the biggest hearts. One of their family names was Zhuang (庄), and the other was either Li or Wang; I can't remember. I could still pick them out of a lineup. These wonderful souls took turns and had to backtrack a long way by bus or walking from their homes to pick Gina up before heading to school. Paul and I would often prepare breakfast for Gina's new friends, knowing they'd been up since 6 a.m. to meet her.

The move left Eddy and me with a much longer commute to his elementary school and my clinic. Initially I asked him to take the bus on his own and I would hop on my bike, but I quickly realized that even at age ten, he was small for his age. The bus was insanely crowded, and he'd be mercilessly pushed and shoved until he was pinned in the middle of the bus. So we changed the plan. We began to commute together, leaving around 6:30 a.m. I'd prop him on the back of my bike, where Gina used to sit, and I'd pedal. During this period, I began teaching him English again.

"I'll bet you've forgotten all about a-b-c-d-e-f-g," I said as he sat in the back.

"Oh, I remember—a-e-i-o-u—right?"

"Yes, great memory! It has been a long while since Mommy taught you English."

"Let's do it again," Eddy said, and pronounced, "Yes, ma'am," in English. He tapped excitedly on my shoulder, wondering if I'd heard him with the wind whistling by.

"I hear you, Sonny Boy. Yes, we surely will." I was delighted to hear his enthusiasm. "What is your name?"

"My name is Edward Richard Perkins. I guess I should add

Hsiung?" and he tapped on my shoulder again.

"That was perfect. What a great memory you have! Yes, you can add your father's family name, Hsiung. Okay now, what grade are you in, Edward?"

"Yes, ma'am, I'm still in elementary school." Eddy proudly answered in English.

"That was good! And your pronunciation is good too! But my question was, 'What grade?'"

"Oh, sorry. Fifth grade, but really, I'm not sure what grade I'm in right now. How do I say that, Mommy?"

Eddy was actually in his sixth year in elementary school. But by 1976, the educational system throughout China was out of whack. When Eddy was five-and-a-half in 1970, he entered elementary school, which China had just decided would be a five-year program. Then they decided elementary school should be for six, rather than five, years, and many kids got caught in the middle, like Eddy.

"I don't know, Eddy," I shouted. "Maybe just say you're in the sixth grade."

"Okay." Eddy suddenly put his arms around my waist and his head on my back. His show of affection touched me, and I gently patted him on the head and said, "Amazing, my boy is now a sixth-grader."

"Mommy, why do you want me to learn English? You promised you would tell me where you learned English when I could speak some."

I knew this would come up again, and I still wasn't sure I wanted to tell him. "I remember saying I would explain everything when you've *mastered* the English language?"

A few minutes later, Eddy gently tapped me on the back. "Mommy, how come you never talk about your mama and papa? And how come I've never met them? Are they dead, like

Papa's dad?"

I was hoping the subject would go away. "Yes, that's it." I was not lying. I believed both Day-Day and Mother had already left this world.

"But how come I've never heard any stories about them? I can tell that Wang *Nai-Nai* is very special to you, and I love her very much too! But she told me that she's not your mother. I think she knows something about your mama and papa. But she wouldn't tell me, even when I begged her. She said you would tell me someday."

"We are almost at your school, Eddy, so how about we pick this up tomorrow or another time?"

"Yes, ma'am," Eddy said in perfect English as he hopped off the bike and waved at me.

83

I'D COME to love our balcony. One cold evening in January 1976, I stood there remembering Mother, Day-Day, and the aunties, who had all left China twenty-five years earlier. The crisp, cool air felt good, but different this time. It was another new year, the Year of the Dragon on the Chinese lunisolar calendar. There was some snow on the ground, and I felt drawn to go down and stand on the street.

"Jeanie, where are you?" Paul's voice reverberated from the room across the hall. I didn't answer, and a moment later, I heard, "Homesick again?" Paul joined me on the balcony and placed a thick jacket over my shoulder.

"Yes, but what's the use? They're all dead."

"Your aunties may still be alive. They were much younger than your parents. Don't give up hope. This could be a very different year," Paul said.

News of the death of Premier Chou En-Lai (周恩来) came on January 8, 1976. The nation mourned the loss of a statesman who was even-keeled, in the face of so much adversity. He was a man who paid meticulous attention to detail and had immense knowledge of the West. Another subdued Chinese New Year came and went, and we had even less food and fewer goods during this so-called festive period. I managed to collect enough cotton to make the kids new winter coats, as promised. As I pedaled away on her sewing machine, my mind drifted to Qiu-Shuang. We had half a pound of meat that a surgery patient insisted on giving me for New Year's dinner.

Paul skillfully shaved off the fatty part and fried it until it became crunchy pork rind, as the kids looked on, salivating. The lard was as precious as gold and had to be carefully rationed over months. Paul marinated the meat in soy sauce and salt and hung it on the balcony, where it was cold, so it would last. He then took two pounds of sticky rice (糯米), another gift from my patient, and patiently pounded it into rice cakes (年糕), a process that takes days. The kids couldn't take their eyes off him, as if he were performing in a show. Sticky rice cakes can be made into ravioli-like dumpling soup (疙瘩汤), stir fried with vegetables or meat resembling fried flat-rice noodles, or steamed for breakfast pancakes with a few sprinkles of brown sugar. And it's dense, so you can only eat so much in one sitting, meaning it lasts for a long time.

Paul and the kids were happy together, and we felt like a family. We had conversations at the dinner table for the first time in a very long while. Eddy ate his meat quickly and was eying my bowl. I ignored him, even though it could have been my opportunity to make up to him. Minutes later, Gina finished eating, picked up half her meat, and put it in Eddy's bowl. Eddy looked very sheepish and thanked her. Paul was mum. So I spoke up, "Gina, that was *your* share. Don't spoil your brother."

"I am not into eating meat, Mommy, and I had enough."

"Don't get me wrong, Gina. I appreciate the way you care about your little brother. But he needs to learn to leave the best for last instead of eating all his favorite things first as if there's no tomorrow." After saying that, I felt terrible; the poor kid hadn't had anything good to eat since he was born. And Eddy had been so much better at managing money than I ever was at his age. So I quickly put my uneaten half in his bowl.

Eddy leaned over and said, "Thank you, Mommy! Mommy

is the most beautiful woman I've ever seen. Am I right, Papa?"

"Aren't you sweet, Eddy," I said, feeling so much better about myself.

Paul sipped his liquor and said, "No, Eddy. Beautiful is not a word to describe your mother. She used to be the sweetest, warmest, and kindest human being."

I didn't know how to respond because Paul had just summed up my life in one sentence. After an awkward pause, Eddy asked, "Papa, what do you mean *used to be?*"

Paul didn't reply, and I stayed silent.

Paul and I both felt it was time to teach Eddy to ride a bike, so I began teaching him as part of our morning commute. But the only bike that might be small enough for him to learn on was mine. Eddy was a small ten-year-old, and even placing the seat at its lowest setting was too high for him—his feet couldn't reach the ground. So, I put him on the seat, held the bike upright, released the kickstand, gave him a push, and told him to start peddling. Off he went in a beeline, and I ran after him with one hand holding onto the back of the bike. It helped him get the feel of balancing and steering. And after we began to make progress, I added English lessons to our morning commute.

"You're making real progress, Eddy!" I shouted from the back.

"Are you okay, Mommy? Am I going too fast for you?" Eddy turned his head around.

"Not at all! You need enough speed to keep the bike upright but keep your eyes on the road. Don't turn around to look at me!" I said, continuing to shout. This was on sidewalks; he wasn't ready for actual streets, with thousands of bikes going in both directions. So, we needed to watch for pedestrians.

JEAN TREN-HWA PERKINS

"Mommy, where did you learn English?" Eddy shouted.

"I'll tell you sometime, but let's wait until you get really good at riding a bike." I prided myself on my new stalling strategy.

"Okay, what should I be learning today?" He turned around again.

"Watch the road, Eddy, please! We're coming to an intersection."

As we stopped at the curb waiting for the light to turn, I noticed many people looking at us. I guess they were wondering what language I was speaking, mixing English words with Chinese. When the light turned green, I started pushing the bike forward again as Eddy pedaled. "Well, Eddy, what are you studying in school these days?" I asked.

"Chinese, math, and geography. And a gym teacher showed us how to sprint and how to dribble a basketball."

"You must be good at running," I said. "You've been running with Mommy since you were seven."

"But I'm not very fast. Actually, quite slow."

"Do you like basketball?"

"No, Mommy. Dribbling the ball is boring and silly."

"Has he taught you how to shoot the ball into the basket?"

"What does that mean? What basket?" Eddy felt confused and turned around again.

"It's called basketball because there's a basket hanging on a post, and you have to throw the ball into the basket to score," I explained.

"What?"

"Ask Papa to explain. He was an outstanding basketball player in college."

"Really?" Eddy turned around again, excited.

"Watch the road! Don't look at me! You're about to hit someone!" I screamed.

SPRING FLOWER: TORN BETWEEN SHIFTING WORLDS

Eddy turned his head back and veered quickly to the left to avoid the person and somehow sped up his pedaling as well. The back rack slipped out of my hand, and off he went. "Eddy, watch out for the tree! Squeeze the brakes!" But before I could finish, the bike, the tree, and Eddy collided. His hands weren't big or strong enough to clamp down on the old, rusted hand brakes. I biked him to the hospital with his nose bleeding and his right eye and cheek swollen.

Paul was furious when he learned that I'd been teaching Eddy English while learning to bike. "I'm not sure why you're teaching him English, but please teach one thing at a time! You just don't seem to be content when he's not cut, slashed, burned, in a crash, or beaten by you!"

I felt sad that Paul had to bring up all of Eddy's traumas in one sentence. But I deserved it. So, I said, "I told him not to keep turning his head back."

"But you were talking to him. Okay, Dr. Pei, I'll teach him to ride a bike, because I'll be taking him to school." Paul's mood suddenly changed.

"What?" I asked, truly curious.

"Chang *Lao-Shih*, Gina's old homeroom teacher, asked if I could go to their elementary school for a week and teach the kids to plow and plant rice," Paul said in an excited tone.

"Why?"

"Schools across the country are trying to educate kids where food comes from and how precious rice is and how hard farmers have to work to produce the food that we eat every day."

"Which brilliant leader of ours came up with this idea, now that the nation is facing starvation again? Teaching kids to plant rice will get us out of this famine? Do they intend to send the kids to the countryside for *Rustication–Reeducation* too?"

Paul sighed, "Well, Dr. Pei, you do have a point, but I think there's another way to look at it. It's important to teach the next generation how precious food is and how much hard work farmers have to endure to feed the country. It will teach them to appreciate and not waste the fruits of other people's labor."

I was shocked he would agree with any of our Great Leaders' programs.

"But of course I understand your skepticism," Paul said, still quite animated.

"Okay, he's your bike-riding student then. Let's see how good an instructor you are."

"I accept the challenge, Dr. Pei. In a week, he'll be riding your bike as though he's been doing it for years."

"I hope so, Professor Hsiung!" I laughed. "Have a go at it."

Two weeks later, not one as Paul had predicted, when Paul was finally done going to Eddy's elementary school to teach spring planting, Eddy knew how to ride a bike! Paul taught him how to put his left foot on the ground to push the bike, the way you would a kids' scooter, then lift his right leg over the crossbar (all bikes in China at that time had crossbars, with women's bikes being lower in overall height). It wasn't pretty and could be dangerous if he got his leg caught on the crossbar when hopping on or off, but riding a bike in China was a necessity of life, and so beauty was less important than getting from Point A to Point B.

Eddy was happy as a bird and kept shouting, "Look, Mommy, look, I can ride—I am free!"

"Yes, dear, but still watch out for traffic and people. Freedom comes with greater responsibility, kiddo. You're responsible for yourself, other riders, and pedestrians. Do you understand?"

"Yes!" Eddy turned his head back.

"Hey, kiddo, slow down. Mommy can't run that fast."

"Sorry, Mommy! Papa taught me some English words, and

he said that whenever you seem to be serious about anything, I should just say, 'Yes, ma'am!'"

"Your papa is very funny!"

"Papa made me a celebrity in our school," Eddy said.

"How so?"

"After Chang *Lao-Shih* introduced Papa to our entire school, my classmates knew he was my papa! Papa drew his plan on the blackboard. He and several teachers then dredged up the mud from a big square ditch to prepare the ground before Papa arrived. Then they filled the ditch with water and made it a pond, and Papa showed us how to plant rice seeds into the muddy pond. We had a lot of fun walking around barefoot in the rice paddy!" Eddy's face had lit up.

"Watch the road, Eddy! Yes, that does sound exciting!"

"Papa also gave us lessons on the history of rice planting in China and the importance of water, irrigation, and plowing. He talked about the spacing between each plant and how deep we should plant, and about pests and weeds."

"Papa is a good teacher, huh?" I, too, was proud of Paul. He was a born teacher but, sadly, his talents had been wasted all these years.

"My classmates loved him, and now I'm a celebrity."

"Okay, my dear celebrity son, how about a few English sentences?"

"Yes, ma'am!"

"When people ask, 'What does your father do?' you can answer, 'My father is a teacher. He teaches rice planting because he is an agronomist, which is like a farmer.'"

"Are *farmer* and *agronomist* different? Papa said that your mama and papa were farmers and that Papa is an agronomist because he researches rice."

"How did you know the word *research*?"

"Papa taught me! So, will you tell me now where *you* learned English and about your papa and mama?"

"I thought Papa taught you everything?"

"No, he told me to ask you."

"Okay, my dear celebrity, please give me the bike back now and hurry to class. We'll talk more tomorrow."

I was happy to hear about Paul and Eddy's time together, and that evening when Paul came home, I complimented him for being a great teacher.

"Oh, they're kids," he said. "It doesn't take much to get them excited."

"Well, Eddy is proud of you and happy to be a celebrity in his class."

"Actually, there is something we need to discuss. After meeting with many of Eddy's teachers, I learned that Eddy's been doing poorly in school!"

"Really? Am I to blame for not paying enough attention to him? And whenever he asks about Chinese texts, I tell him to talk to you and Gina."

"I haven't been around much. I also heard they may reinstate entrance exams for junior high. The quality of the junior high school one attends depends on scores from these exams. I think that's more important than learning English just now."

"What should we do?" I asked, trying to focus on the issue at hand rather than dwell on the latest blow he'd just delivered.

"His math is average. He's not doing well in geography, and he's practically failing social sciences. Surprisingly, unlike his mother, Eddy's Chinese writing is good." Paul grinned at me, and I chuckled, not knowing whether to laugh or cry.

"Chang *Lao-Shih* recommends that we find Eddy a tutor."

"How will we pay a tutor?" I asked, and Paul had an answer ready.

SPRING FLOWER: TORN BETWEEN SHIFTING WORLDS

"I know a couple who might be perfect. I don't know how we could pay, but let me take Eddy to meet them and see if they're willing to help and if they are, we can see what they might need. You never know, maybe they need a highly skilled ophthalmologist and surgeon." Paul grinned again.

"Okay," I smiled and nodded my head in agreement.

The couple were former college professors who were forced to stay at home during this Great Revolution. The woman had taught math and the man had taught water painting, Chinese literature, poetry, and classics. He had shared a dingy room at the *Cowshed* (牛棚) with Paul. According to Paul, they were probably poorer than we were—no small accomplishment! They were ten years our senior, with two young-adult kids living at home, the four of them squeezed into a tiny, dark second-floor apartment (more like an attic) of no more than a hundred square feet.

Paul took Eddy to see them, and it seemed like a good fit, although it was still unclear how we would pay them.

"Please tell them to come to the clinic, and I can check their eyesight, but that's not a payment. What else might they need?"

"The mother complained that they don't have much to eat."

"So they need stamps for rice, oil, meat, and cotton?"

"No, Jeanie, the father hinted that they don't get out much, even to buy food. Next week when I go back to the farm...how much money do you have?"

I took out two wrinkled bills, a ten RMB (*Yüan*, 元) and a five RMB sandwiched among cloth stamps, food stamps, meat stamps, sugar stamps, salt stamps, and oil stamps.

"That's all you have?" Paul looked shocked while taking the ten RMB bill.

"Wait, it's only the middle of the month. I'll need that for the kids' lunch. Aren't you getting a salary now?"

"No. I get a tiny payment for shelving books. We're still living off your salary." Paul paused a second and said, "Okay, give me all your food and cloth stamps. I'll exchange some eggs and meat from farmers on the black market and bring them to this family. They seem to be under even greater duress than we are. Perhaps they're still under house arrest."

"Do you think you and Eddy visiting them may be bad for them?"

"Maybe, but they said they would tell people we're relatives."

I fell into silence as it was hard to imagine a worse situation than ours, but that was the case. I never met this family, since they never came to the clinic despite my offer.

When we got into bed, Paul said, "Dr. Jean Perkins!" His playful tone took me aback. "The kids are asleep, and I want to tell you something that will get you excited."

"Not tonight." I pushed him away.

"Seriously, I have some news. But if you're not interested," he stopped mid-sentence and rolled over, turning his back toward me.

"Okay, sorry, Paul. Please do tell! I apologize for my rudeness."

Paul rolled back over and smiled, "President Nixon visited China again, maybe a month ago; I'm not sure when."

"Are you certain? What was the purpose of his visit?" I was really excited.

"It must be about reestablishing diplomatic relations. If that's his mission, good for him, and good luck to him. With the American war in Vietnam over, anything is possible."

"I don't want to dream about it anymore. The less I feel hopeful about returning to America, the more I can cope with life here—at least life here is with you and the kids."

After a pause, Paul added, "It doesn't hurt to dream." He then turned over and fell asleep, leaving me wide awake the whole night.

SPRING FLOWER: TORN BETWEEN SHIFTING WORLDS

A few months later, on July 6, 1976, Secretary of Defense General Chu Teh (朱德) died. And on July 28, the earth shook again, this time a magnitude 7.8 earthquake with the epicenter in T'angshan (唐山), a city of nearly two million people northeast of Peking and not far from Tientsin. The tremors traveled more than 500 miles, and we even felt some of the aftershocks in Hangchow. Many buildings in T'angshan were poorly designed and built with cheap materials, and the city was leveled. Close to half a million people (250,000 reported, but probably more than that) died from the quake, and the numbers were kept a secret. It was one of the most destructive earthquakes in modern history. Hunger and disease followed. People were displaced without shelters or sanitation for months. By the summer of 1976, only Shanghai and Peking still had adequate resources for healthcare, so doctors were sent from those cities, including some of my former colleagues from the Eye and ENT Infirmary.

Once again, China's leadership arrogantly refused Western and UN help. More lives could have been saved, but we had only ourselves to rely on, and by 1976, even the term *ourselves* had been stripped to its bones by the Great Revolution. Day-Day and Mother would have been saddened to know that China was *still* unable to respond to a huge natural disaster.

Two months later, on September 9, 1976, Chairman Mao died. The nation expressed the deepest grief I'd ever witnessed. We all had to stand for hours outdoor beneath a flag to show our emotions while holding his *Little Red Book* and wearing a black armband. I watched those around me and those still crying on street corners and in alleyways. I was baffled. My eyes were dry; I did not have a single teardrop. Years later, I realized that the tears I saw that day may well have been for different reasons than mourning the death of Chairman Mao.

JEAN TREN-HWA PERKINS

A few weeks later, on an early October morning in 1976, I was called into Jade's office to receive a phone call. It was my brother, Yan-Feng (延豐). I hadn't heard from him in years. He was calling from Kiukiang to tell me that my very own dear Wang-Sao had just passed away. I slumped to the ground and Jade helped me to her chair. I wailed as if there was no tomorrow. Her last words to me had been "I think my job is done. I feel ready to see Dr. and Mrs. Perkins without remorse. But somehow I'm still worried about my girls." The next day, I couldn't get out of bed or find any reason to keep on living, at least in this country. I'd never felt so alone in the world. Wang-Sao was my last link to Day-Day and Mother—and to my treasured past.

In deep mourning, I became oblivious to the world around me, and that's when the big news came: The *Gang of Four* (四人幫) had been arrested by the army to prevent a coup against the heir-apparent to Chairman Mao, Mr. Hua Kuo-Feng (華國鋒). The infamous gang was led by Chairman Mao's last wife, Ms. Chiang Ch'ing (江青), who had been an actress before her revolutionary days; his other consorts were Chang Chung-Ch'iao (張春橋); Yao Wen-Yüan (姚文元); and Wang Hung-Wen (王洪文). A few other cohorts such as Lin Piao (林彪) and Kang Sheng (康生) had died earlier.

Overnight, Chairman Hua rose to power, and his portrait was plastered everywhere next to Chairman Mao's; and the *Gang of Four* was soon prosecuted for crimes again humanity. Various key figures who had been condemned and persecuted during the Cultural Revolution, including Teng Hsiao-Ping (鄧小平), were rehabilitated and brought back into the central governing body. Chairman Hua turned out to be a centrist, one who recognized that China was heading toward a complete collapse, economically and politically. The Great Revolution, initiated by his predecessor, was killing the nation. He was sincerely

SPRING FLOWER: TORN BETWEEN SHIFTING WORLDS

concerned and had the grit and resolve to change course. In a temporary alliance with Mr. Teng, they pronounced the end of the Cultural Revolution, and the Cultural Revolution's atrocities were conveniently blamed on the *Gang of Four*. They admitted that Mao's Great Proletariat Cultural Revolution had been a catastrophic mistake that set China back by decades, if not a century. This is no exaggeration. Regardless of how history will be written about Chairman Hua, he should be given full credit for turning the tide, and China owes much of her future fortune to this man. He might not have lasted long in power, but neither did Gorbachev. A leader's legacy can be defined by a singular event that changes history, like Nixon opening to China.

But how many decades does one life have? With irretrievable losses in culture, art, history, science, literature, and even basic literacy, China was in the dark ages, staring at its own ashes, in a tragedy of its own making. No one invaded us, no one enslaved us, and no one force-fed us opium this time. We did all of this to ourselves behind closed doors, in a holocaust of our own making. A colleague of Paul's, a history teacher named Yuan or Li, I believe, said to him, "How does one assess a mother who gives birth to a beautiful daughter and then kills her in infancy? Should this mother be celebrated as a creator of life or prosecuted as a murderer?" This question runs deep. While we were grateful to be alive, people's collective hearts were ripped out and stomped upon. Paul's heart certainly was, although he remained mum about what went on during his years spent at the labor camp living in a *cowshed* (牛棚). I've never been able to get him to share more than a few sentences before he has to stop, tears in his eyes. It was true of most people I knew. They would sigh and become tearful whenever the topic came up.

Strangely, despite these euphoric changes, people became more cautious. No one expressed joy, for fear that things would revert back overnight. Oppression has a way of silencing people permanently and forcing us to willingly accept the unacceptable and live in a fractured reality. And at the same time, changes were taking place at the speed of light. Within months, the *Worker's Declaration Team* (工宣隊) was disbanded, and their members were investigated for atrocities they'd caused at the hospital. The position of hospital superintendent was reinstated, as were the deans of various departments and division chiefs. I ran into Dr. Zhou in the hallway and saw that the smile and color had returned to his face. He had become the Chief of the Department of Internal Medicine, and his family was about to move out of their slum compound.

Jade was promoted to Chief Attending Ophthalmologist (主任-主治醫生), and I was finally given the rank of Full Attending Physician (主治醫生), retroactive to 1965, as noted in a formal letter of apology. Jade asked me to be her Associate Chief and the Head of the Clinical Research, for which I was grateful. But to be honest, I had lost interest in titles. The positions *Shu-Chi* and Vice *Shu-Chi* remained, but those holding the positions nearly all changed. One afternoon, I saw Li *Shu-Chi* being escorted out of the building by two policewomen, and I shouted, "Oh wait, Li *Shu-Chi*!"

She was startled and said, "Oh, Dr. Pei, I am no longer the *Shu-Chi* here. Please don't call me that." The policewomen were kind, even humane. They let go of her and stepped back a few feet.

"They should know you were very good to all of us these past ten years. If it hadn't been for you...."

She stopped me from speaking and said in a soft voice, "It's okay, Dr. Pei. You don't have to say anything. Hospitals help patients, and so hospitals need doctors. It was that simple for me all these years. I didn't need to treat you any differently from others. I was doing my job."

I felt so sad and wanted to say, "Thank you for saving my life." But before I could say more to express my appreciation, the two policewomen took hold of her and walked her out. I never knew what happened to her next.

The mood at home began to change too. In the winter of 1977, Paul told me he was given two choices. He could resume his faculty position and directorship of the Institute (杭州農科所) or accept a lucrative position as Lieutenant Governor Peng's right-hand man at the Provincial Office. Before he even told me his choice, I already knew.

"I'm honored that Lieutenant Governor Peng (彭省長) wants to nominate me for a position in his office," he said, "and it would be a great opportunity to work with the leadership at the provincial level. But I haven't done anything to deserve such a position, not to mention the comfort and privileges that would come with it. I'm a scientist and an educator at heart. With my mission incomplete and career at the Institute unfulfilled, I can't leave. I mourn the loss of these precious ten years, but you and I are in our mid-forties and still have time to fulfill our careers and help the people of China as we've always wanted."

Not long after, I asked Paul about China's future and why China had been so unlucky the past thirty years. He replied in one word: "Leadership." When I asked him to say more, he became animated. "The fate of a country or even an institute or a hospital department depends on leadership. A sound leader needs three traits."

"Three?" I wondered aloud.

"Yes, vision, the ability to analyze and listen, and the authority to be decisive and take responsibility (有眼光, 能吸收和聽取, 敢決定敢擔當). Having a vision isn't easy, but most leaders manage well enough. The problem is that most are unable to listen or decide, and that's when things go wrong." Paul seemed to be in a trance.

"To be attentive and to listen is a form of respect for those you're working with," he went on. "Doing so, you learn to balance the opinions of dominant but empty voices and the wise suggestions of the seemingly meek, and to discern agreeable but merely flattering chirpings from voices of dissent that ring true. Too many leaders have no interest in listening to others because they already have a preconceived idea. Even if they seem to be listening, it's just for show, with no intent to understand or pursue what others are saying. These leaders are more interested in being boss than accomplishing necessary tasks.

"On the other hand, a leader can't just listen, holding endless meetings and wasting valuable time without problem solving. A leader must be decisive by selecting (or modifying) ideas from the suggestions offered or follow their own instincts based on experience. Too many leaders are gun-shy and won't be decisive because they don't want to take responsibility, especially when things can go wrong. They prefer to shift the blame and move the target. But making decisions always includes the possibility that things will go wrong, and when they do, a leader needs to be the first to accept responsibility. Most leaders underestimate the respect admitting mistakes can engender.

"To mitigate mistakes, especially costly ones, listening can help. But a leader must think carefully about every problem, large and small, and know the issues and tactics thoroughly, including who can be assigned to what tasks. And they must have well-thought-out plans ready for success and contingencies for failure, so-called Plan B. A good leader has to do all this, and it's a thankless, exhausting, and probably life-shortening job that no one should want unless they are truly committed. I cringe when someone *wants* to be a leader, thinking it's about fame or profit."

SPRING FLOWER: TORN BETWEEN SHIFTING WORLDS

To this day, I can feel the vigor in Paul's speech, and I was in awe of his insight. I finally told him that Peng *Shu-Chi* had held onto the letter he sent to the Central Government (中央) in 1957 and had returned it to me. I told him I read the letter, then burned it in fear of our lives. It was no wonder that the Peng couple was taken by him. Paul said that the letter wasn't important unless it could be put into practice. And he finally told me that the night the Red Guards came, he knew they were looking for that letter, and he feared they would find my stuff and I'd be in massive trouble. It all made sense; he went to prison for more than four years and was under an equivalent of house arrest while working in a library for nearly six more years, in large part trying to save me.

The Peng couple went untouched by the *Gang of Four*'s (四人幫) fall because of their neutrality and underground work protecting people like Paul and me. Given that Chekiang Province was predominantly agricultural, food production became their focal point for economic recovery. They were determined to provide Paul and his Institute (杭州農科所) with all the resources needed to improve and maximize rice production. There was hope in the air. It seemed China had finally been liberated, and Paul couldn't wait for spring planting to begin!

84

OUR EUPHORIA was short-lived. It didn't take long to recognize that the road to recovery would be long and winding in every facet of our lives. The nationwide fear of backlash was endemic—every time we raised our heads, spoke a word, or took a step toward recovery. This fear had been tattooed onto our minds and hearts after suffering in silence for ten years. We'd become cautious, if not paranoid, as well as self-protective, self-obsessed, suspicious, and distrustful of one another.

At the same time, Gina was excelling in tenth grade, and I couldn't contain my joy and pride that my baby girl, who nearly everyone had given up on, would be graduating from high school in a year! High schools in China were structured with a two-year system (高一 and 高二, an equivalent of American tenth and eleventh grades) during Gina's time, but changed to a three-year system when Eddy was about to apply. With the reinstatement of stringent entrance exams, though, Eddy struggled and failed to enter a good junior high. So we registered him at a school that had many kids who were caught between grades (as he was) or who hadn't qualified for the better junior high schools. The tutoring was only a short-term fix, because Eddy—as were almost *all* kids in China—was paying the price of society's devaluing education.

Eddy's new school was a little farther away. In part because he was feeling depressed, I shared his long daily commute to school, then biked back to my clinic. I really wanted to teach him English, not just a sentence here and a word there, but complete sentences without resorting to Chinese. Besides, after ten long years of those dreaded daily Mao quotation classes (which had mercifully been terminated), I had more time in the mornings. At the clinic we were still asked to remember words of wisdom from the *Little Red Book*, but Mao's quotations were no longer a substitute for accurate diagnoses, skillful operations, and proper medications. As a nation, we had a little more time for breakfast, getting our kids ready for school, and commuting to work. We had to relearn "normal."

"Eddy, you're almost twelve. Have you thought about what you want to do when you grow up?" I asked in English one day as he was pushing my bike and not riding.

"We're practicing English again today, Mommy?" Eddy stumbled for words, mixing and matching his two languages.

"Why not? The more you speak, the more you'll learn."

Eddy thought about it for a while and said, "Well, to answer your question, I would like to be a writer someday."

"That's what Mommy wanted." I was pleased to hear those words.

"Then how come you became a doctor?"

I wasn't sure what language we should speak in, as the topic had become complicated. So I switched back to Chinese. "It was my dream to become a writer, but many things happened in my life, and some dreams die. I was hoping you'd become a doctor, too. Would that be interesting?"

Eddy shook his head. "I see you tired and busy every day. I'm not sure that would be a great job."

"Well, it's great to help other people."

After a moment of silence, he asked the big questions again: "Mommy, you still haven't told me why you want me to learn English and where you learned English. And who is your mommy, and is she related to Grandma Wang?"

"Whoa, slow down, kid. That's a lot to answer!" I blurted out in English, to distract him.

"Why don't you teach me Japanese? My classmates said Japanese is becoming the most useful language," Eddy pressed on.

My sonny boy was no longer a kid. His comments made me think about Taka. I had received another short note, saying he'd moved to Aomori, the northernmost province on Japan's main island, Honshu. The name on the envelope appeared to be that of a woman, and the envelope itself seemed to have been around the world, covered with fingerprints, ink, and even a bit of mud.

I wasn't sure what to say to Eddy about Day-Day and Mother, or my charmed past in Kiukiang and Yonkers, so we fell into an awkward silence. Then Eddy looked up and said, "Maybe it's a dream to become a writer. But you know what? I do love poetry, and I love to write."

"That's fantastic, Eddy! Please show me your poems."

"Okay, when you tell me who your parents are," Eddy said with a grin.

"That's a fair trade. Poetry can be quite private, and not all poems are written to be shared."

Eddy didn't say anything, so I added, "You'll do well with languages. See how quickly you've been able to learn some English! You have a gift."

That turned out to be the last lengthy, meaningful conversation Eddy and I had, and the last time we commuted to work and school together.

When I arrived at the clinic, Jade pulled me into her office and asked, "Where have you been, Tren-Hwa? What took you so long getting here?"

"I walked with Eddy. He's been low, and I wanted to spend the time with him. What's up?" I asked.

SPRING FLOWER: TORN BETWEEN SHIFTING WORLDS

"The superintendent has been looking for you."

"Oh, dear. Am I in hot water with the new leadership already?" I probably looked terrified.

"No, I think he has a favor to ask," Jade said and smiled.

So off I went, unsure what this was about. Outside the new superintendent's office, I was offered a seat in the waiting area by someone I thought must be his secretary. She seemed kind and poured me a mug of tea. Fifteen minutes later, Superintendent Wen (文), an obstetrician new to hospital leadership, invited me into his office. He was only about my height and perhaps fifteen years older. He smiled and shook my hand.

"Thank you for coming here, Dr. Pei. I have an important question to ask you," and he smiled again.

I moved close to the edge of my chair, anxious I'd be accused of Americanism or some other crime. And indeed, he began that way.

"Did you live in America when you were a child? Were your parents Americans? I mean, were you adopted by Americans?"

My face must have turned ashen because Superintendent Wen quickly added, "Dr. Pei, don't worry. The reason I'm asking is that I'd like to know if you are still able to speak fluent English."

I tried to exhale and speak at the same time, and managed to get out only a few sentences, but remarkably I found myself saying them in English. "Yes, Superintendent Wen, I can speak fluent English, although I haven't spoken much in years. But I'm confident I can remember. To be honest, it's my mother tongue."

Superintendent Wen simply looked shocked. "I know quite a bit of English," he said, "and I know you were speaking English just now, but I could never speak like that! There is a team of medical professions from Egypt currently touring our country, and we are extremely short of people who can speak English. So there was a notice from the Central Government's Ministry of Health in Peking seeking people with English-language skills. I am going to submit your name as a candidate to meet with this delegation."

"Oh, really? You think they'll accept me with my undesirable family background?" I tried not to show my apprehension, but probably failed at that.

"Undesirable family background? Where have you been the last six months, Dr. Pei? Things have changed, at last for the better!" Superintendent Wen was so excited his hands were shaking. "The only issue is whether you are willing to help out."

"Of course, Superintendent Wen. I would be honored to help. What are their medical specialties, and when are they coming to Hangchow?" I tried to express enthusiasm, but my terror had not yet subsided.

"Actually, they're not coming to Hangchow. Hangchow is too small to have the resources to receive delegates of such importance from the West. The primary issue of whether you can help depends on whether you can travel. I understand you have two children and that your husband commutes a long way to his Research Institute (杭州農科所)."

"Oh, of course, I hadn't even thought about that."

"Please go home and discuss this opportunity with your husband, and if he agrees I will submit your name. The delegation will be presenting recent advances in obstetric medicine, which is my area of interest, and so if things go well, you, I, and another colleague from my department will depart in two days to meet the Egyptian physicians in Peking, and then we'll travel to Shanghai with them before they leave China."

I finally showed a natural smile, and after walking away from the Superintendent's office, I felt a big *Yes* inside, not only because I might get a chance to speak English in broad daylight

SPRING FLOWER: TORN BETWEEN SHIFTING WORLDS

but also because I recognized where this might lead.

When Paul came home that evening, he was immediately excited. "Oh, you've got to go!" he exclaimed, his voice reaching a high pitch.

"Please calm down, Paul. I don't want the neighbors to hear."

"Who can speak English better than you and your sister, Chum?" It was funny he brought up Chum, and suddenly I wondered how she was and if she had been tapped for similar duty. She would be a great translator, because she knew English better than I did, having lived in the US longer than I did, completing junior high there.

"You seem more confident than I am. I still speak and understand English, but I haven't spoken it for so long."

"Your concerns are not unfounded and maybe you can use a little polishing, but it's like riding a bicycle. You'll remember within minutes. English is your first language, your mother tongue."

"Thank you for your vote of confidence and for your enthusiasm. But who will take care of the kids while I'm gone and you're only around once or twice a week, right? I will be away for two weeks."

"No problem. I'll take responsibility for Gina and Eddy. They can practically take care of themselves now. What do they do besides eat, sleep, and study?"

With that assurance, I packed up the only presentable suitcase we had and joined Superintendent Wen (文) and his colleague Dr. Song, a senior resident from the Department of Obstetrics, for a two-day and three-night, slow-moving and shaky train ride to Peking. My bed, a very thin mattress—if you could even call it a mattress—was next to the bathroom, and the stench was just nauseating. On Chinese sleeper trains, anyone can sit on your bed and use it as a dinner table, so I tried to make my bed look messy so people would sit elsewhere. Unfortunately, that didn't deter everyone.

We made quite a few stops along the way, scheduled and unscheduled, and of various lengths. Some stops weren't even near a station; perhaps the conductor needed a nap. The country's railway system was, by now, horribly outdated, and I found myself complaining, rather than feeling grateful to have such an exciting task and opportunity. I tried to calm myself and brighten my thoughts. And as the train labored ahead, I was able at last to reach back into my memories and see the shadow of my younger self heading to Harbin. I remembered the fire hydrant shower we took at the Tientsin Train Station and the conversation I had with Professor Ma. I recalled that we hopped off the train in Peking and managed to find enough time to tour the capital city before changing trains. I wondered if I could climb the Great Wall this time, something I'd never done.

By the time we arrived at Peking Railway Station (北京火車站), which had not changed much since 1955, the three of us were dusty, dirty, and oily. We were already a day late. Fortunately, there was a small van waiting for us, but instead of taking us to a hotel for a quick wash-up, we went directly to the conference center to meet with two other physicians, one from Peking Union Medical College Hospital (北京協和醫院) and the other from Shanghai Municipal Hospital (上海市醫院), presumably also English speakers. Then we were to be introduced to the delegation.

The Egyptian delegates had already toured Peking and met with government officials. They were twelve highly regarded medical scholars in several areas of medicine focusing on obstetrics. There were no ophthalmologists among them.

After shaking hands with each of us, the delegation leader, Dr. Said Ibrahim, a warm and humorous man, made a short speech. When he told a few self-deprecating jokes, I was the only one on our side who laughed. Superintendent Wen gave me a gentle nudge. "Dr. Pei, please translate for us. What's so funny?"

I hesitated for a second, and then took a deep breath and said, "Dr. Ibrahim, would it be okay if I translate your words to our team of translators? Sometimes it can be difficult to get a joke in another language."

He turned to me with a big smile and apologized for speaking too quickly and acknowledged that he had a thick accent. As he spoke, everyone on both sides kept looking at me, and I began translating for the translators. Superintendent Wen looked on with proud eyes, and with his affirmation and support, I became less nervous and more daring and began to translate the essence of stories and humor coming from both sides. With that, the atmosphere, and my heart, became alive.

From that point on, everyone on both sides sought me out, whether during lectures, conference presentations, or interactions with physicians at site visits, including Peking Union Medical College Hospital (北京協和醫院). They all asked me what certain words meant and their equivalents in Chinese. It felt odd, because the other translators' English was quite good and more than sufficient to communicate. In any case, I took my job seriously. Everyone seemed so sincere to learn and to find out the meanings of words, and I was very glad to teach and help, although I had to search for many words and expressions that had been buried in my memory.

This was the first time I'd ever translated for anyone. I got used to Egyptian ways of pronouncing certain words and which expressions they liked to repeat. As the week went on, it became easier to capture their intended meaning. But as an ophthalmologist and not an obstetrician, many of the medical terms they used were difficult for me to translate. My colleagues, and especially Superintendent Wen, were far more qualified than I in this regard.

All in all, it was wonderful teamwork, and I enjoyed the camaraderie. The Chinese team thoroughly enjoyed interacting with these experienced physicians and accomplished scholars. And because of their friendliness, humility, and eagerness to learn about our nation's state of healthcare and the medical profession, my first trip as a medical translator was deeply fulfilling.

My only regret was that I failed to see Shou and Peng when we went to Shanghai. We didn't stop at the Eye and ENT Infirmary, and there wasn't time for me to break from the delegation's full schedule of activities. We were also shorthanded in Shanghai, because the Peking team did not travel with us. Even so, it was satisfying to see my Shanghai again. It had been twelve years since I'd been back and *so much* had happened in those years. I was flooded with memories. My life there seemed a lifetime ago—life was simpler and more hopeful then—so it felt as though it had all been a dream.

We traveled by minivan, and I bit my lips as I looked out the window, keeping the tears inside. Nearly every street had my footprints, reminding me of particular people or events. On one stretch, it was impossible to contain my feelings. While riding in the van with the group to see the storied Huang-P'u River (黄浦江), I saw the grassy patches with a few trees along the river where Taka and I last sat and watched Gina crawling, standing up with determination, and then walking a step forward before flopping to the ground with joy. That was where we shared stories of our lives while looking out at countless boats of different shapes, sizes, and colors. I turned my head toward the window and closed my eyes. Superintendent Wen thoughtfully separated me from our inquisitive, excited visitors.

When the trip finally came to an end, we cordially exchanged gifts—and our team was mostly on the receiving end. Dr. Ibrahim took a small colorful cube from his briefcase and said, "This is a small token of my gratitude especially for you, Dr. Pei, or perhaps you also have a different name! It's called a magical cube or Hungarian puzzle cube, something your kids will love to solve." Later, after the inventor Erno Rubik sold rights to an American company, it became known as a Rubik's Cube. Gina and Eddy loved it, and so did Paul.

I was taken aback by his kind gesture, so while sitting next to Dr. Ibrahim at the farewell dinner, I told him I'd been to Egypt and climbed the pyramids when I was fourteen, in 1945. He was speechless.

Finally he said, "That's why I love to travel. One unexpectedly encounters wonders of life on these journeys. I sensed you were different from the others, that perhaps you'd had a different experience. I hope we will meet again, perhaps in Egypt, and you can tell me more."

85

I WAS GONE for only three weeks, but it felt like a year to Paul and the kids. They surely were happy to see me back, and the three of them were fighting to play with this magical cube and move the squares so that each side was all the same color. I was happy, too, because the kids, especially Eddy, never had any toys. He was almost beyond the age of playing with toys now, but this one was unique, not just a toy but something that required intellectual and math skills. And it was a gift for me to remember this fond trip forever.

Paul was more capable than I, it turned out, of taking care of the home and the kids, and the apartment was tidy. He even got Eddy and Gina to help with housecleaning and Eddy to help with cooking.

Then Paul told me about something strange that had happened while I was gone. He asked Eddy to do some errands, buying breakfast in the mornings from the street vendors who had begun to set up on our corner (reminding me of my Shanghai years) and getting provisions for dinner, including salt, soy sauce, vegetable oil, and yellow cooking wine (紹興黃酒), so Paul could prepare the vegetables he'd brought from the farm. He would give Eddy five cents a day for these errands, and one time the "yellow" rice wine used for cooking was a third gone by the time Eddy got home. "I could smell it on his breath," Paul told me, "and I knew that if I asked him why the bottle wasn't full, I'd be forcing him to lie."

SPRING FLOWER: TORN BETWEEN SHIFTING WORLDS

I was shocked. "He's way too young to be drinking alcohol, Paul! Please tell him to stop!" Then I asked Gina if she knew about Eddy drinking the rice wine, and she confessed rather quickly that she and Eddy *both* had been chugging away on it.

"What?" I didn't know whether to laugh or cry. So I discussed it with Paul. "Gina is old enough," I confided, "but she's disabled. Alcohol can't be good for her. And Eddy's only twelve."

"Hear me out, Jeanie. With both of us gone most of the day, I figure the best strategy is to have an open policy."

"Meaning what?"

"Well, let them have some, but under my close watch so it doesn't get out of hand."

"Under your 'close watch'? Who's going to watch *you*? How can you promise me that this won't get out of hand, Professor Hsiung?"

"We'll see if my method works. I have a big glass of rice wine, and the kids each can have a tiny glass at dinner."

"Paul, that is *not okay*. After my next trip, what will I find when I get home? Three drunks lying in bed!"

Paul laughed. I was serious. Still, I knew if another translating opportunity came up, I'd jump at it, and that's what happened. A small team of ENT physicians from Greece would be visiting Shanghai, and I joined two ENT doctors from our hospital and off we went. Before I left, I hugged the kids and told them this trip would be shorter. I encouraged Eddy to study hard and retake his entrance exams, so he could get into a good junior high (seventh through ninth grades in China: 初一到初三). I didn't mention the drinking. That conversation would take more time. I wanted to understand what prompted him to try alcohol at such a young age.

It was a densely scheduled two-week trip, and when I got home, I barely had time to unpack before leaving for Hsiamen

(廈門) or Amoy, to help another team of visitors from Greece. As I had done with Dr. Ibrahim, I made a deep impression on their team leader, Dr. Antonis Stathopoulos, who asked if I could help a friend of his who would soon be heading to China with a team of visitors. I agreed, before discovering that these visitors were physicists, not physicians. I had to ask Jade and Superintendent Wen for a short leave, since this wasn't a hospital-sponsored activity. Unexpectedly, I was allowed to go, while being gently reminded that I should save my energy for medical-related delegations.

At that moment in time, these kinds of activities were considered an honor, not just for the individuals involved but also for their institutions. Interactions at an international level were being promoted to the fullest. I was getting carried away by the excitement of these trips, and why not? I got to see parts of China I'd never seen before and could finally learn and retain some of the history of my country of birth. And encountering these wonderful foreigners while speaking English with no bounds brought back so many memories of the past. I felt hopeful for the first time in decades.

Within days, formal invitations arrived from the City of Hsiamen (廈門) or Amoy and even from the president of Hsiamen University. I finally got to visit dear Old Man Ni's hometown. But, boy, did I regret accepting, in terms of the translation work. I had never translated anything beyond simple conversations and medical terms, certainly not physics. It was nearly impossible!

I traveled with the group from Hsiamen to Canton in Kwangtung (廣州, 廣東), the mainland's southernmost province. Canton was where I'd wanted to flee in 1951, and while I was there, I learned how far the city actually is from Hong Kong Island—about 84.5 miles, or 136 kilometers. As I stood by the shore of Chu-Kiang (珠江), the Pearl River that flows into the

South China Sea, I wondered what might have happened if I'd tried.

Despite its rich history and involvement in revolutions led by Dr. Sun Yat-Sen and his *Kuo-Min-Tang* Party against the crumbling Ch'ing (also called the Manchu) Dynasty and rising warlords at the turn of the century, Canton looked pretty shabby, as if it were still the Ch'ing Dynasty. In contrast, Hsiamen was clean, well-organized, and stately. Although the food was fantastic in Canton, I wasn't sure why it was a part of the journey.

We then went by train to K'unming in Yunnan Province, which reminded me of Taka's uncle and aunt and their Chinese Traditional Medicines. We saw Shangri-La (香格里拉) and Li-Kiang (麗江). I had a very positive impression of Yunnan and the people there.

Although I came close to sailing the Seven Seas as a teen, I'd never traveled like this — going to a new place every few days. The train rides were much more comfortable, as we were booked in "softer-seat (软坐)" cabins, the equivalent of first class, decorated with linens and equipped with a kitchen cart that was open at mealtimes. And the bathroom, oh the bathroom, was a whole different world — it had a *toilet* (although it was made of cold stainless steel). The conditions almost rivaled the Pullman Coach to upstate New York. I smiled while seated on the toilet, having a moment to myself. If it weren't for someone knocking on the door, I could have fallen asleep there, it was so clean and comfortable and I was so tired.

Soon we were heading to Ch'engtu, the capital of Szechwan Province in the southwest of China. All along the way, at these stops and during train rides, the guides were explaining the landscapes and history, so I had to translate. Although the visitors were as warm, courteous, and curious as the Egyptian and the Greek doctors, they stayed quite to themselves. Because they were physicists rather than physicians, I seemed to have little in common with them. So during this long trip, I became more of a professional translator and then a physician who happened to know English, which was good training for me, not to mention that I learned a lot of Chinese history from the tour guides, information that finally stuck.

So, rather than conversing with the delegation, I spent my time talking with the guides, finding out where they were from and what made them pursue this line of work. Many came from the countryside and with this job, they were able to make a reasonable living and send money to their families at home. I was amazed how much they knew. One of them smiled as she told me, "Dr. Pei, it's not difficult. You just buy a book and memorize it!" Another said, "Our grandparents told us these stories when we were growing up."

As the train rambled into the mountainous Szechwan region, I thought about Wang-Sao—how she would tell Eddy and Gina stories from *Romance of the Three Kingdoms*. Just then, one guide stood and began to explain what these mountainous areas were during the Chou and Han Dynasties. Words such as Ch'in Kuo (秦國), Liu Pang (劉邦), Shu-Han (蜀漢), and Chu Ko-Liang (諸葛亮) started to creep into my ear. Although I'd heard these words before, they made little sense until that trip when I began translating. And I thought about Lian, my colleague when I first moved to Shanghai, and her stories, and wondered if she was still in Ch'engtu.

Once in Ch'engtu, the physicists went to their rooms to prepare their lectures. By then, I was far less nervous, because I'd heard their lectures many times and figured these presentations would be about the same, even if they changed a few words here and there. It would be about atoms, electrons, and different kinds of energy. So I spent the day roaming Ch'engtu on my own. I remembered Day-Day saying that a group of Methodist missionaries, who had been stationed in Kiukiang before Day-Day and Mother arrived, had gone to Ch'engtu to build hospitals and schools (Hart Memorial College, today's West China School of Pharmacy affiliated with Szechwan University). I was unable to find it, as I dared not say "missionary hospital" explicitly, and so people were confused by my inquiry. Most responded, "Hospital built by foreigners in the 1850s (洋人建造的)?" It turned out we weren't staying too far from it; it had become part of West China Hospital (成都華西協和醫院).

Then as a group we went to the famed Huang-Lung (黃龍) and Chiu-Chai-Kou (九寨溝) with an array of shimmering colorful ponds. The altitude at Huang-Lung (from 5,500 to 18,000 feet) was a bit of a problem for some of the visitors, but I was okay. After that we went south of Ch'engtu and climbed Mount Le (樂山) and Mount E-Mei (峨眉山). As beautiful as all these places were, the moment that truly captured my heart was when we took a boat ride on the Min River (岷江), which flows into the Great Yangtze River near its origin. As the tour guide chattered away, I was lost in thought. From here, the Great Yangtze River winds downward, passing Kiukiang and Nanking before flowing out of Shanghai into the Pacific via the Huang-P'u River—a total of 4,000 miles. Once again, though, I was wrong; the Great Yangtze actually splits near the city of Chungking (重慶). The higher fork is the Chin-Sha River (金沙江), while the origin flows from the Tsinghai-Tibet Plateau (青藏高原) in the Province of Tsinghai (青海省). The Min River (岷江) we were sailing on was just a tributary.

When someone suddenly shouted something about Tsinghai, my thoughts went to Chum. I hadn't realized we'd be this close to Tsinghai. The stop in Sian was canceled, owing to insufficient resources to host foreigners. Instead, we went straight to Peking and then back to Shanghai, where the delegation would depart from Shanghai Hung-Ch'iao Airport (虹橋機場). Those last two stops were a blur, although I enjoyed finally trotting up a portion of the Great Wall, and I never tired of seeing my beloved Huang-P'u River. All in all, I saw more places in China than I'd ever seen before and came to understand why Day-Day and Mother loved the country so much.

A month later when I finally got home, I found a note saying that Paul had taken the kids to his Institute for a few weeks leading up to the fall harvest. The emptiness and exhaustion of traveling made me weep alone that evening, and for the next few weeks I found it difficult to stay focused at the clinic. Part of me was still somewhere on those trips, part of me wondered when the next opportunity would come, and part of me wondered if Americans would finally make their way here. After three weeks, Paul and the kids came home, and I felt better, especially when Gina seemed really glad to see me. But Eddy tried to act like a grownup, and he'd grown taller than before I left. Paul told me that Eddy had been accepted at Gina's high school for the coming term, officially becoming a 7th grader. And to my great relief, he would have the same math teacher, Ma *Lao-Shih*, who had been so kind to Gina when we were battling for her right to attend school, and he would also be Eddy's homeroom teacher.

"Do you think Eddy will be okay in this high school?" I asked Paul.

"I think so. I met with Ma *Lao-Shih* when Eddy and I went to register, and he seemed to be fond of Eddy and even said, 'This kid is a child prodigy in math. Just look at how he answered some of the exam questions. Amazing!'"

"Really? Are you joking? Eddy barely made it to junior high. If he can graduate, I will be satisfied."

SPRING FLOWER: TORN BETWEEN SHIFTING WORLDS

"I wondered the same. Ma *Lao-Shih* seems to say that about everyone," Paul laughed, but added with confidence, "After being admitted, all the kids had to take another round of exams administered by the school. I was told Eddy did well in the language exam. So let's give him a chance."

Paul then looked straight at me and asked, "Dr. Perkins, what are we going to do with Gina when she finishes twelfth grade?"

"I don't know. I heard they might be reinstating college entrance exams. Maybe Gina should try; she's certainly qualified."

"And facing another lengthy and exhausting battle?" Paul interrupted.

I paused, not sure what to do. The rumor was that there'd be a mad scramble for permission to participate in the first round of college entrance exams since the Cultural Revolution, and the number of people who wanted to take the exams was huge. It wouldn't just be physically normal kids right out of high school. Some would be older, even in their twenties and thirties, having been out of school for a decade or more.

Getting permission to take the exam would be an exhausting battle for a disabled student. Having a high school education was unheard of for kids like Gina in 1970s China; so demanding a college education for her seemed out of reach. China was just beginning to resurrect a higher education system that collapsed under the destructive weight of the Revolution.

But my attention quickly turned toward a team of Polish physicians visiting Shanghai. The time I spent with them was engaging, but these translating assignments were getting tiring, and especially the train rides, even in first class. I was able to appreciate more what Paul went through to take the train from Hangchow to Shanghai to see Gina and me. Afterward, back home again, a weary traveler, I tried getting closer to Eddy, but he seemed even more distant, except when he'd shout, "What do these sentences mean, Mommy?"

I would take a quick look and explain, "Those are in the old style of writings (文言文) or Chinese idioms (成語). You'll have to ask Papa."

"Mommy, my English teacher said I sound funny."

"You're studying English in school now?"

"Yes, Mommy. It's part of the junior high curriculum. We have to choose between Japanese and English, and I chose English because you already taught me so much."

"How are you doing in English, then?"

"Quite well, except my teacher keeps trying to correct my pronunciations."

"Say something in English, Eddy."

"On the way to school, today, I heard a car honking at me, and so I stopped before crossing the street." He was speaking in a loud voice, almost shouting in my direction.

I corrected him on the pronunciation of a few words and then said, "That sounds good. I wonder what your teacher means."

When Paul got home, I asked him that question, and he said, "I don't understand why his teacher is saying that either. With you teaching him, his pronunciation is probably standard English."

"Maybe I should meet with him and see where he thinks Eddy is wrong?"

"Don't, Jeanie. Let's not interfere," Paul said, and went back to his studies.

"Well," I said to myself. "If his teacher thinks Eddy's pronunciation is off, how does this *teacher* pronounce these words? I'd like to find out."

"What are you working on?" I asked Paul.

"We're about to submit an article describing the enhanced

SPRING FLOWER: TORN BETWEEN SHIFTING WORLDS

yield we observed this past harvest using hybrid rice, a topic we had to drop ten years ago," Paul explained, looking up from the papers on his desk.

"I'm so happy for you, being able to do your research again."

"Well, only delayed ten years! You should pick up your clinical research, too, especially your passion for glaucoma. Don't forget that research will make you an even better clinical physician, because you'll become a better observer. Research trains us to think more precisely on a problem and its solution."

"I've heard that before," I responded, "like, eighteen years ago, before Gina was born—centuries ago! My professional life has become unfocused, and I'm not sure I can be an ophthalmology surgeon for the rest of my life."

"I'm sure you can pick up your research. I know you have well-organized files on the glaucoma patients you've treated. You should write that up. Please think about it, particularly in terms of what you want for the future. Right now, you're a highly skilled ophthalmologist, and that's not going to change anytime soon. But when you get older and your hands start to shake, you may need to pursue something else. These opportunities to translate and travel are great and eye-opening. Meeting these people is almost as good as traveling around the world again. But I don't think you should make a career of it."

I paused for a moment, and said, "I wonder why there haven't been any ophthalmologists visiting China, or why no Americans have come yet."

"They will. Be patient. And speaking of translating, will you help me with this English abstract we'll be submitting along with our article?"

"My pleasure, Professor Hsiung!"

In autumn of 1977, Hangchow was finally open to foreign visitors, and a team of Hungarian ophthalmologists arrived. Jade, I, and a few residents went to their lectures, held in a hotel conference room, and afterward my colleagues were speechless. It was the first time they'd heard me speak in English. The Hungarians' tour included our clinic, and as Jade spoke to them, I translated, which was great fun for me. Paul was right. Three of the eight lectures they gave were on glaucoma, which piqued my interest. Listening to their latest surgical and nonsurgical approaches, I became re-enthused about studying this pernicious eye disease.

The Hungarian ophthalmologists were quite friendly, and I felt bad that they'd picked a poor time of year to visit Hangchow. Hangchow gets cold and rainy in October and November. But their spirits were high, despite their getting drenched by cold rain several times while touring the West Lake. We were surrounded by Chinese adults and children wherever we went; they were looking at these foreigners with eyes wide open. Perhaps this had happened during the other recent trips, but it was the first time I noticed.

The Hungarian delegation did not seem to mind. They found it fascinating and even posed for photos with some of the kids. And they were especially fascinated to hear that I'd received a Hungarian Magical Cube from our Egyptian visitors. When the team left, they presented me with a gift, a green plastic disk. They said my family would enjoy playing with it outdoors when the weather got warmer. They also extended me an invitation to visit Budapest to attend an ophthalmology conference in late 1978. I gratefully acknowledged their kindness, although I knew it wouldn't be possible. But I could dream!

A few months later, the mystery of Eddy's English pronunciation was solved. A group of British physicians specializing in tropical disease arrived in Hangchow right after Chinese New

Year, 1978. I hadn't heard an English accent since my days in India in boarding school, and when I got home, I read a few paragraphs to Eddy in a British accent, and asked, "My dear Sonny Boy, is this how your English teacher says you should speak?"

Eddy's eyes opened wide, and he screamed, "Yes, that's *exactly* what he sounds like, and he says it's the proper way to speak English, not the way you taught me."

"Great! Tell your teacher that the way you pronounce is *American English*. It's not wrong, just different. His is the original English."

"Mommy, how did you learn American English? Isn't it time you tell me your stories? I'm in high school now."

I didn't respond, and thankfully he didn't persist.

86

AFTER THE British team left, winter in Hangchow continued for months. Just before spring 1978 finally arrived, we received delegations from both Australia and Brazil that specialized in internal medicine. Their presence made the long winter more tolerable. There had been no Australian missionaries at the Water of Life Hospital. We had Brits and Germans, and of course Americans, but I'd never met anyone from Australia. As for Brazilians, I felt a keen connection with this small group of doctors. And they, too, were shocked to learn that I had been to Brazil in the summer of 1942. I told them that I was in Rio, then Brasilia. Although I was vague about why, that brought us closer.

On a warm Sunday afternoon in March, I asked Paul and the kids if we could go to the park along West Lake. After seeing these sites with visitors, I wanted to go with my family so we could play to our heart's content.

"Paul, Eddy, Gina, are you up for it?"

Paul's first response was, "I can't. I have so much writing to do before tomorrow."

Eddy barely looked up from his books and papers.

"Papa told me you're now excelling in school, and so why not take a break?" I asked. "We won't be out long. The sun is still going down early these days." Eddy didn't reply.

But Gina said, "Papa has become such a grouchy old man and a party pooper. Let's go without him."

And Paul perked up. "Jeanie, I *could* use a break before the busy season starts again. We can buy some sweet bread and make a picnic out of it!" Paul began to sound enthusiastic, and Eddy looked up when he heard the words "sweet bread" (which are more like scones or cakes).

"How about it, Eddy? Be a sport," Gina nudged Eddy. He still looked hesitant.

"How about we take that green disk from the Hungarians and figure out how to use it. I think it's some kind of sport," Paul suggested, patting Eddy on the shoulder.

"Mommy, what is that thing?"

"Well, kiddo, like Papa said, let's go to the park and find out."

"Okay," Eddy agreed, and grabbed his jacket and the disk, which was still in its original packaging.

And off we went to the bus stop. When we got to West Lake, the kids and I headed to the park, while Paul went to see what he could buy. The weather was still cool, but it felt warm in the sun. And while looking out at the lake, I took a deep breath and closed my eyes, trying to hold onto a few seconds for myself. I had come to love this lake. It wasn't a river, like the Hudson or the Great Yangtze River, but it was a huge body of water that ultimately flowed into the Pacific Ocean.

"How about here, Mommy? There's plenty of grass," Eddy shouted, breaking my reverie. The place he'd found was a mix of fresh green and dried grasses surrounded by blossoming plum and peach trees, plus a single cherry tree.

Before I could respond, Paul found us and was running in our direction. He had found a bigger grassy area a few hundred yards away with fewer trees. He thought the trees might interfere with playing with the disk.

"Okay, let's figure this out, Mommy!" Eddy tore open the packaging and took out the Day-Glo light-green gift.

"They told me it's a flying disk." Then I saw the Hungarian

word "*Frizbi*" on the torn packaging. The instructions were in Hungarian, and I was able to figure out that it said, "Throw it into the air and it will float on its own."

"They told me to try it, that it's simple."

Off Eddy and Paul went to the center of the lawn and began to toss the disk, but despite their best efforts, the disk would either wobble a few yards or crash-land and roll on the grass away from us. After a few minutes, Paul and Eddy were panting from chasing the disk, reminding me how Mother had played with her dog.

"This isn't working, Jeanie!" Paul shouted.

"Join us," Eddy added.

"Maybe you can enlighten us, Dr. Perkins. After all, you brought it home," Paul said.

"I'm no good at sports," I confessed.

"Just try!" Paul waved at me with his left hand, his right hand pushing up from the ground.

"Okay, okay, here I come," I laughed.

Well, I didn't fare any better, and soon I was panting heavily too. I recalled them saying it would glide gently like an airplane.

Just then, a voice from behind offered, "Do you need help?" A young man about twenty was walking toward us.

Paul asked him, "Do you know what this thing is?"

The young man nodded, and Paul handed him the disk.

"It's called Fu-li-si-bee in English. I don't think there's a Chinese word for it." His Chinese reminded me of Taka's English.

"I've been watching you for a while, but I didn't want to interfere," the young man said.

"Thanks for offering. Yes, please help us." Paul asked him.

"Okay, thank you. You have to flick your wrist as you throw." He let it fly with a gentle twist of his right wrist, and the Fu-li-si-bee just flew sky-high and far, like a bird set free.

SPRING FLOWER: TORN BETWEEN SHIFTING WORLDS

"Ahh...." Paul and Eddy sighed. "Thank you so much for saving our lives!" Paul said, and the young man laughed. "Would you like to play with us?" Paul asked.

"I would love to, but I have to get going. My parents and my sisters are on those bridges waiting to meet our relatives." As he spoke, he pointed to two ancient bridges over the Su-T'i (蘇踢) and Pai-T'i (白踢) causeways.

"Well, thank you again for teaching us. The technique is obviously critical."

"No problem, sir. You can now throw this to each other, and the receiving person will try to catch it at all costs, even jumping or diving for it. Or you can aim at a target like a tree. These are some of the games we play with the Fu-li-si-bee." Paul nodded and ran off with Eddy.

They learned fast, and before long they were really letting it fly. The twenty-year-old stayed for a few minutes to watch them. After working up my courage, I asked, "*Do-ko ni shushing wa desu-ka? Ni-Hon desu-ka?* (Are you from Japan?)?"

"Oh, you could tell from my accent?"

"Your demeanor reminds me of someone I knew."

"Do you know Japanese?"

"*Oh, ie! Sukoshi desu. Chūgoku wa hajimete desu ka?* (Is this your first time in China)?" I laughed.

"Ah, *Osaka desu*, I am here to visit my grandparents, my mother's side of the family. My mother is Chinese, and my father is Japanese. I was born in Japan."

"Oh, I apologize. I didn't mean to be so nosy."

"Not at all. I'm glad to meet someone who can speak very good Japanese. My Chinese is quite limited. Oh, I'd better get going. My family is walking this way. It was nice meeting you. Enjoy the Fu-li-si-bee." He gave me a quick bow and ran away. I didn't even ask his name.

"Mommy, come and play. It's lots of fun!" shouted Eddy.

An hour later, exhausted from tossing the Frisbee the right way, we all sat down to take a break. Paul didn't ask what I was talking to the young man about, except that he said, "The kid sounded foreign, like you.... Well, okay, you speak a lot better than he does."

I could barely focus on his words, as my mind was wandering again.

"A penny for your thoughts, Dr. Perkins?" Paul said it in English, a sentence I had taught him while we were dating.

"Perfectly spoken, Professor Hsiung," I replied as I leaned my head on his shoulder. "Why do you think no physicians from Japan have visited China yet?" I asked.

"How do you know that they haven't?" Paul said, while stroking my hair. "If they have, you probably wouldn't be the first to know. They're not going to ask you to translate Japanese."

"Of course. What was I thinking?" I laughed. "Well, how come there haven't been any *American* physicians visiting?"

After a long pause, Paul said, "Homesick again? They'll be here. I don't have faith in much of anything anymore, but I do believe you'll see Americans again."

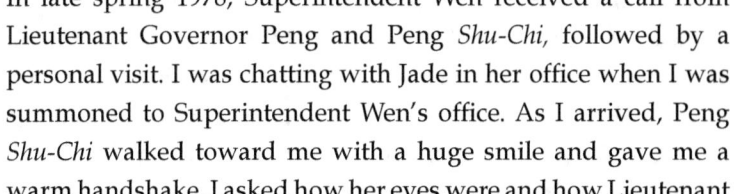

In late spring 1978, Superintendent Wen received a call from Lieutenant Governor Peng and Peng *Shu-Chi,* followed by a personal visit. I was chatting with Jade in her office when I was summoned to Superintendent Wen's office. As I arrived, Peng *Shu-Chi* walked toward me with a huge smile and gave me a warm handshake. I asked how her eyes were and how Lieutenant Governor Peng was doing.

Peng *Shu-Chi* pushed me down onto a chair and said, "This meeting is not about me but about you. I'm here to ask

SPRING FLOWER: TORN BETWEEN SHIFTING WORLDS

Superintendent Wen's permission to let you go to Peking for a few weeks. There is going to be this international conference on acupuncture and Chinese traditional medicine. It's a very important meeting for China and can elevate our status on the international stage, not just for healthcare, but for the country as a whole."

She was simultaneously serious and excited. I hadn't seen her since the *Gang of Four* (四人幫) was arrested in late 1976, and her enthusiasm, optimism, and passion for China hadn't changed a bit.

"Dr. Pei, I've recommended you to the Central Government (中央) and Ministry of Health to be an English translator for a number of high-level officials, including Chairman Hua Kuo-Feng (華國鋒主席), who will be chairing this important event. I hope you will accept this honor and task."

I was floored. Superintendent Wen added, "This is a great opportunity, Dr. Pei. Please do accept." I nodded my head and said, "Yes, of course, I would be honored." Even as I spoke, I was wondering: "Would I, at last, see Americans? Would Americans be interested in Chinese traditional medicine? Day-Day had compared Chinese medicine to the folk medicines of American Indians, but I couldn't recall Day-Day ever mentioning acupuncture."

Peng *Shu-Chi* and I walked out together, and when we reached her jeep, the driver peeked out and smiled and waved at me. That was the same driver the Peng couple had since I first met them in 1969. Peng *Shu-Chi* shook my hand and said, "So that's our plan. Please get ready for traveling, Dr. Pei. We are lucky there are people like you available for international relations. Thank you!"

This would be the first such gathering in China in my lifetime, or perhaps ever, with delegates coming from around the world.

JEAN TREN-HWA PERKINS

Paul representing Chekiang Province and speaking at Chairman Hua's national meeting for China's future in agriculture, science, and technology in 1978

When I told Paul, he was floored; and he had equally good news for me: he had just been nominated (also by Peng *Shu-Chi*) to be one of a handful of representatives from Chekiang Province to attend a national meeting on science, technology, and agricultural development, also the first meeting of its kind.

The Communist Party Chairman, Hua Kuo-Feng (華國鋒), supported by Mr. Teng Hsiao-Ping (鄧小平), the supreme leader of the People's Republic of China, pushed hard to focus on economic and technological development. Suddenly, China was trying to dig itself out of the abyss. The slogans had changed from those of the Great Revolution to promoting higher education, research, efficient production, skilled manufacturing, and international relations. Paul's and my own conferences were set for different times, so we couldn't meet in Peking, but we could take turns staying with Eddy.

So, I was on the road again! This time it wasn't a long train

SPRING FLOWER: TORN BETWEEN SHIFTING WORLDS

trip; I flew for the first time in my life. When I arrived a few days before the conference, the place was already bubbling with energy. There were hundreds of translators of English, the official language for the conference. Most of us stayed in the same hotel, walking distance from the conference site. So I strolled among the crowd in the hotel lobby, thinking I might just see Chum. I thought the chance would be high; she was more qualified than I, or probably anyone here. Unfortunately, I didn't see her, and we got busy quickly. There was no time for social engagement among the translators.

For the first few days, we were instructed on how to behave and how to interact with foreigners of various cultures. At first, I felt bored, but when I tamped down my arrogance and began to pay attention, some of the information was really useful. Although I had been surrounded by Westerners as a kid and had sailed around the world at fifteen, I'd never been to much of Europe.

My assignment turned out to be complex. No two days on the schedule were the same, and it didn't say anything about interpreting for high-ranking officials, let alone Party Chairman Hua. I was a little disappointed but tried to keep my spirits up, because my focus was on meeting Americans, or at least spotting them from a distance.

For the opening ceremony, we were divided into smaller groups, each group led by a government official and a uniformed official. There was little opportunity to wander; our movements were closely monitored. My seat was close to the stage, and the translations for Chairman Hua's opening statement and the words of the other high-ranking officials seemed to have been scripted and translated well before the meeting. Still, the translators did a fantastic job.

Although I was honored to be sitting near the stage wearing

a badge on a red string that hung from my neck, the opening statements were, to me, quite boring, and my focus was on the audience, scanning for reincarnations of my dears Day-Day, Mother, and the Aunties. Of course, I didn't see them, and I realized that I might not even know who was American rather than Canadian, Australian, German, French, or British.

After a standing ovation for the opening speakers, I heard someone say, "Dr. Pei, please come this way." Our group leader was frantically waving at a few of us, and we quickly followed him, weaving among those who were standing and applauding. Soon we were by the side door, and I noticed Chairman Hua and the other officials walking off the stage. The group leader gestured for me to lead the way, and for five or six others to follow.

"Here is your first assignment," he said, "and perhaps the most important. Please follow these leaders as they come off the stage, and stay closely behind them—you first, Dr. Pei. We're heading to the Greeting Hall, where delegate leaders from each country are waiting to meet and shake hands with Chairman Hua. Please do your jobs!"

And off we went, my heart pounding. After a signal from our group leader, an array of armed security guards created a small opening for us to join Chairman Hua. Later I reread the instructions we'd received, and this was all in there. I obviously hadn't paid attention.

I became more and more anxious, as I was just a few feet behind Chairman Hua. He was taller than I am and walked briskly. I didn't know where the Greeting Hall was or how far a walk it'd be, I was just trying to keep up with him.

And then, suddenly, the Chairman of the Communist Party for all of China turned around and said, "Oh, I'm sorry, you must be Dr. Pei. Look at my manners! I didn't even stop to greet you."

SPRING FLOWER: TORN BETWEEN SHIFTING WORLDS

I was taken by his down-to-the earth way; after all, he was the leader of a nation, and I replied, simply, "Uh, Sir, Chairman Hua, it's okay, I'm right behind you."

He then slowed down to my pace, and said, "I heard you were brought up by Americans?"

I was speechless. He not only knew my name, he knew my history! "Well, um, yes, Chairman Hua, that's true. My parents were Americans, and I lived in America when I was a child." I managed to squeeze out actual sentences.

"That's wonderful. They say your English is essentially that of a native speaker, so I asked them to assign you to me for these casual, nonscripted occasions, which are equally if not more important, so that I understand what they're saying and how I should respond."

"Oh, thank you. I'm truly honored by this request and opportunity."

"No, the honor is mine, actually, Dr. Pei. I am fortunate to have a real English-speaking person, let alone native-speaking, translating for me. Your presence may shock them that we have such talent hidden behind our Forbidden City Walls!" And he laughed.

And so, I learned the phrase "behind the Forbidden City Walls" from him, whose equivalent in English might be "in an Ivory Tower." His warm and casual demeanor put me at ease.

"You're very kind, Chairman Hua. Thank you!" I smiled nervously while trying to stay a step behind him.

"I'm serious. Thank you for being here to help with this important event. Establishing excellent global relationships will be of the utmost importance for China's future. It's a long and challenging rebuilding process, and we can use all the help we can get. And you will be glad to know that we are working hard with America to reach a peaceful and friendly accord that will be

JEAN TREN-HWA PERKINS

Chairman Hua Kuo-Feng (華國鋒) visiting the country formerly known as Yugoslavia in 1978: The photo I had standing next to Chairman Hua while translating for him was unfortunately lost, but he was an affable man as shown in this image.

mutually beneficial for decades to come."

With those words, he flashed a wide and genuine smile and then hustled a few feet ahead of me as we were about to reach the Greeting Hall. Two army-uniformed security guards swung the doors wide open, and cameras began to flash. The bright lights covered the entire room and bounced from my face to the ceiling and back as if we were looking straight at the sun. Suddenly I remembered being at a theater in Yonkers, and hearing the words: "Lights, camera, action; it's *showtime!*"

English words and accents began swirling around the two of us. Questions were coming at us at blinding speed, and I felt buried under by a language I was so familiar with yet felt so foreign. I had very little if any time to react, think, or form my phrases, except to let it all out, all twenty-seven years of English being my first language, even if long ago.

SPRING FLOWER: TORN BETWEEN SHIFTING WORLDS

Regardless of his stature as the nation's leader, Chairman Hua was one of the kindest human beings I'd ever met. I was grateful for his innate ability to put me at ease. All these years after sitting behind President Chiang and Madame Song Qing-Ling in the Methodist Church on Gu-Lin Mountains, or sitting across the aisle from Eleanor Roosevelt on a Pullman Coach, or staring at a frail and fasting Gandhi in India, or glancing at Chairman Mao when he visited the Yangtze River Valley, I was not just seeing a man of immense historical significance, I had this unique opportunity to translate for the man responsible for changing the fortunes of one billion souls.

The rest of the conference was a blur. I didn't learn much about Chinese Traditional Medicine or acupuncture. On two other occasions, I translated for Chairman Hua, and we managed to talk about the early 1920s when the entire northern part of China was suffering greatly from warlords, famines, and pandemic disease, and I told him that my American father was a physician helping people in the Shantung area. He was amazed to hear my story.

At the conference, I also translated for quite a few speakers from Europe, but no Americans. I caught myself a few times, especially between presentations, scanning for Americans or hoping someone would hear my American accent and seek me out. But despite my not connecting with a single American, I wasn't as disappointed as I thought I'd be, because I was absorbed in the present and soaking up all the English I could for the first time in a very long while.

Then, someone tapped me on the shoulder. I turned around, and a man lowered his head to read my name tag, and then he said, "Ah, Dr. Pei, where did you learn your American English?"

"Oh, uh," I stammered.

"Oh, I'm sorry. My name is Matthew Anderson." He

extended his hand to shake mine. "I am a pediatrician and I'm very interested in alternative medicines like traditional Chinese medicine and acupuncture. I'm from Seattle, in the state of Washington, working at a hospital affiliated with the University of Washington."

Wow! I was happy as a bird, hearing and seeing an American right in front of me! He looked nothing like Day-Day. He was short and skinny, and had an endearing reddish-brown beard, thick-rimmed eyeglasses, a necktie, and a jacket with square patterns.

I looked around reflexively and saw only foreigners holding coffee cups and teacups chatting loudly among themselves, mostly in English, so I felt a bit safer. Still, I lowered my voice as I quickly gave him a brief history of my life.

"This is amazing," he said. "I'm going to tell my colleagues when I get home. What a story!" Then he added, "It's not surprising that there are people like you in China, but meeting someone with a story like yours is quite fantastic. Dr. Pei, your story would make a fantastic book. But I understand this may not be the best time. Perhaps someday, you will seek me out when you visit Seattle and tell me more about it in detail. Here is my business card."

And just like that, I met my first American in twenty-seven years.

Part VIII

The Road to Salvation:
My Deliverance

87

Spring 1980...
I must have dozed off, and when I sat up, I had to wipe drool off my face. Paul and the kids were still asleep, so I looked out the window. 1978 was a long time ago, yet the image of Chairman Hua was vivid and clear. I had wondered if I'd ever visit Seattle, and now it seemed a real possibility. I could complete telling Dr. Anderson my stories.

"Hey everyone, we're almost at Chiahsing (嘉興), and I need to get gas. Let's take a break here." Shan's voice merged with all I was remembering. He pulled off the main road and headed to Chiahsing, a small town midway between Hangchow and Shanghai. We stopped on a noisy and chaotic street, and Shan set off with a big plastic can in his hand to find gasoline.

As I stumbled out of the jeep, my legs felt numb, having been cramped for hours. I said to Paul, "Let's wash our faces and eat some of what Sue and Conductor Hsie gave us and share it with Shan when he comes back."

"Good idea," Paul replied. Eddy and Gina woke up and wanted to use the restroom. Paul said, "You take Gina first, and I'll stay with the jeep and then take Eddy when you get back."

I opened Eddy's green duffel bag and took out my towel, which I'd stuffed there before we left the apartment. Gina and I headed to what appeared to be a public bathroom. I cannot begin to describe how filthy it was; even today I have nightmares about it. Kudos to Gina. Despite being disabled, she handled everything on her own, squatting above that filthy pit. By the time Gina and I returned with clean faces, Shan had already filled the gas tank. I asked where he'd found gas, and he said, "Dr. Pei, I have friends here!" I laughed as I helped Gina back into the front passenger seat.

By then, Eddy was tap dancing, so he and Paul ran to the restroom. I proceeded to open the plastic bag Conductor Hsie had given us and divided the breakfast food five ways. I bit into the red-bean-paste bun just before Paul and Eddy returned, and Shan said, "Let's go. We should press on."

Paul said, "Sure, we can eat while you drive."

So we left Chiahsing (嘉興), and nearly half an hour later, I realized we'd left Eddy's green duffel bag behind.

"What?" Paul said. "I thought you had it."

"No, I grabbed my towel from it and leaned it against the jeep, thinking you'd put it away."

"I didn't," he replied.

"Then we must go back!"

"We can't," Shan said. "Can't you buy a new one in America?"

"That bag has my autograph book in it, with all my classmates' signatures from Yonkers Elementary School," I said in desperation.

Paul thought a moment and said, "Why did you put it back in the bag after I took out Eddy's books and his damn toy gun? Shan, don't stop, please continue; we need to get to Shanghai as soon as we can. That's most important."

"No! We've got to go back and look for it."

Paul grabbed my hand and said, "Jeanie, we must press forward. We can't take a chance being late; we might run into morning checkpoints."

I couldn't believe what a stupid thing I'd done. "It has to be where we stopped for the restroom in Chiahsing."

Shan looked at me in his rearview mirror and said, "Dr. Pei, you left a brown bag on top of the jeep. I figured you'd brought it back in. It could have flown off the roof anywhere along the road."

"Please keep driving, Shan," Paul said. His voice was cold.

JEAN TREN-HWA PERKINS

"How could I lose a book that saved my life many times!" I said, and no one replied. I knew Paul was right, and I slumped back and fell into silence. What else could go wrong on this fateful journey? The more I tried to focus, the more things went wrong. My mind drifted back to 1978, which turned out to be a great year, not just because many Chinese people were truly liberated or that I met Chairman Hua, but also because of Dr. Arthur Grove of Massachusetts General Hospital.

In late summer of 1978, a delegation of ophthalmologists from Massachusetts Eye and Ear Infirmary, affiliated with Massachusetts General Hospital in Boston, arrived in Shanghai. We had just celebrated Gina's high school graduation, a wondrous occasion. Paul and I watched our precious little girl wobble up the steps with the help of her two best friends to receive her diploma. That evening, we celebrated with Old Man Ni, Qiu-Shuang, and three of their kids back at the slum compound— a wonderful feast, better than any Chinese New Year's dinners ever! Paul prepared the food in the old kitchen, and it brought back memories for all of us. Nearly half the families had moved out of the compound by then, including Chang *Lao-Shih*, Gina's elementary school teacher, and Dr. Zhou's family upstairs. Qiu-Shang, Old Man Ni, and their kids had taken over our unit. At the dinner table, I smiled, appreciating the lavish spread, hearing glasses clinking away, and basking in the sounds of celebration.

"What's next for Gina?" I asked myself. Going to college was

Gina graduating from high school, ca. 1978

unthinkable. I wondered what a disabled child could achieve in America. This gathering felt like a walk down memory lane. Was I unconsciously saying goodbye to everyone? Or maybe it was that big gulp of Shaohsing rice wine (紹興黃酒).

Paul's mother agreed to take Gina for a year and tutor her college-level courses. Gina had always loved her grandmother and her Aunt Grace (Paul's older sister). She was a Shanghai girl at heart.

So, days later, Gina and I headed to Shanghai together, she to be with Paul's mother, and I to translate for the Mass General ophthalmology conference. Gina was in a great mood sitting next to me on the train, and I felt happy. It'd been a long time since my baby girl and I had a moment like this together, just the two of us. The last two times she went to Shanghai, Gina was all by herself. It had been more than thirteen years since we roamed the familiar streets of the city where Gina grew up. We chatted the whole way, and the six-hour bumpy train ride went quickly. We laughed, held hands, and even cried. Gina would be eighteen soon. She was so smart and determined.

We took the bus from the train station, and as the bus wound through the streets we knew so well heading toward Huai-Hai Middle Road, Gina nodded her head and pointed at the sign of Tung-Ping Road. I smiled. "Yes, my baby girl still remembers her old home. I'm so happy we're having this time together, Gina."

"Me too, Mother."

"Why do I have the feeling I'll never see you again?" I said, and began to cry.

"Don't be foolish, Mother. What are you talking about? I'll be back, and by then your daughter will be taking college entrance exams!" She laughed and wiped the tears off my cheeks. "Mother, you're behaving like a little girl, and you're embarrassing me."

We stood at the front gate of Paul's mother's apartment

Rapidly changing scenes in Shanghai post-1976 with privately owned stores and small markets popping up along the streets

building, and I decided not to go in. I gave Gina the longest hug and headed to my hotel, the Hope Hotel (好望角賓館), which was ironic and uplifting and not far away on Chao-Chia-Pang Road (肇嘉浜路), also in the Hsü-Chia-Hui District (徐家匯). Since I arrived too early to check in, I decided to take a walk along the riverside. It was a cool, summer afternoon, and the streets were bustling with people and bikes. My mind was flooded with memories of these streets, and it didn't take long before I was standing alongside the Huang-P'u River, staring at the barges heading east and west. I strolled along the river as far as I could, but many sections were blocked off for construction and restoration. I thought about the joys and struggles of raising Gina, and the image of Taka seemed to be everywhere. I was also both apprehensive and hopeful about meeting the American doctors.

The next day, a team of six ophthalmologists from Boston arrived at the Shanghai Eye and ENT Infirmary (上海五官科醫院) on Yüeh-Yang Road. We stood in a small circle, and those on

SPRING FLOWER: TORN BETWEEN SHIFTING WORLDS

the Chinese half included many familiar faces, including Shou. I gently waved at her, and she smiled back. Memories flooded me as we introduced ourselves and I translated. The American team leader, a tall, slender man named Arthur Grove, smiled and asked, "Dr. Pei, are you by any chance from New York? You *do* know you have a New York accent?" The whole room broke out in laughter, and I said, nervously, "Maybe."

Each of the six visitors gave a half-hour presentation on their research or on new technologies for ophthalmological procedures and methods, including new lens materials for cataract patients. Dr. Grove was the last to speak, and then, from the Shanghai side, my former Chief spoke on behalf of everyone. I found that translating at this gathering was difficult, because I was not only trying to find the right words, but also trying to learn the latest advances.

Still, I managed to get through the two long seminar days, realizing how far behind China had fallen in ophthalmology, both technologically and in our fundamental understanding. At the final reception dinner, both sides agreed to forge a meaningful scholarly exchange by having a team of Chinese ophthalmologists visit Boston. That sounded like a dream, but an impossible one, since I no longer worked at the Shanghai Eye and ENT Infirmary. Just then, my former Chief patted me on my shoulder and said, "We'll have to bring Dr. Pei along to translate for us, and she can visit her family, if they're still alive."

I was ecstatic and said, simply, "That sounds like a great plan!"

Dr. Grove agreed and smiled. He had a large dimple on his chin, and it wiggled when he smiled.

The visitors were staying at the Hope Hotel, too, and when we returned there, Dr. Grove pulled me aside and asked, "Dr. Pei, if you're not too tired, would you like to chat a bit in the lobby? I can buy you a drink or cup of tea or coffee."

As the rest of the delegates shook my hand and retired to their rooms, Dr. Grove and I sat in the corner of the hotel lobby, where a busboy brought us a pot of tea. He also brought two glasses of Rémy Martin cognac, and I took a sip of mine, as I was trying to be polite. But it burned my throat, so I pushed my glass toward him and said, "I'll stick to the tea and give this to you."

"Oh, that bad?" he smiled.

"I can't hold my alcohol," I smiled back.

"No problem. But I do want to chat with you a bit longer." Dr. Grove took his first sip and winced, "Rémy Martin is supposed to be smooth," he said.

"Chat about what?" I asked, the teacup in my hand shaking a bit.

"Please, Dr. Pei, it's nothing serious. But I must ask first if sitting here could cause you unforeseen problems?"

"I think we're okay, since they allowed me to ride in the same van with all of you to the hotel." Then I noticed a couple of girls at the front desk staring at us, along with the busboy who had brought us the cognac and tea. The front desk wasn't far, given the relatively small lobby, and it was very quiet with no one there except the two of us. I shrugged my shoulders and said, "Whatever happens, happens. What would you like to talk about, Dr. Grove?"

"Well, I'm a history junkie, and I've been dying to know your story, ever since you answered 'Maybe' when I asked if you were from New York." Dr. Grove crossed his long legs and began to twirl his whiskey glass as if that would make it taste better.

I looked around, and still seeing no one in the lobby, I leaned over and lowered my voice to begin telling my story. I began with the prisoner of war exchange in 1941.

"What? That would be a violation of these Japanese Americans' constitutional rights, and it would be inhumane. I've never heard or read anything about this." Dr. Grove looked distraught. Sensing I had offended him and his beloved country, I thought I might as well continue the assault. "When has war ever been humane, Dr. Grove?"

"Yeah, but this is crazy. We're not like that. We're in the business of saving people—from Nazis, fascists, dictators. Oops, I should lower my voice." Dr. Grove quickly covered his mouth and looked around, then sheepishly smiled, "Sorry, I got carried away."

"It's okay. I don't think these kids understand what you just said. Of course, our conversation in this lobby could be recorded."

"Yes, Dr. Pei. I should be more careful and remember where I am. And most important, I don't want to get you in trouble!" Dr. Grove squinted as he said that.

"Dr. Grove, I'm telling you the truth. When you return to America, please investigate and check my parents' names and the names of my aunts in Michigan. We were on that list of passengers on the *MS Gripsholm* that came into New York Harbor in 1942. Ours was the first of three such exchanges. My little sister and I were probably the only Chinese on the entire ship, and yes, we spoke English with all those Japanese American kids being exchanged for us in Rio de Janeiro."

"I'm speechless. I find it hard to believe we Americans would hide and remove pages of dark and evil segments of our history from our textbooks." Dr. Grove sighed and continued, "I will check. But I have to admit, Dr. Pei, I think you are telling me all the truth. How else would you be able to speak so flawlessly?"

"Thank you for being generous, but I speak like a thirteen-year-old," I said, fumbling for words.

"Well, I mean, some of your word choices are outdated, if I may be permitted to say so. But there's no doubt you sound like a native speaker, based on your pronunciation, your instincts, and your understanding. That's very hard to fabricate." Dr. Grove nodded his head, and I suddenly realized he was about my age, although he looked older. We talked for another two hours. I wanted to know about America over the past twenty years, and he, too, seemed curious about my life.

"To be fair," he said, "the world has undergone a significant shift in the past twenty years, with President Kennedy's assassination, the Cold War, a space race with a man landing on the moon, the Civil Rights movement to enfranchise Black Americans, women being treated as men's equals, the Vietnam War that affected the perception of America in the world, even though I still believe it was worth fighting—I'm in a minority on this, just so you know, Dr. Pei. Then, Richard Nixon stepped down in disgrace, but to some outside America, perhaps including you, he could be a hero."

"Yes, to me he is," I said, getting excited.

Dr. Grove looked at me with an amused expression and continued, "America is not the same as when you left. You should be aware of that. It's a very different world now. And we know so little about what has been going on behind the impenetrable Great Wall! I believe this will fascinate the world for the next fifty years! On that note, Dr. Pei, would you consider, if given a chance, coming to America, at least for a visit?"

"Oh, yes!" I nearly shouted.

"Oh, of course you would!" Dr. Grove affirmed.

With that, we went our separate ways. But the conversation played over and over in my mind that sleepless night at the Hope Hotel and throughout the long train ride home the following day. We also spoke in great detail about how handicapped children were treated in America and how they were able to attend college and work. A few days later, I told Paul about the conversation I'd had with Dr. Grove, and Paul gave voice to a number of practical concerns.

"It's a long shot at best, Jeanie. You're assuming this Grove guy is even going to remember your conversation, let alone find a way to sponsor you for a visit. I heard there might be government-sponsored scholarly exchanges and visits, but I have no idea how you'd get a passport for something not sanctioned by the government. Where would we even start?" He shook his head.

I wasn't disappointed by his reactions, but instead at myself for leaping ahead, as always. I had no answers to his questions.

Paul sensed my disappointment and he said, "Okay, one thing at a time, Jeanie. Let's wait and see if the guy even gets back to you. I wouldn't hold my hopes too high. But things *are* changing, and like Dr. Grove said, America's very different now and you might not even like it. You've been living here for so long and adjusted to many drastic situations, and I'm not sure that Hangchow at this moment is any less of a home to you than Yonkers."

I didn't say a word. Paul was probably right, but my mind was made up. Things might be changing in China for the better, but how did we know they wouldn't change back? Chairman Hua might have the best of intentions, but how long would he remain in power? A backlash could doom us all, because the recent national horrors nearly exhausted our will to survive. For our family, if it weren't for all those angels who mysteriously supported us at just the right moments, we would be ashes in the ground by now. Who would bail us out if there was another revolution? The more I thought about it, the more determined I became to go back to America if I could, even if my intent was selfish or not what God wanted. By 1978, I had little faith in this God who had allowed us to live through all these atrocities.

JEAN TREN-HWA PERKINS

I wasn't afraid to die if I had to stay in China; I was more afraid if, like the two generations before them, Eddy and Gina's generation would also be destroyed by China's policies. Two months went by, and I hadn't heard anything from Dr. Grove or anyone else about going to America. I was slowly giving up hope and getting back into my old routine. Then one day, Jade waved a letter at me and smiled, "If you buy me dinner, I'll give this to you. You're lucky I saw this in the office. It could have been snatched up by someone who covets these fancy American stamps."

"Oh, pretty please, may I have the letter? Yes, dinner's on me, or rather Paul, as always." Jade finally handed me the envelope, and the return address was Boston. I ran into the women's restroom and slipped into an open stall. After locking the wooden door, I opened the letter. It read:

> Dear Dr. Jean Pei (Perkins):
> My apologies for taking so long to write to you, and it might take even longer if this letter has to go by sea. It was wonderful meeting you a couple of months ago in Shanghai, and equally fulfilling to have that fascinating conversation with you in the hotel lobby. Believe it or not, I dug up everything I could about what you said of American history and was simply floored that it all checked out. Yes, everything you told me was true. During the war, executive orders were given by Roosevelt to round up all Japanese American citizens, and we even set up internment camps so we could exchange them for our POWs as needed. What an atrocity, a shameful history we have here.
> Anyway, back to the point at hand, I found your name on the *MS Gripsholm*'s passenger list. I also

tracked down your family—the Perkins family. Believe it or not, I will be meeting all of them next week. They were all shocked when we first spoke on the phone that you are alive. Your cousin Evelyn has retired and is now living with her husband in Hartford in the same house she grew up in. She distinctly remembers you living in their house while visiting her parents (your Uncle Henry and Aunt Olga?). It turned out that you may not know this—but this was exciting for me—as you know, I am a history junkie. In Hartford, your uncle and aunt's house (where your father and his older brother grew up) is next door to the home of the great American author Mark Twain. A daughter of Evelyn's, Olivia, whom I had already met, lives in Cambridge—across a narrow river from us here in Boston. She was very excited to find out that her granduncle's little daughter is still alive in China. And perhaps this goes without saying: Your mother passed away in 1961 and your father in 1958. They are both buried in the same cemetery as your Uncle Henry and Aunt Olga in Hartford.

Here is the more important info. I spoke with my Chief, who upon hearing me tell your story is equally fascinated by it and has agreed to offer you a research fellowship to visit us at MGH [Massachusetts General Hospital]. How exactly we proceed remains a mystery, but where there's a will, there's a way. There are a few things we'll need from you. I have found another excuse to visit China—likely Peking in early December, but I will try flying through Shanghai, and as of now, my flight is scheduled for November 27. I propose we meet at the same hotel on the 28th or 29th to discuss this in detail. My proposed plan to meet in Shanghai may sound sudden and uncertain, but I don't know how else to discuss this with you. Hope to see you there.

    Yours truly,
    Arthur

Tears were streaming down my face as I read Dr. Grove's letter. I had already accepted that my father couldn't possibly be alive in 1978, or he'd be 103 years old. But I did hope that Mother might still be alive and in her nineties. Dr. Grove's news dashed that hope. The finality — the thought of never seeing them again — brought with it an overwhelming feeling of sadness.

But alongside the sadness, excitement and hope were bubbling inside me. I couldn't believe a complete stranger had gone out of his way to track down my long-lost family in America and was trying to find ways to help me get back home. He had typed the letter on September 7, 1978; it was postmarked September 12; and I received it on November 7.

I went home and told Paul, and he came up with a great idea. We could travel to Shanghai together, using the excuse of seeing Gina, and could wait for Dr. Grove while staying with Eve. The plan would be to leave Eddy alone and give him enough food and water. Although in hindsight, he might have been too young to stay by himself for almost a week, he relished the opportunity of being independent. The day came, and I handed Eddy two five-RMB bills to buy additional food if he needed it.

Staying with Eve was a challenge for me, but since Paul was there and since I knew she was very fond of her granddaughter, I managed to smile whenever I could, with a few gentle kicks from Paul beneath the dinner table. Gina was happy in Shanghai. We tried not telling Paul's family why we were there, but when we told them why we were in Shanghai, Bart and Jane were both happy to hear what we were up to. But Eve and Grace were outraged that we dared to plot going to America behind their backs.

On November 28 and again on the twenty-ninth, the two dates Arthur said he'd meet me, we swung by the Hope Hotel, but he hadn't checked in. I was so disappointed and once again losing hope.

"Oh, Paul, why did we come here? It's all a fantasy, as you said when I first told you. Why did you even come with me when you knew it would amount to nothing?"

"I don't know," Paul said softly.

"Let's go home tomorrow," I suggested.

"Why not stay two more days? Maybe he was delayed and had no way of contacting you. Don't lose hope, Jeanie."

"Why do you sound so different now?" I asked, and Paul said nothing as we boarded the bus back to Eve's.

On December 1, the day before we were to return to Hangchow, we went back to the hotel one last time, and the front desk clerk told us Dr. Arthur Grove had just checked in but was not in his room. Paul and I looked at each other with the biggest smiles.

"He's here!" Paul said. "Let's wait in the lobby until he returns."

"Okay!"

We sat down at the far corner, and after a few minutes, Paul stood up.

"Where are you going?" I was puzzled.

"I think I'll sit over there. We can pretend we don't know each other, so you can talk freely in English without having to translate for me and so he doesn't have to think about being polite to me. You can discuss important things. And I won't have to worry about speaking broken English and feeling embarrassed. And most importantly, I can observe him to be sure he's not a con artist."

"None of that makes sense," I said, but Paul nevertheless walked to another table about twenty feet away.

Half an hour later, Dr. Grove strolled into the lobby, and he immediately recognized me and rushed toward me. "Jean, oh my God, I can't believe you're here! It's so good to see you again!" He squeezed my hand and was going to give me a bear hug but stopped halfway.

"Me too. So good to see you too, Dr. Grove. You look great!" I tried to stem the awkwardness.

"I'm so sorry. I had no way of contacting you when my plans changed." He brushed his hand through his curly hair, and the dimple on his chin wiggled. "I thought I'd still come, just in case, even though I had given up on my end. I had much less faith than you. I just came back from the post office where I mailed you a letter."

Dr. Grove then proceeded to sit next to me, and before he completely anchored himself, he leaned over to me and said, "That man is a bit close. Shall we move farther away?"

I was taken aback, then said, "I think it will be okay. I don't believe that man understands English."

"Oh?" Dr. Grove replied, while he took another peek at Paul. Just then, Paul glanced over at us and gave me a dirty look.

Once situated, Dr. Grove took out a stack of papers from his briefcase. "Some of these documents may be too risky to mail, so I kept them and hoped to find another way of reaching you. They contain information about your family that I dug up, and at the very top is a signed offer letter from our Chief at Massachusetts General. I need information from you to prepare a curriculum vitae, or CV, and information to fill out the application for our Office of International Scholars and Exchange. They'll need this to prepare the documents so you can get an entry visa."

I didn't understand everything he said, as this process was completely foreign to me. But I sensed it was all important.

"I don't know how to thank you. We just met and you hardly know me, and here you are going to these lengths to help me!"

"Please don't thank me yet. It's still a long shot, perhaps a fantasy to you and even to me. On my trip home last time, I told myself I'd get to the bottom of that shameful chapter in American history, and if it were true and that I was wrong, I would try to help you go home or at least visit America. Perhaps someday you'll get a chance to tell the world your stories." Dr. Grove nodded his head assertively and then glanced in Paul's direction again to make sure "that man" wasn't eavesdropping.

We spent the next half an hour composing my biography and CV. Thanks to Paul's suggestion, I'd brought a list of publications dating all the way back to 1957. Dr. Grove did not seem to care how much research work I'd done, but he did confirm to me that these publications would be useful to convince the Massachusetts General authorities that I was more than just a clinician and that I had enough experience to be a research fellow.

At last, our conversations came to an end, as Dr. Grove had an early flight to catch at Shanghai Hung-Ch'iao Airport. "So, here's the plan, Jean. Your job is to secure your passport, and I'll get all documents ready for you from the Boston side so you can apply for an entry visa to visit America as an exchange scholar. Most likely, I won't be able to come back again. Getting an entry visa into China is not easy, but more importantly, I'm running out of excuses to be the one in my department who gets all these trips to the exotic Orient!"

"China is considered exotic?" I blurted out. "It's a dump here."

"Well anyway, I'll have to find another way to get the

approved documents to you, and in the meantime..." and he handed me a yellow envelope, which contained important letters and information about the Perkins Family. "Please take good care of this envelope, and I'm hoping it will be useful for your petition for a passport. I don't know how difficult it will be for you, but you'll need a passport to enter the US."

We stood up, and he looked at Paul again and said, "Let me walk you to the door." As we headed to the door, Paul also stood up and followed us.

"Why is he also leaving? I think he's following us. Are you going to be okay?" Dr. Grove sounded anxious.

"I'll be all right, but thank you for your concern," I assured him.

"Right. By the way, my wife, Lois, is also on this trip, but it looks like she'll be back late from this tour she signed on to, so she won't get a chance to meet you. She gives you her best regards. She's heard so much about you from me."

"It's a pity, and it would be my honor to meet her. But, coming all this way, she should enjoy as much sightseeing as she can, especially since this must be her first time in China. I'm sorry you had to miss the tour."

"Oh, Jean, I'm here for work. I have a very short attention span for sightseeing. One more thing. Rumor has it that the first US–China Consulate may be opening soon, perhaps in Shanghai at its pre-1949 residence, where your parents likely went to obtain your official adoption papers for entering the US."

"Oh, do you know when it might open?"

"I don't know, but according to the US news, it may be soon. But what's 'soon'? It may or may not be soon enough to work in synch with your application. You might need to enter Hong Kong or Japan and receive your entry visa there. If needed, you could attend a meeting or give a seminar to enter Japan."

I wasn't sure what all that meant, but I was taken aback that he had thought that far ahead in such detail. And he sounded confident, as if he had gone through the process himself. "Thank you so much, Dr. Grove." I reached out my hand to shake his, realizing that, by now, he had walked me six or seven blocks from the hotel. "Please don't feel you need to escort me further. I'll be okay. But will *you* be okay?"

"China is such a safe place, and I'm tall and burly," he joked. He was actually quite thin, but much bigger than almost everyone on the street.

A few yards away, groups of kids were pointing at Dr. Grove and chuckling heartily. With that, Dr. Grove bade me farewell. "Let's hope we meet again on the other side of the world." I watched his tall, thin figure walk away and suddenly felt sad, as if Day-Day were walking away from me.

"Dr. Jean Perkins, may I escort you from here?" Paul's voice and his broken English jolted me back to reality. I turned around and ran into his chest.

"Where did you go?" I asked. "You walked right past us and disappeared."

"I ducked into that little store. I wasn't sure how far and where this tall American man would escort you, or if he would walk all the way back to Hangchow with you. So I figured if I walked past the two of you, he'd feel safer that I wasn't following you and would allow you to go home on your own."

I chuckled and explained everything to Paul as we took the long walk back to his mother's. Paul was reflective and didn't say too much, except to raise questions about the details.

88

THE NEXT MORNING, Paul and I said goodbye to Gina, and I felt a greater sadness than when I saw her off months ago, wondering "What if the next time is when I leave her behind?" So I cautioned myself not to jump ahead. There would be many challenges, and as Arthur had said, it was a long shot at best.

The train ride home was uneventful except for my conversations with Paul. The train car was crowded, so we invented code words to represent "America," "passport," and "visa." Even then, a few passengers gave us glances and squeezed close to us. We didn't feel safe discussing such an important issue, but how else would we spend six hours sitting side by side? So we called Americans "Native Indians" (印第安國), referred to our passports as "ferry tickets" (船票), and described my visa as a "movie ticket" (电影票).

"No, I don't think boat alone is going to get you to the Indian country, Jeanie. You will need a ferry ticket, but having a movie ticket will be critical as well. I'm just not sure we can afford the movie ticket."

"Yeah, but is the new movie theater even going to open?"

"I think the doctor is smart!" Paul said, becoming animated, while the man next to him seemed annoyed. Nonetheless, Paul continued: "If the movie theater in Shanghai doesn't open in time for you, maybe you can get your boat ticket and buy a fishing license in Shanghai, and then go to the island [Japan] to fish and wait for the real movie ticket to become available." Talking this

SPRING FLOWER: TORN BETWEEN SHIFTING WORLDS

way made our trip back to Hangchow shorter and rather fun.

Back in Hangchow, we were both happy to see that Eddy was still alive. He didn't seem to miss us at all. Ever since I'd hit him, I could never be sure if he was still mad at me. The emotional gulf between us had widened, as if there were an invisible screen between us. I simply couldn't get too close. He showed very little emotion most of the time. Maybe it was all in my mind, since I felt so guilty. He didn't even spend half the money we left for him. To reward him for his maturity and frugality, we let him keep the remaining seven RMB (*Yüan,* 元), which was an insane amount of money for a thirteen-year-old. It was a week's wages for an adult. I gave him a tight squeeze and called him "my grown-up Sonny Boy who is so much better than his mother with money."

Eddy gave me a glance and a slight smile before returning to his books. With the thought that I might be leaving, I decided to get closer to him. I brought back toys and gifts from people I met on these translating trips, but except for the Frisbee, none of the other gifts interested him. Although he'd never had many toys, he seemed to be beyond them.

So I asked Eddy if he'd like to go to a movie, and he agreed. To be honest, it was a movie I had desperately wanted to see, called *Convoy* (车), a 1978 action film directed by Sam Peckinpah and starring Kris Kristofferson and Ali MacGraw. It was the first movie from America permitted in theaters, and the line for tickets was blocks and blocks long. We stood for hours before reaching the ticket window, bought two of the last tickets, and sat in the very last row. Eddy was too short to see the screen and had to sit on my lap or stand, which he did for parts of the movie. I wasn't sure how much he understood, as he kept asking me questions. I was completely enthralled. I had seen Americans visiting China, but I wanted to see *America*, even in a film about moving trucks and not much else, so I savored every moment. As we walked out, Eddy asked, "Why did we have to watch that?"

"You didn't quite understand the movie?"

"I think I understood the movie—a bunch of drivers unhappy about their lives. They look funny with blond hair and pale skin, especially when they try to be tanned. What I didn't understand was why that guy kept asking different women to visit his truck. And then, he would lock the door. Sometimes he would take her clothes off before locking the door, and the movie cut off right at those moments."

"I don't know, Eddy.... They're Americans, I guess." I had no clue how to explain those scenes to him.

I couldn't sleep that night. That terribly made movie only deepened my desire to go home to America. Paul rolled over and said, "Still not asleep?"

"No," I replied with a sigh. "I just realized that whether it's a ferry ticket [back to the code names] or movie ticket, it will be difficult. The whole thing is crazy, not just because it's a long shot, but I don't know if I can face being deeply disappointed again."

"Jeanie, we're not on the train. You can use real words," Paul chuckled. "It is a very long shot, but we can try." He added, "Let's buy some small gifts and visit Peng *Shu-Chi* and Lieutenant Governor Peng."

"Bother them again?" I asked.

"Are you kidding me? They're the only ones who can get you a personal passport, and even for them it will be challenging."

"I believe they would help us, but I feel uncomfortable asking, as if I performed surgery on them to benefit later. Besides, we've bothered them enough. They helped get you released from the *Cowshed* (牛棚). That alone could have gotten them into trouble, even jailed and persecuted. They are already our benefactors. I can't ask them to do more for either of us."

"What you're saying is correct, but it's also a little self-righteous. You would rather die than beg people, or even ask for a favor. But how else will this happen? I've gotten to know them so much better these past few years, and they're tougher than you think. I wouldn't worry about them; they're determined to do good works."

"I still don't want them to get into trouble for us," I cautioned.

"You think we can just waltz into the police department and say, 'I'm thinking about making a trip to America. Can you issue me a passport?'"

"Well, of course not." I thought about it some more. "If I could speak proper Chinese, I would do it my way and not try to bribe a high official and plead for their help."

"I think you speak well enough now. I don't believe it has anything to do with your rhetorical ability, Jeanie. I don't even know how to approach a police officer for something like this. I've never even seen a passport! I just know that's how things have worked in China for the past three thousand years. It's top-down!"

I sighed. "Okay. I'll make an appointment to see them. Please pick a day."

A few weeks later, Paul and I arrived at Peng *Shu-Chi's* apartment. Paul handed her two containers of fresh tea leaves and said, "We're sorry we don't have better gifts, Peng *Shu-Chi* and Governor Peng, but we are here to plead for your help."

Being the best kind of human being who knew how to treat people, Peng *Shu-Chi* quickly opened up one canister and took a quick sniff. She closed her eyes and said, "Professor Hsiung, it's almost winter. Where did you get tea leaves with so much fragrance this late in the season?"

For a rare moment, Paul was speechless.

"*Lao* Peng," Peng *Shu-Chi* said to her husband, "please get some boiled water and let's enjoy this hot tea."

I could feel the love between them. Governor Peng smiled and obligingly stood up and walked to the kitchen. Paul followed him, pretending to want to help, but Governor Peng declined the offer.

"So, Dr. Pei, what can we do to help you? You want to visit America?" Peng *Shu-Chi* went straight to the heart of the matter.

"Paul already told you?" I stammered.

"No, I just guessed." Peng *Shu-Chi* chuckled and continued, "I figured that if Dr. Pei personally called to see me and sounded like she might need some help, it would be the house is on fire or she wants to visit America. I guessed it was America." She continued to chuckle.

Paul and I looked at each other, speechless.

"I guess you will need a passport, which is not easy to get, but I know the process and I can certainly help." That's when I realized this godsend of a woman was on our side. I quickly said, "Peng *Shu-Chi,* I'm not trying to leave China and emigrate to American. I merely want to visit my home — well, once upon a *time* it was my home — and visit my parents' graves."

"I understand, Dr. Pei," Peng *Shu-Chi* said, gently interrupting me. "You don't need to explain yourself to me, or tell me all the details. Actually, the less I know, the better." She continued with so much love in her voice: "How things work out, we will let the process take its course (顺其自然). But I know that as much as we don't want to lose exceptionally talented people like you to help this second try at nation-building, you should go home and pay your utmost respect to your parents who gave you life, who adopted you and brought you up."

I nodded gratefully. Sensing I was being overly respectful

and timid, Peng *Shu-Chi* looked at Paul and then at me and continued, "But you know, Dr. Pei, *Lao* Peng and I think the world of your husband. He has the talent and potential to become a transformative leader on the world stage in agriculture. You might not know that we've been engaged in discussions with other countries, including America, Japan, and others, to establish four or maybe five experimental rice research stations worldwide, with one in China. The Central Government (中央) has selected four possible sites, including Hangchow, which will most likely be the place. We are in the final stages and have nominated Paul to be the first president of this new national and international Chinese Rice Research Institute (中國水稻研究所)! And here you are thinking about leaving! You, too, are an exceptional ophthalmologist and surgeon who could be a Chief Attending Physician (主任醫生) in any top hospital in this country. I just hate to see our country lose truly talented people, even though we've been mistreating them for the better part of twenty-five years!"

I appreciated everything she had to say, even though she was a Communist. I guess one's belief and party allegiance had nothing to do with anything. It was about who had the most decent human heart. At the same time, I knew Peng *Shu-Chi* was doing her best to convince me to stay or to return. But in my heart, I knew if I could have a chance to go back to America and never return, I would.

Just then, Governor Peng came back in carrying a tray with four glasses of hot tea and some small snacks.

"I'm so sorry we have another engagement, or else we'd love to have you stay for dinner. So, this tea will have to do, and it will be symbolic to wish us well and succeed in this next challenging endeavor." Peng *Shu-Chi* raised her teacup and saluted us.

Paul was quiet on the bus ride home. I was still in shock that it had all gone so smoothly. Finally, I broke the silence, "Do you think this will bring them trouble?"

Paul shook his head. "Wait for a week to give them time to contact the key person, and when we do the waltz into the police station asking for a passport, we ask for a specific officer, Officer Liu."

"Oh, did she say that? My Chinese gets bad when I'm nervous." Paul was mum, and I wasn't sure why he was so quiet. I reached out and grabbed his hand. He received mine, gently separated my five fingers to intertwine with his, and squeezed my hand tightly, so tight that it hurt. With that, we sat quietly on the bus the rest of the way, and I'd wince from time to time, feeling the pain of his grip. But I didn't complain, as I began to understand what he was thinking.

Then, on an unseasonably warm December day, Paul and I took time off from work and headed to the Hangchow Municipal Public Security Bureau (杭州市公安局) to apply for a passport. We met with Sergeant Liu, who had been notified by Peng *Shu-Chi*. Everything went smoothly. We were ecstatic coming out of the building and were so excited we decided to sit on a park bench.

Paul said, "This might just work!"

"Even with Peng *Shu-Chi*, I still have almost no confidence in these people or this process," I replied.

"Let's give them a chance. They said to come back in two weeks, and we will. What happened to that girl I knew, full of hope and optimism?"

"That was a long time ago. She's buried among the ashes of the Korean War and so many revolutions."

"We're in a public park," Paul reminded me. He looked around nervously, but there wasn't a soul around. He wrapped his arm around my shoulder and let out a deep sigh.

"Why the sigh?" I asked.
"Nothing," Paul replied.
"Please, tell me," I persisted.
After a few minutes, he said, "Are you sure you want to do this? Have you thought it through?"
"Of course!" I said emphatically. "Paul, you know it as well as anyone. My home is in Yonkers, New York, by the Hudson River, or wherever my parents are. I know they are no longer alive, but I have to go to America and see their graves. China is not my home. It's been hell for the last twenty-eight years. I'll go home and retrieve my citizenship, and then I'll come for you, Gina, and Eddy. It shouldn't take long!"

Paul looked at me and wiped the tears from the corners of my eyes, then said, "I know, and I understand. I'm all for it, and I'll do everything I can to help. I haven't forgotten our conversation at the Nanking Train Station. Of course, at that time, I didn't know you'd have to wait three decades. While I was trying to convince you not to take a risk, I was quite sure it'd be a matter of months, or at most a few years. From that moment on, I knew I was sent here to make sure you live through all of this and are able to return to America. So, perhaps that moment has arrived. But if you're there all by yourself, how will you survive?"

"How will I *survive?*" I asked.

"I know you'll have no problems with the language and that you can find a good job. I know you will reconnect with your cousin Evelyn and her family and be supported by connections with your Aunts Dee and Bessie—and Chum may be there by now, too—along with your high school classmates. But how will you re-adapt?"

"What do you mean?"

"I'm sure America has changed since you left. It's nearly thirty-five years!" Paul began counting on his fingers, and continued, "It's a different world now."

I sat in utter silence, acknowledging that I'd never thought about any of this.

"Whatever America has become, I'll deal with it," I vowed. "Whatever it takes, I'll adapt. I'm sure I will." I couldn't look at Paul while saying all that. I was kicking small stones beneath the bench. "I can't worry about this now. I have to move forward one step at a time until I reach home. You're right, Paul. The moment may be upon us." I finally looked up at him.

Paul ran his fingers through my hair and said, "I'm sure you will, one thing at a time."

"What about you?" I asked.

Paul chuckled, "What *about* me? I'll do my best to hang in here until your lifeboat arrives."

"And in the meantime, Gina will need your care, Eddy is still young, and we no longer have those wonderful neighbors to help us out. How will you handle two kids and still work on top of a long daily commute? I regret making you get rid of that motorcycle, but I feared for your life riding at that speed." Paul had bought a used moped the previous year, but I made him sell it back, which led to yet another big fight.

"We should be okay," he ventured. "I think things will continue to look up here. There's no need to worry about starvation, at least. I will try to find people to help me with the kids when needed. And Eddy can help in ways he never could before." After a moment of silence, Paul said he had an idea!

"What?" I asked.

"Take Eddy to America with you!" Paul said, and his voice sounded firm.

"That sounds marvelous. But how is it possibly going to work? We've exhausted our resources submitting my passport application. Adding Eddy into the mix will never work. And if

Eddy leaves with me, the authorities will be a hundred percent sure we're running away!"

"It may be the opposite," Paul said, now in deep thought. "If half the family is still here, we're like hostages, and they won't worry about you not returning. We can say it's a great opportunity for Eddy to study abroad. No one will think you'd leave him there or send him back to China alone. And since Eddy knows practically no English, it's hard to imagine how he could adapt to a new world and a new education system in just a few months or even a year. So, after having fun for a while, you'll both want to come back. Eddy will appear to be a burden that will force you to come back."

"I'm trying to absorb your logic. And how do we even begin pursuing this? Another visit to Governor Peng?" I asked.

Paul said, "Maybe we can go to the Police Department and ask them if this is even possible."

"Then let's do it before they complete the processing of my passport."

"All right, let's go now!" Paul stood up.

We hurried back to the Hangchow Municipal Public Security Bureau. The person at the front desk just waved to us. We scanned the big room and saw Sergeant Liu. "I said two weeks, not two hours," he repeated.

"Sergeant Liu, we're so sorry to bother you again, but we have a quick question."

"Sure, have a seat," he said. We sat on the chairs in front of his desk.

Sergeant Liu quipped, "What's going on? Let me guess. You don't want to go abroad after all (咋麼回事, 不想去美國啦?)."

"No, the opposite," I said. "Is there any chance you could process a passport for our son too, so that I can take him with me to study abroad for a year?"

As we prepared to hear roaring laughter, he simply asked, "Studying abroad? How old is he?"

Before I could say a word, Paul took over. "He's about to enter junior high."

"Studying abroad at that age sounds crazy to me, but maybe it'll good for him," the sergeant admitted. "The key issue is that you want to go and attend meetings and possibly study as an exchange scholar. That's all fine, I guess. But to issue your son a passport as an adult is nearly impossible at this point. He has no reason to hold an adult passport unless he is a college graduate or a physician."

My heart sank, and I began to regret coming back in, thinking this could ruin my chances too. Then Sergeant Liu added, "If your son is young enough, we can add his photo and name to your pending passport. That can be done easily."

"Really?" Paul exclaimed.

"Correct. We can help you with that, but you need to prove your son's age, like with hospital documentation to certify his date of birth," Sergeant Liu explained while fiddling with the wooden knob of his desk drawer. "Damn, are we that poor?" he asked himself. "I could use a new desk or at least a new drawer. This knob is practically coming off (啊呀, 我們都這麼窮呀, 座子也快要破啦, 什麼時候才能有新的)."

"Where was he born?" he then asked, looking up at me.

And before I could answer, Paul replied, "City of Hangchow, Sergeant Liu. And when you say young enough, what age do you mean?"

"Fifteen," the sergeant said, making the number with the fingers of both hands. I wanted to join the conversation, but Paul quickly said, "Okay, Sergeant Liu. We will get you that birth certificate soon."

"Even documentation from his current school would help,"

he suggested. As Paul signaled me to stand up, Sergeant Liu added, "Don't forget his photo or a joint photo of the two of you." We thanked him politely and went out the door, dumbfounded that this was even possible.

"Why did you say Hangchow?" I was filled with confusion and curiosity.

"How are we going to get a birth certificate for Eddy in Shanghai this day and age, Jeanie? It would be next to impossible," he said. Suddenly I woke up to the fact that we wouldn't be able to find anyone to provide an accurate record of Eddy's birth in the 1960s, not to mention our taking another long trip to Shanghai. "But Paul, what do we tell people here the year when Eddy was born, since I officially started working here in 1966?"

"When has it ever been a crime in China to be six months older or younger than your actual birth, not to mention the confusion between lunisolar and Georgian calendars?" Paul asked.

"What do you mean?" I still couldn't follow.

"No one will care if Eddy is six months older or younger. But being younger could help, since the passport processing could take a year, or maybe longer, and by then, he'll turn sixteen."

My head was spinning. While I preferred to write down his actual birthday, I knew Paul had a point. Two months later, in early March 1979, the hospital where I worked provided me with a birth certificate for Eddy, and Paul and I headed to the Public Security Bureau. To my surprise, we didn't recognize anyone in the room. One officer raised his head and said, "Who are you looking for?"

"Sergeant Liu, please," Paul said, wearing a big smile and bending forward in the kowtow posture that I hated.

"We have a couple Liu's here. Which one do you want?"

Paul took the envelope out of my hand and handed it to the officer, with our photos and Eddy's birth certificate, and proceeded to explain the situation to this officer.

"Officer Li, we were here to apply for a passport for both my wife and my son. We spoke with Sergeant Liu a few months ago, and he asked us to bring in my son's birth certificate."

"For what?"

"They may be traveling to America?"

"Why?" Officer Li didn't even look up at Paul.

I was beginning to lose my patience. "We explained everything to Sergeant Liu," I said, "and he told us all we needed were my son's birth certificate and some school records."

Officer Li looked at me from the corner of his eye and seemed agitated. "I'll take these materials and you can come back later."

"When?" asked Paul.

"Another week? Maybe a month? Check back when you think it's time."

I wanted to take back our documents and photos. I didn't trust this man.

"I'll keep them," Officer Li said, and he put them in his drawer.

Before I could say another word, Paul signaled that we should leave. Once outside, I raised my voice, "What if he loses it on purpose, or confiscates it? We may be wasting valuable time."

"Once he said he would keep them, what can you do? Fight with a police officer and get locked up?" Paul looked anxious too, and when he saw my face, he said, "Please don't tell me Americans wouldn't do it this way!"

A long week went by, and we decided to try our luck again. This time I was happy to see Sergeant Liu sitting there! And Officer Li was there too. "I gave your photos and documents to Sergeant Liu a few days ago," he told us, smiling.

"Thank you so much!" Paul said, while I walked right past him.

"Dr. Pei, please come here. I just have one more question, and I think we can submit this application."

"Yes, Sergeant Liu?" I was excited.

"You need to give me your son's full name in Chinese and English."

"An English name is needed now?" I asked.

"Yes."

"Edward Richard Perkins Hsiung," I said after a moment's hesitation, honoring my father and also Richard Nixon, who had opened diplomatic relations with China. "What do you think, Paul?"

"Too long! (太長了吧)," Paul said. Then even Sergeant Liu weighed in, and Paul added, "I agree with Sergeant Liu. Make it shorter. Any name will do. Just write one down so Sergeant Liu can submit the application and return to his important work."

"Dr. Pei," the sergeant agreed, "any name will do, because we don't care what English name you use for your son, just as Americans wouldn't care what Chinese name you write."

"Well..." I said. I couldn't make up my mind

Paul had had enough. "Just write Edward Richard Henry Perkins Hsiung?" he said sarcastically

"Henry? My uncle?" I asked.

"No, Henry Kissinger."

"I want it to be meaningful!" I was becoming nervous under pressure, and I made a quick decision, "Okay, it should be Richard E. P. Hsiung or Edward R. Perkins–Hsiung with a hyphen, because I don't want Eddy to be a Junior or a III."

Paul looked puzzled. "Jeanie, please pick *one!*"

"Okay." After writing down *Richard*, I was already running out of empty boxes on the application, so I quickly jotted down *Hsung* and handed the application sheet back to Sergeant Liu.

As we walked out of the Public Security Bureau, I felt

disoriented, like someone who had just completed a difficult exam. And halfway home, I realized I'd forgotten "Perkins" and misspelled "Hsiung"—I had left out the "i." "Oh no, Paul! I spelled *Hsiung* wrong. We've got to go back."

"No, Jeanie. What's done is done. The misspelled name is going to be his English name, for better or for worse." Paul tugged on my arm.

"This is a total disaster. His last name is going to be different from yours. I was under so much pressure to choose, I botched everything!"

Paul held my hand firmly and said, "It's okay, Jeanie. We're not going back. The key is not to delay this application another second. We have a long road ahead, with many hurdles and challenges more consequential than a misspelled name. Why didn't you just write 'Perkins'? It'd be so much simpler for you."

"I wanted to honor the fact that Eddy is your son."

Paul did not reply.

Months went by with no news from the police department, and my moods would swing many times a day. I was having trouble focusing on work, which could lead to disasters. I decided to find things to distract myself, especially ones I could control. I tried to restart Eddy's English lessons. I had been traveling so much that we'd lost the thread of the lessons for the past year. With his biking skills improved, I told him we could get up early again, and instead of taking the bus, he could ride my bike and I'd run along and shout English phrases at him.

"So, Eddy, what's your name?" I asked in a loud voice one day, while trying to catch my breath racing alongside him. It had been a while since I'd run regularly.

"Edward Perkins. Oh, sorry, Mommy, Edward Perkins Hsiung—yes?" Eddy sounded uncertain, which reminded me that I needed to coach him on his new name.

SPRING FLOWER: TORN BETWEEN SHIFTING WORLDS

Hangchow streets in the late 1970s: Much like the street shown here, while teaching Eddy how to ride a bike, I told him that his official English name would be Richard Perkins Hsiung, honoring Richard Nixon.

"Well, actually, no, Eddy. I changed your English name. You will tell people that your name is Richard Hsiung or Richard Perkins Hsiung."

"Why?" Eddy turned to me.

"Watch the road, Eddy. I wanted to name you after President Richard Nixon."

"Who is Richard Nixon?" Eddy shouted so loudly that people turned their heads.

"Just repeat what I tell you, okay? Focus on pronunciation. How old are you?"

"Fourteen, Mommy!"

I suddenly remembered that his age had also changed.

"Did I say it wrong, Mommy?"

"No, but keep your eyes on the road! Where are you from, Richard?"

"I am from Hangchow," Eddy shouted from the bike.

"Well, Eddy, many foreigners usually do not know where

Hangchow is. But they would know Shanghai, which is a much bigger city."

"*What* foreigners?"

"Just repeat after me: 'I am Richard, and I am from Hangchow, a small city south of Shanghai.' Okay?"

"Okay, ma'am!"

Our simple English dialogues threw me back to 1937 in Kiukiang, when Mother prepared me to answer possible questions from my first-grade teacher.

89

It was late August 1979, and we still hadn't heard back about my passport. Gina triumphantly returned from a year in Shanghai a changed girl, looking rather worldly. My little one had grown up, although there'd be no college for her to attend. China had reinstated college entrance exams (高考) that year, after abolishing college education altogether thirteen years earlier at the outset of the Great Cultural Revolution, forcing two generations of Chinese youth to miss out on a college education. So, millions were rushing to participate in the first wave of exams, some well into their thirties. Some cities were even running out of rooms

A rare family photo, ca. 1979 Autum Moon Festival

to host the exams. It was tragic and moving, at the same time, to see the renewal of higher education. Books for preparing for the entrance exams sold out as soon as they arrived on the shelves. Tutors and teachers were in high demand.

Paul and I recognized this might not be the time for Gina to begin the battle as a disabled young woman to try to attend college. So we encouraged her to study as much as she could to be ready for the possibility of entering a college in a year or two. And I was dreaming of Gina's attending college In America! I was pretty certain America would treat people with disabilities differently from China and that American children would enjoy an equal right to education. Being well prepared could benefit her, so I urged Gina to study English, especially since she seemed to have had a knack for pronouncing English syllables even as a child.

One Sunday afternoon as Paul left for the fall harvest season, I took the kids to a Japanese film about life in Japan and America, titled *Proof of Man* (人證). But when we got there, the tickets were sold out, but then I heard a man not far away say, "You want some movie tickets? (想要电影票吗?)"

"How much?" I asked.

"2 *Yüan* (元, or two RMB)."

"Two RMB per ticket?" I cringed. I was only making 56 RMB (*Yüan*, 元) per month.

"Yes," he nodded, and began to walk away. I followed him into a narrow alleyway. I'd never done anything like this, and I told Eddy to hold onto his sister and wait for me about ten yards back.

"I'm sorry, sir, two RMB per ticket is too high. Would you lower the price?" I was nervous, fearing for my safety.

He looked puzzled and asked, "Are you Chinese? (你是中國人吗?)"

SPRING FLOWER: TORN BETWEEN SHIFTING WORLDS

"Of course I am. But I can't afford your price. How about one RMB per ticket?"

"You don't sound Chinese," he said. "You do seem keen to see this movie; how about one RMB and fifty cents per ticket?" He flashed his fingers. I reluctantly pulled out a five-RMB bill and told him I needed three tickets.

"Ma'am, don't you have fifty cents?"

"Why?" I was puzzled, thinking we'd have to return to the annoying pricing negotiation. "Sorry, I don't."

"Me neither. Okay, the movie's about to start, and I feel for your kids out there. How about three tickets for four RMB?"

"That's great, thank you. You're very kind!"

I took the tickets and change, bought three popsicles for four cents each, and we rushed inside and found three seats in the theater.

Weeks later, Paul was furious. "What movie could be worth that much? It's dangerous to negotiate pricing with a scalper, probably one from the underworld (黑社會)." Paul was right. By 1979, the mafia had begun to emerge in China. I guess I mustered the courage to negotiate ticket prices because of the movie's theme.

Then, one day in early fall, Superintendent Wen told me the exciting news that a group of American physicians would be visiting and they needed me as their interpreter. It would be in Hangchow, and they would visit our hospital. Soon, I received a call from Peking from a Loring Pratt, who told me that he was part of the delegation and that he had something for me from Dr. Arthur Grove. After hanging up, I sighed. It had been almost a year since I'd spoken with Dr. Grove at the hotel in Shanghai, and I still didn't have a passport.

It turned out that I had a wonderful time with Dr. Pratt, a family physician from Maine, and his wife, Janice. What a

JEAN TREN-HWA PERKINS

warm couple they were! He had known Dr. Grove for a long time. Loring and Janice Pratt were so easygoing and pleasant to converse with that I brought Paul along for one excursion, so that Paul could explain the historical sites in Hangchow, which had been the capital of the Southern Sung Dynasty (南宋) from around 1127 to 1279. Meeting them, Paul even seemed to think that my parents had come back to life.

The information from Dr. Grove was paramount to my fate. Dr. Grove confirmed that the Laboratory of Dr. Morton W. Grant, a preeminent glaucoma specialist at Massachusetts Eye and Ear Infirmary, had agreed to accept me as a Visiting Scholar, and Dr. Grove himself was in the process of securing for me a three-year fellowship through Massachusetts General Hospital. All I needed was a passport, and I could apply for an entry visa using the documents Arthur Grove had sent via Dr. Pratt.

Once I received a passport, I would have to decide whether to wait for a US Embassy to open in China or to apply for the US entry visa in Japan or perhaps Hong Kong. Another important letter was enclosed. It was from Dr. Edwin Fisher, former Head of the United Methodist Church. Dr. Grove had tracked him down, too. Dr. Fisher spoke fondly of Mother and Day-Day and confirmed that Day-Day had passed away in 1958 and Mother had passed away in 1961. He told me the United Methodist Church was the executor of my parents' will and that the Church would do its best to help me return to America. He also provided me with contact info and addresses of people to contact in both Japan and Hong Kong.

In late January of 1980, I received a brand-new Chinese passport in the mail that displayed the joint photo of Eddy and me. And the passport had spelled Eddy's English name "Hsung." With our precious passport in hand, what remained was to decide whether to wait for a US Consulate to open in

SPRING FLOWER: TORN BETWEEN SHIFTING WORLDS

Shanghai or head to Japan instead. To be prepared, I registered for an ophthalmology conference in Tokyo and was accepted to give a short talk. I also got in touch with the conference co-host, who had expressed interest in organizing a mini-tour for me. Paul and I made another long trip to Shanghai, this time to apply at the Japanese Embassy for an entry visa to Japan. All that was left for us to decide was when to "pull the trigger." If we missed the Japan window, we could be waiting for an American Embassy to open, which had zero time frame. (The US Consulate in Shanghai reopened in April of 1980, thirty years after it had closed.) Documents from Dr. Grove would expire in October 1980. We could seek entry to Hong Kong, which had become less stringent. The irony was that three-and-a-half decades after Paul talked me out of swimming from Canton to Hong Kong, I might finally get there! But I decided instead to fly to Tokyo, because I wanted to stop in Japan en route to America.

Paul planned a few gatherings to thank and say goodbye to our dear friends, like Qiu-Shuang and Old Man Ni, and Sue and Conductor Hsie. The dinners all ended in tears. We all had gone through so much together! After these gatherings, I was all the more determined to leave quietly, with minimal fanfare. I couldn't take many more alcohol-drenched, emotional goodbyes.

If we decided to leave suddenly, what would happen to my job? Jade said she'd cover for me if I made it to America. And if we did not get further than Japan, I'd simply attend a conference there and try to find someone to organize a month-long tour so I could lecture on my work with glaucoma. Both were completely legitimate activities in Japan, so I'd be able to come back to my hospital and assume my position as the Associate Chief of our Division.

But then I began to get cold feet. "Am I doing the right thing returning to America with reckless abandon," I asked myself.

"Should I wait till Eddy finishes ninth grade instead of yanking him out of class?" And at the time, Eddy was about to participate in the nationally administered high school entrance exam. We thought we should let him complete the entrance exam, in case he had to return for high school. His teachers all spoke highly of his academic aptitude in literature and math. They were certain Eddy would be ranked high in Chekiang Province, and even nationally. What would this sudden change do to him? And what if I didn't *like* what America had become, as Peng *Shu-Chi* and Paul had warned?

Peng *Shu-Chi*'s parting words echoed in my mind: "Dr. Pei, please do go home and see your family in America, and stay if you can. But if America is not what you remember or if America doesn't remember *you*, you'll always be welcome back here. Dr. Pei, you can rest assured of that! To keep on serving the Chinese

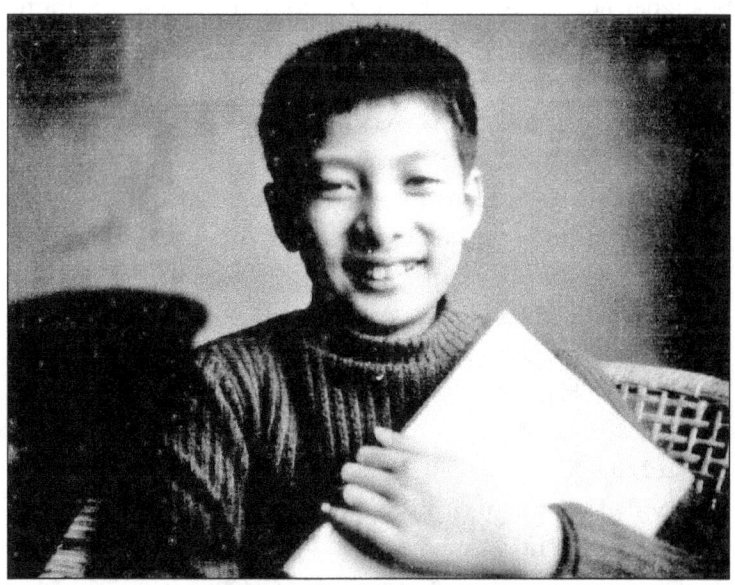

Sitting on his favorite bamboo chair and studying for his high school entrance exam, ca. 1979 or 1980

people would be in the same spirit as the great work your American parents did for China. We're deeply sorry for what happened to people like you and Paul in the past decade; please consider giving us another chance."

Spring 1980...
I was interrupted by Shan, who was driving us to Shanghai.
"Don't worry, Dr. Pei! I'm sure your American classmates will remember you. My elementary school friends still remember me!" He turned around and gave me a broad smile. I tried to smile back, but only an anxious cough came out.

"We're almost there, Dr. Pei," Shan said, looking at me in the rearview mirror. His eyes reminded me of how life's ironies know no bounds. Shan was no longer merely the guard I'd met at Paul's labor camp. I finally smiled and felt relaxed. "Okay, kids, Shanghai, here we come!" Then we approached a long red traffic light. The policeman sitting in the guard tower at the corner appeared to be staring at us, or so I thought. I became more and more nervous, thinking, "My God, not here! We're almost at the Shanghai city limit."

Finally, the light turned green, and Shan said, "Please give me directions to your friend's apartment. I'm not familiar with Shanghai."

I sat up straight and said, "Yes, Shan. I know this place inside out. We need to get to Hsü-Chia-Hui District (徐家匯). Please head toward Heng-Shan Road (衡山路)."

"Okay," he said.

Paul chuckled. "Actually, I know this place well, too! Nearly twenty-five years ago, we lived and worked here together!"

I ignored Paul's comment as I tried to avoid nostalgic thinking, and continued, saying, "That's Heng-Shan Road. Stay on the road till we come to Huai-Hai Middle Road (淮海中路)."

Silence ensued.

"Oh, Shan, there's Tung-Ping Road (東平路). Please make a right," Paul said.

"Why?" I asked.

"Let's take one last look. Shan, please bear left onto Yüeh-Yang Road (岳陽路)." So, we passed another place where I had lived and worked for ten years—the two-story building Gina and I lived in, where Eddy was born. Then we drove past the Infirmary. Except for traveling through Nanking and Kiukiang, this trip to the airport was my life in reverse.

"Now please bear right and follow Fen-Yang Road (汾陽路)," Paul continued.

I looked out the window with little outward emotion as memories flooded in. It had affected me less on those tours as a translator. A glimpse of Taka's smile flashed in my mind. I wondered if our paths would cross again on this fateful journey and how he was doing after returning to Japan. I thought about his comment, "Jean, learn some Japanese; it may come in handy someday."

We passed Fen-Yang Road and turned onto Huai-Hai Middle Road (淮海中路), and within minutes, we were at the Shous' front entrance. She and her husband, Mr. Liu, started unloading our things. Shan suggested we might leave the two bigger suitcases in the jeep.

"No, please," I said. "We should bring them up." I was not going to take any more chances losing stuff. And so Paul grabbed them.

Shan said, "Suit yourself. I'll park the jeep somewhere safe and meet you upstairs."

As it was already afternoon, we were tired after the long trip. Lunch was waiting for us. "Shou, you shouldn't have," I said.

"Are you kidding? When did we become so formal! We've

SPRING FLOWER: TORN BETWEEN SHIFTING WORLDS

Street-level stores reappearing on the first floors of Western-style buildings in Shanghai. While that was a sign of returning prosperity, people were still using tricycles like that on which Old-Man-Ni had pedaled us umpteen times.

eaten already, so you guys go ahead." Shou pushed me toward the table.

I saw Shou's two kids peeking out from behind a curtain, and I waved to them. They were about Gina and Eddy's ages.

Shou said, "Come quickly and say hello to Auntie Pei."

They waved and ran back behind the curtain, each grabbing one of my kids to play with. Shou's apartment was very small, divided into three "rooms" using curtains.

Mr. Liu said, "Paul, shall we drink now or tonight?"

Paul replied, "How about a little bit now? I'll have too much responsibility tomorrow."

Mr. Liu said, "Okay, it's time to celebrate!"

And Paul told him, "We're nowhere near that yet."

Shou said, "Please, *Lao* Liu (老劉), this is a serious trip."

Shan entered the apartment and shared his two cents: "Any drinking would have to be now for me. I need to be sober to take you to the airport tomorrow." Shan helped himself to a beer and asked, "What is it about cold beer and summer?"

"What's the plan for tomorrow morning?" Shou asked. She'd always been detail-oriented, like Paul.

Shan said, "Are we all going? That will be way too many people in the jeep, and if we get caught? No way!"

Paul said, "If we leave early, maybe it'll be okay. It's Sunday." Shan just sipped on his beer.

Shou said, "One or both of us should go. You'll need all the help you can get tomorrow. And Shan will have to stay with the jeep."

"What about your kids?" I asked.

"They're grown up and can stay home by themselves," Mr. Liu said. "Okay, it's decided. We'll both go to the airport with you."

Shou turned to me and suggested, "Tren-Hwa, why don't you take a nap? We could probably talk from now until you depart, but you have a long journey ahead."

I probably looked exhausted and didn't participate much in the discussion of tomorrow's plans. I wanted to chat with Shou, but she was right. I asked Gina and Eddy to take naps too. Eddy shouted, "We just began a new game."

Shou gently said, "Eddy, you can play some more this evening." Reluctantly, Eddy went to the floor, where four blankets were laid out for us. That's where we'd be spending the night.

I slept for hours. When I finally got up, Paul was still at the table with Mr. Liu and Shan. "You didn't sleep?" I asked.

"Nope," Paul said. "Just having a couple of beers with the guys."

Mr. Liu added, "Dr. Pei, don't worry; we'll serve dinner soon."

"*Lao* Liu's been at it since yesterday," Shou added. "Think of it as Chinese New Year, half a year early," Mr. Liu chuckled. Soon, the nine of us crowded around their tiny dining table, barely big enough for four.

"It looks delicious!" Eddy exclaimed.

"Eat up, Eddy!" Shou said. "You may not have a chance to eat real Chinese food soon." I doubted that comment registered with Eddy. We'd been so poor, my kids never knew real Chinese food, at least not a spread like this.

"Cheers! Have a safe journey, Dr. Pei!" Our beer glasses and tin cups clinked.

Shou said quietly, as I stood next to her by the sink helping with the dishes, "If it's too difficult, Tren-Hwa, just come back. Things will get better here."

"Maybe," I said, "but I don't trust even these changes or that they might last. If I make it to America, I'm not coming back."

Shou continued to wash our bowls. Night came, and she said, "The blankets on your beds are thin, but I think they'll be enough. If you get cold, you can close the front windows."

I nudged Paul and asked softly, "Are you asleep?" He was already snoring. I'm not sure how much beer and white liquor he'd had. I, on the other hand, felt restless and kept rehearsing what to do when Eddy and I arrived in Tokyo.

Morning came at last. With little sleep, I was even more focused and running on adrenaline. "To leave today at all costs" became my motto. I washed and got dressed, and I dressed Gina swiftly as Paul was packing everything we'd taken out. I double-checked to make sure all my documents, passport, proof of conference registration, and visas to enter Japan were in my handbag.

Paul asked, "Are your passport, plane tickets, entry visa, meeting invitation, and all documents relevant to picking up your visa in Tokyo, information regarding your parents, and invitation to be a visiting scholar at Massachusetts General

Hospital, and Eddy's school records — all in your handbag?

I checked them off mentally as he spoke, and replied, "Yes, all here."

Suddenly, Eddy ran in from outside and said, "Mommy, Gina is crying hard."

Shou also came in and said, "Come quickly, Tren-Hwa. Gina is refusing to go." I went outside, and Gina was holding onto the railing by the stairs and wailing, "I don't want you to go, Mommy. Please don't leave me."

I held her firmly and said, "Oh, my dear Gina, you're not a kid anymore. You were born here in Shanghai twenty years ago, and you're a young lady now, the exact age I was when my parents left." With her tiny figure, it'd be hard for anyone to believe she was twenty. I continued to plead, "Please, Gina! Crying isn't going to help Eddy."

Then Eddy grabbed Gina's arm and expressed his solidarity: "Please don't cry, Gina. I won't leave you."

I knew I had to be firm, and I said, coldly, "Let's go, Eddy!" By then, Paul and I had loaded the jeep and gone back up the stairs. In a swift motion, he carried Gina down the steps, while I grabbed Eddy's hand. Shou's children stood at the top of the spiral stairs motionless, watching it all.

Shan was waiting by the jeep and said, dryly, "I hope it all goes well. Here's the plan: Whenever we stop at a traffic light, the kids need to crouch as low as they can so it looks like there are just five of us in the jeep." So, with Eddy and Gina practically sitting on the floor, off we went toward the Hung-Ch'iao Airport. It all went well, clearing one light after another, until we reached one long stoplight. Eddie and Gina were crouching low for several minutes.

"Mommy, my legs hurt."

"Please, Eddy, just a moment longer," I said, pressing his

head down.

At that moment, the policeman in the intersection said through his loudspeaker, "Will the driver of the jeep please pull over and come here."

Shan turned around and said, "Just be sure the kids stay down, and I'll be right back." Shan grabbed his documents and headed toward the officer. We watched his body language. Shan and the policeman seemed to be going back and forth. "Is this conversation ever going to end?" I muttered.

Paul squeezed my hand as if to say, "Relax, Jeanie."

Shou grabbed my other hand. Mr. Liu was sitting up straight in the front passenger's seat and, without turning his head, said, "I'm not sure what they're talking about, but if it were bad, the police would already be shouting and telling us to get out of the jeep. That's a good sign."

Shan lit a fresh cigarette for the policeman and walked back with a grin. He started the engine, and none of us asked what happened. And soon we arrived at the airport. After driving around a long stretch of barbed-wire fence, we came to a red brick building built in the 1930s, got out of the jeep, and headed in. Guards came over to us right away and asked who among us would be on the flight. They sensed that Shou and Mr. Liu were not part of the family and asked them to leave immediately. Shou knew this was the moment to burst into tears, tears she'd been holding back ever since we arrived at her home, if not for thirty actual years. She gave me a big hug and whispered, "My dear Tren-Hwa, you are finally going home after all this time!" Just that. And she headed out with Mr. Liu, who held up two fingers in a "V" for "victory" sign; I'm not sure where he learned that.

Next, they asked Paul and Gina to leave. Gina held my arm tightly as Paul pleaded, "Please, we won't leave or run away. My wife and son are boarding a plane for Japan. Can you allow us to escort them until they board?"

An officer came and asked what the commotion was. Before the guards could say anything, a female officer said, without affect, "They are family. We can let them see each other off." She then led us to the checkout and security lane where three more uniformed officers were standing, two of them young girls. The older one, a man in his forties, examined my passport and visa and asked, "What is your reason for going to Japan?"

I told him, "To attend a meeting," and showed him my conference invitation and the Chinese translations. He nodded his head and said, "For how many days?"

"The meeting is for one week," I said, "but the visa is for two weeks because I will visit several hospitals and have exchanges with their glaucoma specialists."

"Oh," he said. Then the dreaded question came. "Why are you taking your son?" Then he chuckled and asked, "Is he also attending this international conference?"

I caught Paul's eyes, who was standing a few feet behind us holding Gina.

"It's summer vacation, a great opportunity for my son to see the outside world."

To my great surprise, he grinned. "It sounds wonderful. Lucky kid," and he nodded at Eddy. Then came the surprise. "If you're just leaving for a couple of weeks in Japan, why did your husband and daughter insist on seeing you pass through security? That isn't what we usually do, except my colleague felt sorry for your daughter, who appears to be handicapped."

I was dumbfounded. I could never think fast on my feet. Paul quickly intervened, saying, "Officer, our disabled daughter has never left her mother, even for a single day, let alone leaving the country, and so this is a special moment for her."

The Border Patrol officer said, "Oh, okay," and turned to the two young girls working with him and said, "Please go ahead and check their bags." So, they opened everything under the watchful eyes of the older officer, fumbling through clothing, a book on glaucoma, my photo album, and the folder containing all the other documents relevant to going to America.

My heart raced faster with each passing item, fearing they would open the album or the document folder. It felt like years, although it'd been less than half an hour since we entered the building.

"The suitcases are okay," one of the young officers said.

Paul came over and helped me repack our belongings. We handed them one maroon and one blue suitcase to check in and headed to the door at the rear of the brick building.

A few more guards came over, checked my plane tickets and passport, and signaled that we could proceed, but not Gina and Paul. Paul tried to talk his way into continuing with us and turned around, trying to get the attention of the other officer. But these guards wouldn't budge, and Gina fell down and began to cry. Paul quickly picked her up and said, firmly, "Gina, please, not here."

Eddy went over and held onto his sister, perhaps for the last time. Paul pleaded some more, and one guard softened and said, "Okay, but just to the fence outside the departure gate and not a step further!"

We walked through the gate, and there it was — a huge Japan Airlines jet plane sitting on the tarmac, gleaming under the sun and the deep blue sky, just a few hundred yards beyond the fence. I held onto Eddy, my other hand clutching the duffel bag and a big handbag, and began to walk toward a gate in the barbed-wire fence. I turned around to hug Paul and Gina, but my knees somehow gave out and I collapsed onto the ground, tears streaming down my face. Paul looked startled and reached out to grab my arms, and accidentally let go of Gina, and she fell hard and lay there in a heap. Eddy rushed over to pick up his sister.

Sobbing out of control, I grabbed Paul's leg and whispered, "If it weren't for you, I wouldn't have been alive today. I owe my life to you. If we never see each other again, I'll repay you in the next lifetime (我下輩子來還你)!"

Paul pulled me up quickly, fearing this would draw too much attention. Trying to lighten the mood, he said, "My goodness, Jeanie, your Chinese has finally improved after three decades! Please, you need to get going now. We can't have this conversation, it's neither the time nor the place. Any more of this could ruin everything."

I bit my tongue and went over to a standing Gina. I gave her a firm kiss on her forehead, grabbed Eddy's arm, and we headed straight to the mobile stairway anchored on the back of a small truck next to the Japan Airlines plane on the tarmac. By then, other passengers were heading out too. I quickened my pace and felt Eddy trying to pry free of my grip. When I looked at him, I was surprised to see his face covered in tears. I couldn't remember when he cried last—perhaps as a three-year-old saying goodbye to his grandmother.

"Mother, I don't want to go! I want to be with Gina and Papa. Please trust me. I'll be a very good brother to Gina. I'll take very good care of her and listen to Papa about everything. I will do everything to help him. Please don't take me. I don't want to go."

The mobile stairway was just twenty feet away, and I began to walk faster.

"Mommy, I know I haven't done enough for Gina and Papa. And I haven't done well enough in school, but please don't punish me. I really don't want to go!"

Just then, Eddy's hand slipped out of my sweaty palm, and he turned around and ran back toward the fence, where his

SPRING FLOWER: TORN BETWEEN SHIFTING WORLDS

father and sister were standing. I dropped my duffel bag and raced after him. Boy, could he run! He had dropped all his bags along the way and was shouting as he ran, "Gina! Papa!"

Paul quickly came to his side of the fence and frantically gestured to Eddy to turn around. Then the guards came out shouting, trying to prevent him from going any further. A sudden fear came over me that this could turn into a disaster, and I picked up my speed and finally caught up with him. I yanked his arm so violently he nearly fell, and I shouted at him, "You listen to me now, young man! We have to go. Now! Please, Edward!"

I looked at his tear-soaked face, and my heart was broken. So, I wiped his face and quickly changed my tune. "Please be a good boy, Eddy, like you always have been. You've always listened to me, all your life. Mommy needs your help right now, at this moment, please!"

His resolve broken, I dragged him back to the plane, picking up his bags and my duffel bag along the way. We walked briskly toward the mobile stairway and went straight up the stairs and into the plane without looking back.

The stewardess at the door smiled and said in a sympathetic tone, "*Kon'nichiwa* (こんにちは, Good afternoon)." I saw her eyes swelling up and realized they'd been witnessing our drama. I nodded my head and quickly turned to find our seats. I gave Eddy the window seat so he'd be trapped and couldn't run away again. Another stewardess came over and helped me place our bags in the overhead compartment. As soon as I sat down, Eddy collapsed onto my lap, quietly sobbing away, "I don't want to go, Mommy. Please, I don't want to go!"

Another stewardess handed me two warm, moist towels and, smiling kindly, asked, "*Daijibu desuka?* (だいじぶ ですか, Is he okay?)"

I nodded my head and said, "*Daijibu, desu, aigado* (だいじぶ,

です, あいがど, He should be fine; thank you)." Then I turned to face the window so no one could see my tears.

"Why haven't they closed the doors?" I thought, and looked around nervously. Most people were minding their own business. Then I looked out the window, hoping there'd be no unanticipated security inspection, especially given the commotion we'd just created. It seemed like years till the doors finally closed and the plane began to move. As it made a U-turn, I stretched my neck to look out the window, sensing the metal fence where Paul and Gina might be standing. I looked and looked, and a few hundred yards away, I saw two stick figures, one tall and slim, the other short and crooked, with their hands clutched against the fence. As the figures began to fade away, I waved, knowing they couldn't see me, and then they disappeared from sight. Within minutes, we were in the air, and I could see only dots of buildings and lines of streets, and then the deep blue ocean below. I was leaving China for the second and last time. I finally exhaled.

90

Eddy was asleep with his head on my lap, exhausted from the whole ordeal. I tried to rest too, but couldn't. Every moment of the past few days was replaying in my mind, mixed with events of the last three decades, along with memories of Yonkers and all the people I knew. My heart raced faster and faster, and I tried to focus on the tasks at hand—what I needed to do when I landed, and what to say in which language. I was completely on my own; Paul was no longer with me. I missed him already, and Gina too. Tears began to roll down my face.

"Excuse me, ma'am, would you like something to drink?" I was startled by the stewardess, who spoke in Japanese.

I tried to answer in Japanese, but English came out. "Orange juice for my son, and just water for me, thank you."

"No problem," she replied in English, politely nodding her head. I woke Eddy up to hand him the juice, and then the stewardess gave us small trays of food. Eddy's eyes lit up!

"What's this?" he asked.

"It's called a salad," I explained.

Eddy looked shocked. "Raw? Not cooked?"

"Yes, some vegetables can be eaten raw. Just mix them together with this sauce, which is called salad dressing. It's really tasty, try it."

Eddy took a bite of dressing-covered lettuce and made an excruciatingly pained expression. "Yuck," he said.

"Okay, but please don't spit it out. That's not polite. You don't have to eat any more, but swallow what you've taken," I told him sternly. For a kid who hadn't seen much food in his life, I thought he'd gobble down the whole tray. But I couldn't blame him, as there were too many sudden changes, and now I was asking him to eat raw vegetables, till now unheard of. I apologized when the stewardess came to take our trays. I wholeheartedly enjoyed my first real Western meal in a very long time. Then, just a few hours after we took off, the pilot announced "Dear passengers, we are about to land at Narita International Airport," which was about forty miles east of Tokyo. Eddy and I were both looking out the window at a brand-new world.

"From here on, always carry your own bag, plus one of the three suitcases, unless I ask you to carry two or watch all of them, okay? And Eddy, please *never* let me out of your sight. Do you hear me? This is important." Eddy nodded, and we deplaned and headed toward immigration. I was rehearsing in my mind whatever I might need to say in response to their possible questions. At last, our turn came. The officer behind a small window looked carefully at our joint passport, checking our faces.

"Purpose of your visit?" he asked in perfect English, perhaps seeing our English names.

"To attend a weeklong conference and visit a few hospitals to meet with experts." I was relieved that I didn't need to say it in Japanese.

"You plan to return to China in a few weeks, and so there's no need for a long-term entry permit, correct?" he asked.

"I would still prefer a standard sixty- or ninety-day permit, as it would give me flexibility to attend additional visits arranged by people at the conference," I told him.

He looked at me for a second, then turned around to look behind him, and soon a female officer about my age came out of the office. The two exchanged a few words, and the woman gestured to Eddy and me to follow her. Eddy began to drag the two bags I'd handed to him as we approached the window, and I suspect we looked like refugees.

I reached over and took the heavier bag back, while swinging the other one onto my shoulder and using my free hand to grab his arm so we wouldn't fall behind following her. Once we sat down in her office, she said in English, "My colleague tells me you need to stay longer than the standard fourteen- or thirty-day single-entry visit. Why? You'll just be attending a meeting and visiting a few hospitals."

I'm a terrible liar and always have been, so I blurted out, "We are trying to get to America and will need to apply for an entry visa here in Tokyo."

"Oh, please explain," she said, looking surprised.

I showed her my other documents from Massachusetts General Hospital/Mass Eye and Ear Infirmary and proceeded to tell her a three-minute version of my life story.

"Really? It sounds like you could write a book," she said in all seriousness. Her eyes lit up and a smile flashed across her face.

"Yes, all this is true." I wasn't sure how to read her smile, but she opened her desk drawer, took out a rubber stamp, and stamped firmly on our passport. "I hope this is enough time for you. On this date, you must return to China. Best of luck getting your visa to enter the United States."

I nodded in appreciation and thanked her profusely in both English and Japanese. After we exited her office, I saw that she had granted us a special 120-day stay! We gathered our belongings, and after going through an additional spot-check of our suitcase, we entered Japan.

"Mommy, why are there so many policemen?" Eddy asked. I was reorganizing all our stuff, struggling to stack it all onto a small luggage cart, and was completely unaware of my surroundings. Eddy's comment made me look up. "I don't know, dear. Can you help me steady this bag so it won't fall off? I guess it's normal to have lots of police guards at an international airport, to protect the airport." Eddy continued to look in all directions, in awe of his new surroundings. Once outside we saw even more guards, some heavily armed. A few were pacing back and forth. It felt more like a prison than an airport. I didn't have the leisure to worry about it, as I needed to make a call. With all these people, it was hard to push the cart.

"Eddy, you stand here with our bags. I need to find a phone and make a call. Please don't move one inch. I won't be far, and I don't want you out of my sight."

"Yes, ma'am," Eddy answered.

I quickly ran to a phone booth, nervously turning my head twice to keep an eye on Eddy. I took out a sheet of the paper and some Japanese coins.

"Hello, is this Ms. Tiyo Nishiyama? This is Jean. How are you? (こんにちはTiyo Nishiyamaさん ですか? わたしはJean - uh - です. お 元気ですか)?" I shouted into the phone.

"Yes, Jean. You've arrived! I've been expecting you. Welcome to Japan."

"I look forward to meeting you, Ms. Nishiyama. Can you instruct me how to get to your place?" I asked.

"Take the express bus to Tokyo Station, and then a taxi. That's the easiest way. Do you have my address from Dr. Fisher?" Perhaps sensing my shaky Japanese, Ms. Nishiyama began to speak rather good English.

"I understand, and yes I have your address," I replied, using the word *adoresu* (アドレス), unsure if there was a better word I should have used. Taka had told me that many Japanese words originated from British English and even if they contain an "r" are pronounced without the "r" sound.

"Be careful. See you soon," By now Ms. Nishiyama was shouting, and my voice grew increasingly loud too, as if we'd understand each other better with the volume turned up.

I hung up and hurried to get back to Eddy. Trying to see him through a forest of tall people with tree-trunk legs, I started to worry, "Where is he? I told him not to move." Just when I was about to shout his name, I saw him with two stewardesses. He was sitting on the bag that kept falling off the cart, and the stewardesses were standing with him talking to him.

"Eddy!" I called his name, and both stewardesses turned toward me. One of them said, "Is this your son? We were hoping he wasn't lost."

"Thank you, and sorry if he caused you any trouble. I had to make a call." I bowed slightly from the waist, as Taka had taught me, and apologized.

"It's no trouble at all. He's very cute. He told us he was waiting here for you." Then they walked away, waving to Eddy.

"Come on, kiddo, let's find the bus to Tokyo." I began to push the cart.

"They're very pretty, Mommy," Eddy said, looking up at me as if comparing my face with theirs. "Well, what do you know?" I thought.

Looking out the bus window at neatly aligned rice fields with patches of hills, I thought of Paul. This looked like where he worked, which was now a world away. I began to feel my exhaustion. Eddy was asleep again. I tried to doze, but still couldn't. I was thinking of all the remaining hurdles, the first of which would be to make our way through the Tokyo crowds I had been warned of. But to my great surprise and delight, despite thousands of people filling every imaginable space, things were phenomenally orderly. People waited in a line at our taxi stand,

and as the driver closed the door, I gave him the address in the Shinjuku District.

He wound through the narrow streets of Tokyo, and I realized that Japan had been rebuilt from the ashes of its own creation. I was bedazzled by the contrast between where I'd just come from and where I was. As we were weaving in and out of a series of neighborhoods whose streets were even narrower, we saw old two-story buildings on both sides, some with rusted metal roofs. I spotted an elderly woman holding an umbrella, and sensed that was Ms. Nishiyama, and before I could say a word, the driver slowed down, and pointed to an old building. "This is the address," he said.

"Thank you very much."

As the driver helped us get our luggage, Ms. Nishiyama walked over. "Welcome, Jean, welcome!" and held her umbrella over my head, since by then it was raining.

"Please say hello to Ms. Nishiyama, Eddy." Eddy bowed slightly and greeted her with a big smile. Ms. Nishiyama chuckled, "Cute, very cute. A very handsome young man."

Ms. Nishiyama must have been in her seventies, or at least her late sixties. She was tiny but sprightly! She grabbed two of our bags and headed up the stairs, where she showed us our tiny yet very clean room.

"Sorry, not very big, but hope it's okay," she said.

"This is plenty big. It's very nice. Thank you," I replied.

"I have something for you. I will be right back," she said.

I didn't want to completely unpack; I wasn't sure how long we'd be here. Eddy and I sat at the foot of the bed, staring at our suitcases.

Ms. Nishiyama returned with a packet of mail. "This is from Dr. Edwin Fisher of the Methodist Mission in New York, and some mail from Boston. I believe Dr. Fisher and the Mission

Office also sent some money for you to use during this time." She pointed to a separate envelope, and said, "If it is not enough, please let me know."

"Oh yes, Ms. Nishiyama. How much do I need to pay you for the room?" I asked.

"Call me Tiyo, Jean. You don't need to worry. It has already been taken care of. You must be very tired. Please rest, and I will have a simple dinner ready in an hour. You must be hungry." She walked over to a small table and poured us two cups of tea. "This thermos has hot tea." It was strange; you could push on the top of it, and the hot liquid came out the spout! "Please help yourself. Tomorrow morning first thing I will go with you to the US Embassy." I loved the way she blended both languages.

The next day, we went to the embassy, telling an officer at the front desk "Dr. Jean Perkins is here in Tokyo to attend a meeting, and she has been accepted for a fellowship at Massachusetts General Hospital. She would like to submit an application in Japan for a J-visa to enter the US as a visiting scholar. Here are her papers," Ms. Nishiyama explained, handing the envelope with my documents to a man whose name tag read "Jeffrey Ishihara," an embassy staff member in his thirties who was probably Japanese American.

"Oh, this is unusual, but it is a legitimate request," Mr. Ishihara said, speaking fluent Japanese as he scanned through my documents and passport. He turned straight to me and asked in perfect English, "When do you need to begin your fellowship position at Massachusetts Eye and Ear Infirmary?"

Ms. Nishiyama began to translate the question to me in Japanese, but I nodded and replied directly to Mr. Ishihara, "There is no specific starting date, but as soon as I arrive, preferably by October 1."

"For how long will this fellowship be?" he asked. Ms.

Nishiyama then chuckled and patted on her own head, "I'm so sorry. I'm getting old. What was I thinking? I don't need to translate for you. You speak English!"

"One year but renewable," I answered.

"Please fill in the areas I've checked," he asked, handing me two forms.

I complied, and then he inquired, "What is your son going to be doing?"

"I will try to enroll him in a junior high."

"Where?"

"People at Mass General who are sponsoring this fellowship submitted an application for him to Milton Academy in Boston."

"And your husband and daughter...?" he asked.

"Yes, they are living in China," I replied. "How long will this take?" I then asked as I handed the forms back to him.

"A few weeks, maybe a month or two. We'll call you. Do you have a local address? Shall we use yours?" he asked, turning to Ms. Nishiyama."

"Of course," she said with a big smile.

As we walked out, Ms. Nishiyama said, "That went smoothly," and she seemed delighted.

"I hope the application will be accepted soon," I said, more subdued that she was.

"It will be. Have faith, my child!"

"I feel bad about taking so much of your time and energy."

"Dr. Pei, this is an important duty Dr. Fisher has bestowed upon me, and it is my pleasure to help. I learned about your parents from him, so in fact, this is an *honor* for me. Not to mention you two are going to keep me company for a little while."

We headed toward a café diagonally across the street. Eddy clung tightly to my shirttail as we crossed. He had probably never seen so many cars.

SPRING FLOWER: TORN BETWEEN SHIFTING WORLDS

"No need to be afraid, Eddy; we have the walk light. When it's green, they'll all stop for us," I assured him.

"How did you meet Dr. Fisher?" I asked as we sat in the café.

"He and his wife came here about twenty years ago to help us establish a Methodist church, the way missionaries would. They're a lovely couple, and it was great fun working with them," Ms. Nishiyama replied. "This Sunday, I hope you and Eddy will come with me to church."

"Oh yes, we certainly will. It's been a long time since I've been in a church! And Eddy has never been to church," I told her.

"That reminds me. We should call Dr. Fisher and report our good progress on this end."

"Is there a post office near your home?" I asked.

"Post office, why?" she wondered aloud.

"To make a long-distance call," I replied.

"Oh, just use the phone in your room."

"But that's expensive," I explained.

"Please don't worry about that," she said emphatically. "Do you have plans to see Japan while waiting for your visa approval?" She tried to change the subject.

"From the bus yesterday, I got a glimpse of how beautiful this country is. How far away is Hokkaido?"

"Quite far, but a beautiful place, although it can be very cold in winter," Ms. Nishiyama said. "What makes you want to visit there?"

"My parents visited Lake Onuma many times and stayed in Hokkaido. They spoke highly about their stays," I said, and then after a brief pause, I told her about my old friend Taka Mori.

"Really?" she exclaimed. "I wondered how you learned some Japanese! Do you have his address?"

I took a piece of paper out of my backpack and handed it to her.

"Oh dear, this is in Aomori, just south of Hokkaido." she said. "Oh, I only guessed, since his father and grandmother were from Chitose, Hokkaido."

"Aomori is far but it's not difficult to get there. I can help you map out a train route. And since it's far, you may want to take the journey now." After a brief pause, she said, "Eddy, let's go home. I'll make another fish dinner tonight, since you loved last night's so much." Eddy looked pleased as he loudly sucked on the straw finishing his chocolate shake.

With Ms. Nishiyama's meticulous directions, we headed north toward Aomori (青森) and also to Lake Onuma (大沼湖).

"This train is fast, Mommy!" Eddy said excitedly.

"Yes, dear, not like the ones in China," I replied. "Ms. Nishiyama said we will be riding on one that's even faster when she takes us to see her daughter in Shin-Yokohama. It's called a bullet train (*Shinkansen*, しんかんせん)."

"Really?" Eddy said, half-believing, while literally sticking his face on the windowpane, fascinated by seeing the trees, fields, and hills flying by.

"Japan is beautiful, Mommy, but I miss home," he said.

I didn't respond, but glanced out the window of the fast-moving train and couldn't help thinking about the long train ride to Harbin twenty years earlier. The scenery was no less beautiful, and while I lived with fear of uncertainties, I hadn't lost hope. Perhaps that was true for many people at that time. We were grateful for our education and glad to use our skills to help build a new China. Then, there were the years in Shanghai, when I unexpectedly met Taka. I took out his last letter and thought about how much catching up we had to do. I wanted to know how he'd survived the dreadful years of the Great Cultural Revolution, an era that destroyed most of us spiritually and some also physically. I wondered if he'd gotten married and had children and what hospital he was working in. I would surely visit that hospital. After all, that would be the professional part of my trip to Japan. I would need evidence that I'd followed through.

"Mommy, where are we going?" Eddy's question broke through my thoughts.

"To see a dear friend of mine, and also to see where your grandma and grandpa visited," I told him.

Evening was approaching as we arrived in Aomori, a small coastal city. It was July, but I could feel an evening chill. I told Eddy to put on his jacket, and we headed to the small hotel Ms. Nishiyama's travel agent had arranged, not far from the station. Once we got settled in, I asked Eddy, "Hungry, kiddo? Let's get a bite to eat." This was one of few times we walked outside in the dark after arriving in Japan.

"Why are there so many lanterns, Mom?" Eddy asked.

"I don't know. I believe it's their tradition. When the light is on at a restaurant, it means we are welcome to enter and eat," I replied.

"Hangchow has lanterns too, but only for the new year, and they're all red," Eddy said observantly. "Most of these are white or colorless."

"How about this place? Shall we get some noodles?" I put my hand on his shoulder and we walked into a small ramen restaurant.

"*Irasshaimase ira sa yaimase* (Welcome, いらっしゃいませ)," an older woman wearing a headscarf said in a friendly tone, while an old man behind the counter smiled at us, perhaps her husband.

I nodded and we sat down at a table in the corner. The woman came over with two cups of green tea and a menu, which was completely in Japanese and had no pictures.

"Great!" I thought. "This will be the biggest test yet. I think I can read the menu, order some ramen, and brag to Taka about it tomorrow."

When the woman returned to our table with a pencil and a small pad of paper, I was prepared: "Two bowls of ramen, please, one with soup and salad, and one just noodles, and an order of fried mini-fish (ラーメン2杯、1つはスープとサラダのセット、もう1つはラーメンだけ.小魚揚げもひとつ)."

She nodded and repeated my order.

"Gosh, she figured out what I'd said despite my terrible accent and grammar," I thought.

"You speak Japanese, Mommy?" Eddy asked.

"A little, my dear. You heard me speaking some with Ms. Nishiyama already, no?" I rubbed his hair.

"Yes, but she speaks English well, but I hadn't heard Japanese come straight out of your mouth. Where did you learn that?"

"A good friend taught me, and I learned on my own."

The food came quickly, and the woman refilled our hot tea. I asked for a cup of sake and Eddy had a small taste. We were both hungry, and I began to wonder whether the address I had for Taka would still be correct.

The next morning, I became anxious about visiting a friend unannounced. I decided to forge ahead. "Okay, Jean, what do I wear? I should have bought a new jacket. But I wanted to save money, as I'm not sure how long we'll be in Japan."

"C'mon, Eddy. Let's go."

"Where are we going, Mommy?" Eddy looked confused.

"Mommy wants to see an old friend." I tried to be brief.

"Okay," he said, jumping up. Then I looked at my watch. It was 7:30 a.m., and the only train back to Lake Onuma was in the late afternoon, so I thought we'd wander around and head to Taka's after nine. Moments later, we were walking toward the shoreline. It was really quiet and peaceful, although the cool morning air penetrated my bones. "Are you cold, Eddy?" I feared he wasn't wearing enough.

"I'm okay. What ocean is this?" Eddy asked.

"I don't know. Your mommy is terrible at geography," I chuckled. It turns out we were standing at Aomori Bay looking out at the Pacific Ocean. We walked slowly down the rocky shoreline along an old boardwalk. There were two piers in the bay where a few ferries and boats were docked, and several fishing boats were anchored just beyond. Taka's letter had said this was a venerable fishing village. Now standing on one of the wooden piers, I looked as far out to sea as I could under the overcast sky. I shivered, unsure whether it was due to excitement, uncertainty, or sadness. All of a sudden my mind was spinning and my heart a ball of tangled yarn.

"It's getting colder, don't you think?"

"A little," Eddy said, obligingly holding onto my hand as we walked away.

By then it was almost nine, and some stores were opening. "Maybe I can buy a new jacket," I thought, looking at the shabby one I was wearing. We went into one store, where an old man gestured that we come right in. Shopping did not seem to calm my nerves, though, and after walking around several racks of garments, I lost interest, and Eddy and I walked out.

Following the map to Taka's house, we came to the front door. With my heart pounding, I rang the bell and zipped up my jacket.

I hoped against hope this would still be his address, but there was no sound or motion from inside. So, I rang again, and then heard a voice, "One moment, please (ちょっと待ってください)!" A woman about my age opened the door and asked, "Hello, may I help you? (こんにちは、どういったご用でしょうか?)"

"Does Dr. Taka Mori live here (森隆博士はここに住んでいま

JEAN TREN-HWA PERKINS

すか)?" She stared at Eddie and me for a brief moment, grinned and nodded her head, and said, "Please come in (どうぞ、お入りください)." We followed her into the house, a simple two-room flat with a low ceiling.

"Please have a seat (どうぞ、お座りください)," she said, and walked toward her kitchen. Then she turned around and said, "I'm sorry. By the way, I am Taka's wife. Do you prefer English or Japanese?"

I was relieved and replied, "English, please. I am Jean Perkins, a very old friend of Taka's in China...in Shanghai."

"I know, Dr. Perkins. Please give me a moment, and I'll get some tea." Minutes later, she came out with a kettle, three mugs, and some pastries with an envelope beneath her arm. She kneeled down by the coffee table in front of our sofa and looked toward Eddy with a very interesting expression. "Your son?" she asked.

"Yes. Please say hello, Eddy," I asked him.

"I hope you'll like these cakes."

"Thank you. I'm sure he will. Eddy, please say thank you." I turned to Eddy and he looked especially timid.

"I'm sorry for coming unannounced. I didn't have a phone number, just an address," I explained, "and we don't have much time in Japan. But I promised I'd visit if I ever made it to Japan. I'm so glad this is the correct address. Is Taka at work?"

"It's no problem at all," she said, and continued. "I know you don't know. Unfortunately, Taka passed away nearly two years ago."

"What?" I felt as if someone had punched me in the chest. "What happened?" I was hoping I'd heard it wrong.

"He died of liver cancer. He blamed the cheap Chinese grain liquor he drank to keep warm and stave off depression." She handed me the envelope and said, "There is a letter from him to you. Taka told me about your life together in Shanghai. That's why when I first saw you, I guessed it was you, even before you told me your name."

"He did?" I choked back the tears and could barely hold onto the sealed envelope with my trembling left hand.

"I tried to mail the letter to you, but twice it was returned. And so, Taka thought we would just leave it be and maybe you would show up some day and I could give it to you. I then sent a short note with this address to you." She invited me to follow her into another room. I saw Taka's photo resting on a dresser along with some slowly burning incense. I stood in silence and said, quietly, "It's so good to see you again. I'm so sorry I'm late, again."

Back in her living room, I was trying to regain my composure, despite overwhelming despair and disappointment.

"What is your name?" I asked.

"I'm sorry, I completely lost my manners. My name is Murakami Masako (村上正子). I don't have an English name. I was actually born in San Francisco and came to Japan when I was seven. Thank you for your compliment, but I know my English is about second-grade level." She smiled and went on, "These days I pretty much only speak Japanese, and I grew up speaking Japanese at home. Can you and your son stay for lunch?"

"Thank you, but our train leaves in the afternoon, so we shouldn't take up too much of your time." I was trying to be polite, although I knew in my heart I had so much to ask her. She then turned on her TV and showed Eddy the channel dials and said, "Please feel free to watch anything." And then she said to me, "Maybe we can chat in the kitchen."

After we were seated in the kitchen, I anxiously asked her, "I have a guess, but please tell me how you were born in San Francisco and ended up here."

Masako replied, "During the war, we were interned at a camp after President Roosevelt signed the executive order to round up all people of Japanese ancestry, citizens or not. I was a third-generation American, you see, but that didn't matter. It was a war, and we were considered prisoners of war."

"America did *that* to its citizens?" I shook my head.

"They spared my grandparents, who were too old to travel, but my parents and my little brother, who was four at the time, were sent to the camp. I was too young to remember, but I think it was in Utah, or perhaps Colorado or Arizona. Then in 1943, we were shipped to sea and exchanged with American POWs on the *Gripsholm*. It was the second exchange. Taka told me you were part of the first exchange."

"I was young and didn't grasp the meaning of it all," I replied. "I had imagined those were real Japanese prisoners, although I saw kids my own age and even spoke with some of them. They all spoke perfect English," I sighed. "So why are you here and not back in America?" I asked.

"I visited America a few times in recent decades," she replied, "and I thought about going there for college. We went back to see my grandparents, who were ill at the time. And I could have reclaimed my citizenship when I turned eighteen. But I decided to stay in Japan."

"Why?" I was surprised.

"I no longer felt I belonged there. I belong here more." That was hard for me to understand. To me, there could be no place better to live than America, the land of the free.

Masako quickly prepared a scrumptious lunch and spread it out on the table, a unique mixture of East and West.

"Eddy, please turn off the TV and wash your hands," I said in a raised voice. As he sat at the table, I encouraged him to eat everything, even the salad.

SPRING FLOWER: TORN BETWEEN SHIFTING WORLDS

"Sake, Jean? It's good-quality rice wine," Masako offered.

"Maybe a few drops," I replied. "I apologize in advance if my face turns beet-red."

"Me too, so a few drops it is. You're in Japan now, and this is their favorite spirit. Everyone turns beet-red, trust me!" Masako chuckled and poured me a glass, then she sat down, placed her palms together, and said, "*Itadakimasu* (いただきます)."

"I wonder how you and Taka met," I inquired.

Masako smiled. "We met in a bar. If he were here today, he would argue otherwise, but I know for a fact he was drunk that day. I was living in Kyushu, and he was in town for some sort of meeting. He walked in and sat next to me at the bar counter, and asked, 'So, where are you from?'" Masako laughed and continued. "His Japanese was not very good and the way he said it meant something else, so I thought for *sure* he was drunk. I replied, 'I'm an American from San Francisco (私はアメリカ人です、サンフランシスコからです),' and he nearly fell off the bar stool! That wasn't what he was expecting, and it caught his attention. That's how we met," Masako said with a chuckle.

"That's fascinating and romantic. It must be fate, Masako!"

"I like to think so." Masako took a sip of her sake and continued, "He had been trying to look for another job, thinking Kyushu could use a bilingual Japanese or at least be more open to people like him."

"People like him?" I was confused.

"In Kyushu and on the other islands in southern Japan, there's more Chinese heritage—language, food, culture," Masako said. "It was difficult for Taka after he returned to Japan. Japan never gave returnees from China their citizenship back, and they could work and live here but not as citizens."

"I had no idea," I interrupted.

"Taka's Japanese language skills were that of a primary school child, or worse. Culturally, it didn't matter how much his mother had taught him. He had never lived in Japan. He was recognized as different the moment he opened his mouth. At least I came here when I was young, and even in America we spoke Japanese at home. When Taka returned, he was already over forty. He was seen as Chinese, not Japanese. It was hard for traditional folks to accept him at work, or sometimes even in his own home with distant relatives. It was very sad. Those settlers sent to Northeast China to occupy the invaded territories were casualties of war, forced to leave their homes and resettle, and then not welcomed back to Japan." Masako took another gulp of sake. Her cup was almost empty.

"His medical degree was not recognized in Japan," she went on, "and he didn't have enough language skills to take the medical board exam to qualify. So he bounced from job to job at different hospitals. The best one came right before he became ill. He was a physician's assistant, and they trusted his knowledge and valued his experience and instincts, so they let him see patients, make diagnoses, and give treatments. But he always needed a physician to sign off."

"He was an outstanding ophthalmologist, Masako," I assured her.

"By the end, he accepted that this was his fate in Japan," Masako said with a half-smile.

I wanted to ask how he became ill but held my tongue.

"Are you here just to attend meetings or are you on your way to America?" Masako asked.

"America, I hope. It's been thirty-five years," I replied.

"And you are taking your son to America. How old is he?" she asked.

"Almost fifteen," I replied.

"Great timing! He's still young and will adjust well. I hope it

SPRING FLOWER: TORN BETWEEN SHIFTING WORLDS

works out well for you, and it should," Masako said emphatically.

Our long and heartwarming conversation seemed about to come to an end. Whether it was out of politeness or if Taka had told her many things about me, Masako didn't ask too many questions. That was fine for me, and I came to appreciate how small the world is and how our lives intertwine and are linked together by the same war. The woman sitting in front of me was essentially the kid I was exchanged for during World War II.

Masako walked us back to the train station. Before we entered the station, she gave me a hug and then cupped hands around Eddy's face and gave him a kiss on his forehead. I saw tears in her eyes.

We boarded the train and Eddy soon fell fast asleep. With the humming sound of the fast-moving train as we headed toward Lake Onuma in Hokkaido, I opened Taka's letter, which was written in Chinese.

> My dearest Jeanie, if a dying man may be allowed to call you by that name... By the time you read this, you will have met my wife, Masako... I fell in love with her the instant she told me the story of her exchange. She, too, has an amazing past... Yes, war may be a terrible thing—as your mother said—but there's always redemption in every atrocity, like a cactus blooming in the desert... During these past few months, I thought about many things, and I had a lot of time between the poisons and radiations they gave me. So, my dear Dr. Perkins, my teacher, and my soulmate, thank you for the memories by the river... If you're indeed returning home at this very moment, I wish you the best in finding happiness in the land that you've always loved... I know you don't believe in that, but I'll see

you in the next lifetime. Please don't feel sad for me, because I feel rather relieved. I believe my journey to real freedom has just begun… Love, Taka

To avoid making a sound or moving my body, I pressed my head against the window, tears streaming down my cheeks. I looked up toward the sky and soaked in all the sunlight I could through the window. I believed it was Taka's light shining on me! He was right; his journey to true freedom had just begun, and so had mine. As the tears on my face dried, I quietly said a prayer of goodbye to Dr. Taka Mori. Knowing him was a memorable and important chapter of my life, one that no one knew and yet one that would always live in my heart.

When we returned from Lake Onuma, there was a note from Ms. Nishiyama that she'd gone to Kobe to be with her youngest sister, who was ill. She left dinners for us, including Eddy's favorite fish. Days began to seem like years, waiting for the visa.

One day, when Eddy's eyes were glued to TV cartoons, I said, "Let's go out for walk, Eddy. It's a beautiful day out. Too much TV will fry your brain, and I don't think you understand a word of what they're saying."

"Pictures say a lot," he explained, and reluctantly he stood up.

Wandering through the narrow streets while being ever so careful not to get lost, I spotted a small café.

"How about we go there?" I suggested.

"Okay," he said, appearing quite happy.

"*Konnichiha, ira shaimase* (Good afternoon, welcome, こんにちは, いらっしゃいませ)," a woman behind the counter greeted us and gestured that we could sit anywhere.

I took Eddy to the counter. "Let's see what they have."

"What's this?" Eddy asked, pointing to a row of glass bottles in the refrigerated case.

"Coca-Cola, dear."

"How much for one lemon cake and two Cokes?" I asked, wanting to be sure I had enough money, given that I didn't know how many more days we would be in Japan.

"And what's this?" Eddy asked, pointing to a thick slice of pie.

"It's called lemon meringue," I answered.

"Lemon *what?*" Eddy asked.

Just then I realized that Japan had adopted many cultural elements from America.

When we returned home, Ms. Nishiyama was already back from Shin-Yokohama, and she handed me a letter from the US Embassy. My heart quickened as I opened it.

"Great! We got the visa, and we can pick it up as soon as possible."

"See what I told you! It'll all work out," Ms. Nishiyama said with a big smile.

The next day, the three of us arrived at the embassy and met with Jeffrey Ishihara, the man who had originally handled our application. After checking my passport again and placing a small sticker on one of the pages, he shook my hand as we stood up and said, "Please allow me to be the first to welcome you back to America! I read your files, and your story could be a book."

I thanked him and walked out, feeling an immense amount of excitement. Back at Ms. Nishiyama's, I immediately phoned New York to report my visa progress to Dr. Fisher. He was equally excited: "Great news, Jean, and welcome back home soon. Please call the Pan Am office and reserve two seats on the next available flight. I will notify Evelyn, and we'll pick you up at JFK," the airport in New York.

Things moved quickly over the next few days, and with our

bags packed, we called a taxi and bade farewell to Ms. Nishiyama.

"I should go with you to be sure everything goes well," she said.

"We should be fine," I replied.

"No, really. Narita is chaotic and can even be dangerous. I want to go with you," she persisted.

"Dangerous? We saw more heavily armed guards at the airport than one sees in China."

"Well, there are protestors. After purchasing the land in Chiba to build that airport, because Haneda had no room to expand, several families refused to sell their land, so the airport was built around them. Those families are still protesting! My job isn't done until you are in the air," she said emphatically. And soon we were on the road heading toward Narita. Ms. Nishiyama insisted on paying the taxi fare, which wasn't cheap. Then the three of us headed to the Pan Am ticket counter.

"Next, please. Can you I help you? Where are you flying to?" the ticket agent asked.

"New York, JFK Airport, please."

"Sure thing," she smiled and nodded.

Our bags were tagged, and with tickets in hand, I nearly forgot to say goodbye to Ms. Nishiyama. I turned around to give her a big hug and said, "Thank you so much for everything! I'm sorry we won't be making the trip to Yokohama, but maybe someday."

"Oh, we will meet again, child," she said before disappearing behind the security wall. I never saw her again, and we never got to visit Yokohama.

We went through immigration without fanfare, and soon we were sitting in the waiting area by the gate. The plane was already parked at the gate with Pan Am's blue logo painted on the gleaming tail. Staring at this logo, I was reminded of seeing the Statue of Liberty for the first time, nearly forty years earlier.

"Are we coming back to see Ms. Nishiyama?" Eddy's question broke my musing.

"We will, you heard her."

"How long are we going to be in America?" he asked

"I don't know."

"How far is America from Japan?"

"Very far."

We finally boarded, and the plane door closed, but we weren't moving. I was becoming anxious again, wondering if the plane would ever start moving. Finally we pushed back from the gate, then we sat on the runway for what seemed like an eternity.

"Stop it, Jean," I reminded myself. "Be calm, be grateful, and be patient. Whatever happens happens."

I closed my eyes and in my mind's eye reviewed our beautiful stay in Japan. It was hard to fathom that thirty-eight years ago, we sailed for America while trying to stay away from Japan, the enemy at the time. But today Eddy and I went right through it. At last, the engine roared, and the mighty Pan Am jet turned onto the runway. She sped up and took off into the blue air. I was going home at last.

91

THE PLANE ascended into deep violet space. As the white clouds rushed by, I gripped an armrest to brace for the skyward pull of gravity. I was becoming anxious again, and I searched for something in the plane I could focus on. When I saw the Pan Am logo on the interior walls of the plane, I thought, "That's a good image to focus on. It's a Pan Am flight, and it's not sending us back to China!"

Eddy was staring out the window at the ocean below, and I peeked over his shoulder.

"Mommy, how far is America from home?" he asked.

"America *is* home, honey," I replied.

"China is our home," he queried, "in Hangchow, where Gina and Papa are, isn't it?" I knew it'd be too complicated to talk about on the plane, so I said, "A person can have many homes. I will explain it all when we get to New York." I hadn't told him *anything* yet, apart from dragging him around. He had to be overwhelmed by all the changes and new places, but with my brain firing at a mile a minute, anything I'd say now would just confuse him. So instead, I reached out and held his hand as we cruised over the vast Pacific Ocean.

As long as this flight was, it was nothing compared to the voyage we'd made in 1941. Eddy fell asleep, stretched out on the floor in front of the seats. I leaned over to make sure he was covered, and then I raised the window shade slightly to see the sun rising on the eastern horizon. The deep orange-red blush tracing the earth's curvature was stunning. Hours later, the captain announced that we had reached North America and were about to fly over San Francisco. I looked out the window but couldn't tell if what I was seeing was the Golden Gate or another bridge. As we jetted across America, tiny twinkles of light began to burst skyward from the towns and cities below. A few hours later, I woke Eddy up, and, disoriented, we both sat up to receive our wake-up meals before landing.

"Wow, Mommy, look at all those lights!" I leaned over and spotted the Empire State Building at a distance.

"Yes, that's New York, honey! We're almost there," and my heart began to pound much more than even before. After a turbulent descent, our wheels struck the runway, and we were in America! The plane swirled left, then right, before speeding straight ahead. I looked up to the sky and said, "Thank you!"

"It's raining in New York, Mommy," Eddy said, pointing to the streams of water on the window.

"Tears of joy from God!" I said.

"What?" Eddy asked.

On an early fall day in 1980, I finally came home, returning to the cradle of the civilization I loved. It had been thirty-five years, and this time I brought Dr. and Mrs. Perkins's grandson with me. I was now fifty years old.

We spent what seemed like an eternity on the runway, and two eternities waiting in line at immigration. "What's another hour after thirty-five years?" I wondered. "Be patient. Who cares how long it takes! This is the home stretch."

Finally, Eddy and I collected our suitcases and dragged them toward the exit, the gateway to America and the last barrier between us and true freedom. As soon as the automatic doors opened, we were blinded by a huge crowd of people, many holding signs with names of people and companies. I'd never met Dr. Fisher and had only seen photos of Evelyn when she was a teenager, so I nervously scanned the various faces.

"Jean! Here, Jean!" a female voice called.

I followed the sound and saw a tall, elegant woman in her sixties. She was wearing an ivory-colored dress coat and a light blue scarf, and she waved her arm vigorously while elbowing a tall, handsome man, almost like Day-Day, standing next to her. I figured they must have been Dr. and Mrs. Fisher, and I wondered where Evelyn was.

I waved back, and the woman jumped up so I could see her. "Jean, come here. We're over here!"

I told Eddy to follow me, and soon I realized it was Evelyn herself, with Dr. Fisher!

I ran toward her and she ran to me, and we embraced for several minutes, both of us crying. She squeezed me as my mother would have, and said, "My goodness, Jean, we should have, but we've never met, although I feel I've known you all my life! I learned so much about you from my favorite uncle and aunt." Her warm body instantly made me feel that I was home at last. I could sense Day-Day and Mother looking on with smiles, as were Uncle Henry and Aunt Olga in the flesh.

At last she let go of me. I wiped away my tears and said, "Oh, come here, Eddy. Please say hello to your Aunt Evelyn!"

Eddy was shell-shocked and said in broken English, "Uh, Aunt – uh, Aunt – Eve – lyn — how are you?"

"Hello, Edward, so nice to meet you at last!" Evelyn stood up straight, and surprisingly, she gave Eddy a soldier's salute. Then she turned around and said, "I'm so sorry. I should have let Dr. Fisher present himself before I grabbed hold of you. Here he is, Jean — Dr. Edwin Fisher, the former director of the United Methodist Church and the man responsible for making all this happen, the man who essentially rescued Dr. and Mrs. Perkins's only daughter, my cousin, from China!"

"So nice to meet you in person," Dr. Fisher said, "Jean, or rather, Dr. Perkins, and it's my honor to meet with the legendary Dr. and Mrs. Perkins's only daughter at long last."

He reached out his hand and leaned forward forty degrees as if we were in Japan. I grabbed his hands and said, "I am eternally grateful for everything you've done for me...for us!"

"Ah, this must be Edward Junior, or the Third," Dr. Fisher said, looking toward Eddy.

"Yes, Dr. Fisher, this is the grandson of Dr. and Mrs. Perkins. Please come here, Eddy, and say hello to Dr. Fisher." Eddy was struggling to hold onto two big suitcases, standing a few yards behind me, clearly overwhelmed and probably confused. I took the suitcases and pulled him forward.

Eddy made a quick bow to Dr. Fisher, and upon acknowledging him with a big smile, Dr. Fisher immediately said, "Eddy, you're a very strong boy, taking care of all of these suitcases! Please allow me to help. Mrs. Fisher would scold me for not having better manners." He smiled and took most of our luggage.

"Let's head to the parking lot, shall we?" Evelyn said.

"Yes, indeed, or my wife will think I've gotten lost again." Dr. Fisher laughed, and then quickly turned to me to say, "My wife is waiting for us near the parking lot, guarding our little car." We walked out to the parking lot and met Mrs. Fisher, another warm human being and a beautiful woman, also in her sixties. The car was parked nearby, and not in a legal spot.

"Jean," Evelyn said as we rode out of the airport, "we don't have a place in Cambridge for you yet, and Mass General has not provided the final documents for your employment, so you'll have to stay in New York for a week or two. I hope that's okay. For the next few days, we've settled you at the Empire Hotel at 63rd and Broadway."

"Oh, anywhere will be fine. I hope it's not too expensive. We'll be happy at a simple place."

"Don't worry about that, Jean, it's all taken care of. It's the least we can do for Dr. Perkins's daughter and grandson," Dr. Fisher interjected, while looking straight at me in his rearview mirror.

"Thank you so much, Dr. Fisher. We appreciate all of that, but we don't want to be a burden to you, the Church, or the Perkins family in any way."

"What are you *talking* about, Jean, what 'burden'? We are *family*." Evelyn gave me a happy-yet-disappointed push.

Mrs. Fisher then turned around from the front passenger seat and said in the warmest, friendliest voice, "Jean, I think I speak for everyone here, and maybe even for the entire Church if not everyone in the United States. We were simply shocked to find you and discover that you are alive after all these years. God only knows what it was like!"

"Thank you," I murmured to acknowledge what she was saying. Mrs. Fisher reached to squeeze my hand before turning back around.

Silence ensued, and we were soon on the highway from Kennedy Airport to Manhattan, the city lights flashing behind the trees. I was flooded by memories, and the past thirty years seemed as though it had all been a nightmare from which I was waking up. If Eddy weren't holding my hand, I would have thought it had all been a dream or perhaps something from a past life.

Just like that—in a flash—my life in Mao's China was far away, as if it were a different universe. I began to squeeze Eddy's hand to help ground me in time and space: I was in a car with Eddy on our way to the city I loved, with my parents' niece Evelyn. And the other half of my life was still, in my mind's eye, clinging to

SPRING FLOWER: TORN BETWEEN SHIFTING WORLDS

a metal fence at the airport in Shanghai, hoping and waiting to hear from us. I squeezed Eddy's hand harder, as my tears flowed faster than the rain. Then I pressed my face onto the car window, as I had on the train in Japan, staring at the reflections of light through the splattering raindrops. This physical touch—with Eddy—and seeing what was going on outside me—the rain and the lights—were what I needed to keep from losing my mind.

A sudden car horn and the screeching of tires brought me back. Evelyn chuckled, "Welcome back to New York, Jean!"

"New York taxi drivers think they own the world," Dr. Fisher added.

I strained to look through the windshield. We were in Manhattan! "More Yellow Cabs than I remember," I said to myself.

"So many lights, Mommy," Eddy said, waking up and becoming very animated.

"We're here, Jean. This is the Empire Hotel, where you and Eddy will be staying for a few days. Evelyn will be staying with you, and she'll help you check in. Mrs. Fisher and I will meet you for lunch day after tomorrow, and we'll get things squared away at the Church headquarters."

"Yes, there's a lot of red tape here too, even at a church," Mrs. Fisher added, reaching out to shake my hand and pat Eddy on the head.

"Where is the church office?" I asked.

"Oh, thank you for reminding me. Here's a map I drew for you. It's on Riverside Drive, a block east of Broadway, near Columbia University. It's just a quick taxi ride, or you can take the #1-train uptown. Did you take the subways when you were here? Evelyn may be able to draw you a better map, or the front desk should have directions."

Evelyn, Eddy, and I got out of the car and the Fishers rode on. We walked into the glittering lobby of the Empire Hotel, and I told Eddy to look after the bags, but before he could even move, a bellboy came over and put them all in a cart. Evelyn went straight to the front desk, and I shuffled behind, asking how much it would be. I took out some US dollars and wanted to give her money.

"No, Jean. Dr. Fisher has taken care of it. I just need to get you signed in and get the key."

"Wow, Mommy, a palace!" Eddy exclaimed. As we entered our room, I was speechless.

"Evvie, this has to be expensive!" I shook her arm.

"It's a bit on the high end. It wasn't easy to find a room this time of year on short notice. But, all things considered, it's not unreasonable. There are three of us, and my husband, Amyas, will be joining us tomorrow. We won't stay here long. And, last but not least, this is a fantastic way to welcome you back in style!"

"Okay, thank you." I was still taking in the surroundings, a beautifully furnished suite.

"I'm sure you and Eddy are tired and jet-lagged after the long flight."

"Jet-*what?*" I heard a new word.

"Oh, you know, the time-zone difference. It's now morning in Asia," Evvie chuckled.

"Why don't you both use the bathroom first," she said. "There are three rooms. Eddy can have his own."

"I can't sleep with you, Mommy?" Eddy tugged on my shirt.

"A teenage boy, and he still sleeps with you, Jean?" Evelyn looked surprised.

I thought about explaining how little space we had in China and how Chinese people are used to having three generations squeezed into a single room. "I guess this is all new to him, and he's a bit shell-shocked."

I pushed my son away and said, "Eddy, listen to Aunt Evelyn.

You're a big boy, and you've been assigned to your own room."

Suddenly, I wasn't tired at all. I had so much to talk to Evvie about, so many things on my mind I wanted to ask. I was flat-out excited to be back in America—in New York!

So, after I took a long hot shower, Evelyn and I sat on the couch and began to chat. She handed me a glass of white wine and formally welcomed me home.

"Evvie, I have so much to say and ask, I'm not sure where to begin. I'm so excited that I doubt I'll sleep tonight! So maybe you could tell me something about Uncle Henry and Aunt Olga, you, and your four children! Also, maybe Cousin Harry—yes?"

"Oh, Jean, I understand. I don't know where to begin, either. It *is* rather strange. We've heard so much about each other, but we've never met until now. And all this time, we were sure you didn't make it in Red China, with all the tragic stories we heard."

Just then, the doorbell rang. Doorbell in a hotel room? I thought. Evvie opened the door, and a tall, handsome Black man wearing a coat and tie asked, "Good evening, Madame, is there anything we can do for you?"

"Did you call for room service, Jean?" Evelyn looked surprised.

I shook my head.

The man walked in and pointed to a white service button on the wall near the door, saying, "Someone pushed the service button, and we came to see if you needed anything."

"Eddy, did you?" I turned my head and found Eddy standing behind a cushioned chair, looking guilty.

"Yes, Mommy," he said, his face turning red.

"Oh, we're sorry, sir. The young man probably pushed the button by mistake," Evelyn quickly explained. "So sorry to have troubled you. We don't need anything."

The man smiled. Evelyn tipped him and closed the door.

"It's okay, Jean. Eddy was probably tired and bored."

"Go to bed, young man! Please don't push any more buttons. You should be asleep by now, Eddy!" I had the impulse to slap him.

Eddy reluctantly went to his room, and Evelyn and I talked way into the night.

I don't remember when Evelyn and I went to bed, but in no time at all the morning sun was shining brightly, penetrating the window shade. I got up and heard the sound of the shower, thinking Evelyn was using the bathroom.

As I waited in the living room, an ear-piercing alarm went off. The sound was deafening and sent me right back to World War II. Then Evvie grabbed my arm and said, "Jean, it's the fire alarm! We need to exit the building now, and we must use the stairs."

"Okay. Where's Eddy?" I asked, anxiously.

I looked to my left and saw him standing by the door, his face alternating between red and pale. He looked petrified.

"It's okay, Eddy, let's go. It's a fire alarm. We need to leave the room now!" He didn't budge as though his feet were planted on the floor. He was shivering in fear. And then I saw broken glasses by his feet. I looked to the wall and saw that the glass was broken and the fire alarm was in pulled-out mode.

"Did you pull the alarm, Eddy?"

He nodded his head, aware he'd done something terrible.

I rushed over and was ready to tear him apart.

"Let's just go, Jean. Quickly! There's no time to scold him now. We need to go down and explain it to the hotel manager."

So the three of us joined the other hotel guests rushing down the stairs. Someone sighed and said, "Damn, another fire drill—so early in the morning!" Once in the lobby, the New York Fire Department was already there to direct us, and I could hear sirens wailing and saw fire trucks pulling up in front of the hotel.

SPRING FLOWER: TORN BETWEEN SHIFTING WORLDS

Amid the chaos—shouting from the police and firemen, and shuffling footsteps—I held tightly onto Eddy's hand and headed to the front entrance. I was in complete disbelief that this was our first full day back in America. "And this is so unlike the Eddy I know. We just got here! What do we do now?" I kept thinking.

I'd lost track of Evelyn. Eddy and I rushed out the front door and joined the many people standing outside. We were among the last to leave, as we'd walked down from the penthouse. I felt embarrassed and fearful about what might happen next. Soon we were forced behind a yellow barricade tape as the firemen rushed inside.

Then I saw Evelyn standing around the corner, surrounded by several people including two policemen. She was frantically trying to explain what had happened. Then she spotted us and waved, and soon a police officer escorted us toward Evvie.

By then, I was petrified. "Look, there they are," she said. "That's my Chinese cousin, Jean, and her son. They just arrived last night after thirty years being trapped in Red China. Her son doesn't know a word of English and pulled the alarm by mistake. Please forgive us. We will pay for any damages."

"Mrs. Ames, it's okay," the officer said. "We just need to understand what happened. Please tell them to come over, and we may need to take their names for our records. But we won't press charges."

Another man with a New York Fire Department badge turned to a man that I thought was the hotel manager, saying, "Well, Mr. Barclay, we're glad it's nothing more serious than a false alarm. But please, this can't happen again."

"Of course, sir," Evelyn nodded in agreement.

A New York policeman walked toward Eddy and me, and grinned as he tipped his hat and said, "Welcome to America, kid."

JEAN TREN-HWA PERKINS

When we got back upstairs, Eddy explained to me that he didn't know what the red lever was for, but he saw the word *pull*, which he understood, and I'd only told him not to *push* anything. I was still furious.

By evening, with all the unwanted excitement and attention behind us, we had dinner with Evvie and her husband, Amyas. Amyas laughed, amused at the story, when Evelyn said, "It's not funny! I was afraid they'd take Jean and Eddy into custody, and maybe even send them back to China." I had shared her fear.

"Oh no, that's not happening," Amyas grinned as he sipped his wine. "Perhaps the boy is bored, Jean. Evvie and I are leaving New York tomorrow morning. You have a couple of free days before you'll meet with the Methodist Church. Why not show Eddy around the City?"

"A splendid idea!" Evvie echoed. "We'll be back next week to drive you to Boston. But if your employment at Mass General still isn't settled, Dr. Fisher has arranged for you and Eddy to stay in Brooklyn for a few weeks. The New York Methodist Hospital in Park Slope has a furnished hospitality facility. After that, if it's still not settled, you can stay with us in Martha's Vineyard."

"I'm so sorry for troubling you. I'd hoped we could go straight to Boston, or I could stay with my classmates in Yonkers."

"My God, Jean, what trouble? We are only happy to know that Uncle Edward and Aunt Georgie's daughter has finally come home."

The next day, after Evelyn and Amyas left for Hartford, I had a long and exciting phone conversations with Marie and Jill, my Yonkers High classmates and best friends. They were waiting for Betty to drive down from Danbury, Connecticut, and then they'd all come to Manhattan for a grand reunion.

By then, it was nearly noon, and Eddy was still sound asleep. I woke him and offered to show him the city, but he said he was hungry. So first we headed to what I thought was the lobby restaurant. As soon as we walked in, we were stopped, and an older man with a bow tie told me that no children were allowed in the bar area. Then a younger man with a matching bow tie whispered to him, and the older man came back and said, "Madame, please give us a minute. I think we may be able to obtain a special arrangement for you and your celebrity son." And a moment later, the younger man came back and said, "Ma'am, our hotel manager says that it's quite okay for you and your son to have lunch right here, and the lunch is on us."

"Oh, thank you," I nodded and smiled, then I saw a jacket and tie in his hand. "But we do have a dress code for a gentleman like your son," he said. "Unfortunately, we don't have a jacket and tie in children's sizes, only this adult blazer, if you don't mind."

I looked at the clock and said, "That's okay. My son will need to learn to wear a coat and tie soon enough," and I wasn't sure where else we could get a quick bite to eat.

The maître d' said, "Marvelous, please allow me," and he carefully helped Eddy with the blazer and rolled up the overlength sleeves. Finally, he knotted the tie and fit it around Eddy's neck.

It was quite a sight, and I almost laughed, but Eddy actually looked quite nice, except that everything was way too large. My boy seemed taken by all the attention as we got seated at a high table. He ordered an egg salad sandwich from a very kind waitress. As I tried to coach him how to use a fork and knife and to chew his food with his mouth closed, he asked me, with a mouth full of egg salad, "Mommy, what's that they're playing on the screen?"

I looked up at the TV screen and realized it was the New York Yankees.

"That's called *baseball*. Finish your sandwich, and I'll teach you the rules."

Soon I pulled out four coffee stirrers from a container and lay them into a diamond on the table and proceeded to show Eddy the basics of baseball, exactly as Day-Day had shown me on a fall evening in 1943.

"Wow, that's exciting! How do you know so much about it?" Eddy paused for a second and asked, "Will you take me to a baseball game?"

"Yes, of course. That's a promise," and I ruffled his hair. "How about we go outside now, and Mommy will show you New York?"

After returning the blazer and tie and getting a map from the front desk, we headed out to the 66th Street subway station. And on the way, when I pointed to Lincoln Center, Eddy asked, "But what are *they* doing, Mommy? How come they're not wearing clothes?" I then saw a group of scantily clad young men and women banging away on drums and various instruments; and some of the women appeared to be topless. I quickly pulled him down the stairs into the subway station. But Eddy remained fascinated by what he'd seen. After buying a number of subway tokens, unsure how many our tour would require, we boarded the #1 train downtown and were off to Battery Park to see the Statue of Liberty and Ellis Island. I was surprised to learn that Ellis Island had been closed for quite some time. From there, we boarded the Staten Island Ferry for a quick view.

Eddy was mesmerized by the harbor water and the lady statue, while I thought back to the days after we'd just come ashore from the *Gripsholm*. I was about Eddy's age then, and once again I started to miss Mother and Day-Day terribly, and fought back my tears. Soon Eddy and I were walking along the East River until the Manhattan Bridge and the Brooklyn Bridge both came into view. "What a scenic view, Mommy! It's so beautiful; I wish Gina and Papa were here." I didn't reply. After a brief rest sitting on a boulder staring at the Brooklyn Bridge, we strolled westward toward the Empire State Building.

"Do you like New York City, Eddy? All this walking is good for you. Do you know why?"

"Why, Mommy?"

"So you'll be too tired to push or pull any more things on the hotel wall." I tried to be funny, and Eddy *did* chuckle. "But I too wish they were here. It'd be great to see all this with them."

The line for going up in the Empire State Building was short. "You'll love the view from the top of this tall building! I did this when I was your age. Your grandparents took me straight up."

When we got to the top, Eddy was awestruck, although his first comment was, "It's really windy up here!"

"Yes, Eddy. And you can see everything from here! See those tiny taxis on the street? That skyscraper is called the Woolworth Building, and that beauty over there is the Chrysler Building. You can even see the Statue of Liberty from here." As I shouted with excitement, Eddy asked, "What are those two buildings over there, Mommy?"

"I don't know. They weren't here when I lived in Yonkers." A security guard standing nearby told us, "That's the World Trade Center, the Twin Towers, ma'am. They were built in 1974." I nodded graciously. New York had certainly added more buildings since 1942!

Looking at my watch and thinking about the reunion with my high school girlfriends, I suggested we head back to the hotel. "I'll take you to Central Park tomorrow, maybe even Rockefeller Center and Radio City Music Hall."

At the hotel, there was a message that Betty was delayed, and we'd be meeting much later that evening. I was getting hungry and told Eddy I'd buy him one of New York's famous hot dogs with "everything on it." It seemed like an exciting idea, and we stopped at the first street vendor we spotted. While waiting for the man to dress our hot dogs, an idea suddenly came to me.

We both wolfed down our hot dogs. "You like it?" I asked

"The hotdog is good, but not this sour green stuff!" Eddy said, pushing away his relish.

"Don't waste food, please. Just wash it down with Coke. And when you finish, we can go see the Hudson River?"

"How far is it?" Eddy sounded less enthused.

"A few streets up and then we head west. It's one of Mommy's two favorite rivers!" I tried to get him excited, sensing he might be getting tired, and I was also trying to gauge how far it would be. On that summer day back in 1942, we had to walk back to the Waldorf-Astoria on Park Avenue after watching the sunset at the Hudson River. Soon enough, the river came into view.

But I wasn't sure where to find the 79th Street Pier, or if it'd be still there. After making our way through some junkyards and warehouses near Riverside Drive and trekking beneath the elevated portions of the Henry Hudson Parkway, I spotted an old wooden pier, but it would take some bushwhacking to get there.

"Mommy, I'm scared. There's no one here."

"It's okay, Eddy. New York is quite safe," I said, with zero confidence that it was true.

I could see hints of trails, and we had to fight through some tall plants and bushes, but at last, we were close to the water and near the pier. I couldn't tell if this was the right pier, but at that point I didn't care. We carefully stepped onto the wobbly wooden platform and sat down.

"Is it safe here, Mommy? I don't know how to swim." Eddy's voice was filled with the pent-up trepidation of a lifetime.

"It's okay. Mommy knows how to swim, and I'll save you if we fall through the boards." Then I tried to cheer him up, or perhaps distract him. "Mommy lived just up the Hudson River in a town called Yonkers. I could see the river from my bedroom window."

"This river is kind of dirty, but it's pretty with the sun going down," he said, pointing west toward New Jersey.

"Yes, let's watch the sunset from here. Your grandparents and I did that many years ago. It will make me very happy if you agree." My mind raced back to that very day in August 1942, one of the happiest days of my life. I could picture us sitting on a bench with Day-Day looking at Mother while she was in deep thought looking west.

"It *is* pretty, Mommy. The sun is changing the color of those clouds every minute." Eddy's voice broke my stream of thought. "I still wish Papa and Gina were here. I wish they could enjoy all of this with us."

And again, I didn't say a word. Instead, I stayed frozen in time, imagining an era when I was a carefree teen and life was good. I was trying to see Mother and Day-Day's faces again; I missed them so much.

"Mommy, I miss my papa and my sister. I miss home!"

Those were the very thoughts I'd been trying to ignore. I hadn't recognized the irony that I was doing the same thing with my own parents at that very moment.

"Enjoy the sunset, Eddy. See the boats going by?"

"When are we going home?" Eddy asked, sounding more adamant this time. I squeezed his hands tightly as I fought back my own tears. His words pierced my heart.

"I want to go home, Mommy."

"Eddy, we're *not* going back to China! At long last, Mommy is *home,* and America is now your home too. You need to understand that!" I barely finished my sentence, when thirty years of tears poured out of me like a river.

AFTERWORD

My Parents' Lives After 1950
Mother's Only Letter to Me from Taipei (1955)
1955 Letter from Dr. Edward C. Perkins from Taipei
Epilogue

My Parents' Lives After 1950

At the end of Book 1, I wrote a tribute to my American parents, Dr. and Mrs. Edward C. Perkins. Here I continue their story.

Exodus from China

For thirty years, my mind would often drift back to the days at the end of 1950 when my parents left China, and I always wondered, "What happened? What if I had returned to Kiukiang and joined them? Could I have escaped China, too?" For the next few years, I continued to receive occasional letters from my mother, but I never really knew what happened.

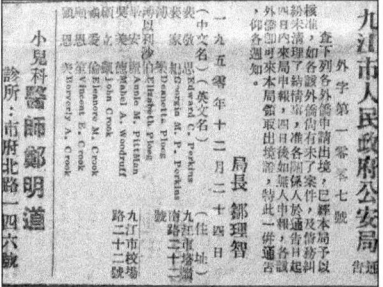

"*Kiukiang Daily Newspaper reporting anti-American sentiments and the raging Korean War and publishing the names of remaining Kiukiang missionaries who were granted exit permits to leave the country.*"

SPRING FLOWER: TORN BETWEEN SHIFTING WORLDS

Now, after reading letters Mother wrote that I never received, listening to memoirs of Aunt Dee and Aunt Bessie recorded in 1978 (courtesy of the Ploeg-Van Laan family, specifically Mrs. Trudy Van Solkema), studying family archives, and having conversations with family members and with my parents' friends and colleagues, I have pieced together most of the story.

On December 24, 1950, the Kiukiang Municipal Police Department issued my parents and eight other missionaries permits to exit China. These papers were valid for only one week, so they had to leave the country posthaste. Mother and Day-Day spent the next four days disposing of the belongings they'd accumulated during thirty-five years of mission work in China, made arrangements for the continuation of the Water of Life Hospital, and then, along with the other eight missionaries, boarded a train to Canton. From there, they'd travel to Hong Kong, then Japan, and finally to America. I think of this group as the "Fellowship of Ten" — Mother, Day-Day, Aunt Dee, Aunt Bessie, Miss Mabel A. Woodruff, Miss Annie M. Pittman, and four members of the Crook family from the British China Inland Mission.

They had to change trains in Nanchang (南昌), stayed overnight with Dr. and Mrs. Wise (Methodist missionaries from the hospital there), and arrived in Canton in late afternoon on Saturday, December 30, 1950. By that time, their luggage and handbags had all been opened and inspected four or five times, and a few items of nostalgic value, including some old Chinese stamps, had apparently been confiscated. Miss Woodruff and the aunties lost full sets of china they'd received as gifts from the residents of Kiukiang.

On Sunday, December 31, none of the official office buildings were open because of the weekend as well as New Year's Eve. Their exit permits were set to expire that night, and, without papers, they wouldn't be able to apply for entry visas to Hong Kong. So they holed up in a downtown hotel waiting for the New Year's holiday to pass. Just as Day-Day had scolded me for peeking out the window at Japanese soldiers in Kiukiang during World War II, he let Aunt Bessie and Mother know how he felt when they looked out the window to watch anti-American parades on the streets of Canton. At one point, they saw a burning effigy of President Harry Truman, and at that moment, they realized how dangerous things had become for Chum and me.

Mother wrote to friends:

"I know Edward was not pleased that we weren't being sensible watching the parade. But I had to watch with my own eyes. As the anti-American demonstrations got louder and more aggressive, we became more frightened and wondered if the mob would come up to our rooms if they spotted Americans in a hotel. My mind drifted to Jeanie and Chum. China and America are at war [in Korea]. Being an American's daughter, how would my precious Jeanie survive when we might not even make it out of here alive without the proper papers?"

Over the years, I continued to wonder *what if* Chum and I had tagged along? While I was 300 miles away, Chum could have gone with them. But neither of us had either a passport or an exit permit, and we might have had to prove that in fact we were American citizens. And if two young Chinese women were with the "Fellowship of Ten," would that have compromised the safety of their own departure?

On Wednesday, January 3, 1951, the city of Canton reopened, and the Fellowship of Ten went to the Municipal Police Department and managed to get their exit permits extended. The officials there, they said, were cordial and diplomatic. The Fellowship then headed straight to the British Consulate, where the staff looked ready to flee at a moment's notice. There were loose papers everywhere, and some documents were being burned in a large urn in the front lobby. The enmity between China and the US extended to the United Kingdom, as both countries were playing major roles in the UN Command in Korea, fighting against the Chinese and the North Koreans. But the UK had been one of the earliest countries to recognize Mao's Communist government (on January 6, 1950), which turned out to be strategic in preventing Hong Kong from being taken back immediately.

According to Day-Day, it was good that he was with the Fellowship, being a man with both New England reserve and an Ivy League persona. The British consular agent seemed undone when Mother, Aunt Dee, and Aunt Bessie began talking simultaneously, and he could barely find the right seal to stamp the entry visas onto their passports. The three American women were asking if they could telegram Chum and me to join them in Canton to cross the border. Mother wrote, "I became very distracted and nervous because the radio on the agent's desk was rather loud, alternating between Voice of America updating the war on Korean Peninsula and Frank Sinatra — I didn't know Frank was still singing! I yelled out to Edward, 'Why did we leave the girls behind?' and that got Dee and Bessie going."

Although she'd been fearless during the Japanese occupation of Kiukiang in World War II, my beloved mother could be distracted and nervous at times. In later years, Aunt Dee confirmed that they were advised that the time-consuming procedure for Chum and me to obtain exit permits while still Chinese citizens could have jeopardized everyone's exits and they'd be better off leaving first and then coming back for us. These *what-ifs* had haunted me until I learned this. Now I see that for them to have tried to take us with them, they would have needed Indiana Jones to succeed! But in their final moments in China, they did make a last-ditch effort to see if they could. The mere thought that they hadn't forgotten about Chum and me gave me a sense of peace and closure.

Just as the Fellowship of Ten was ready to board the train to Hong Kong, Aunt Bessie and Miss Woodruff realized they needed to find a bank to exchange their last US dollars for Hong Kong currency. I never understood why China prohibited US dollars from being taken across the border, but it did. Perhaps war-torn, impoverished China wanted to keep as many valuable US dollars as it possibly could?

It was getting late, and Mother was worried about missing the last passenger train to the border via the Kowloon-Canton Railroad, which had been used to ship Westerners out of China only since fall 1949 (Chum and I most likely wouldn't have been able to get on the train). The extended exit permits were for just twenty-four hours. Luckily, the trip to the bank was uneventful, although no one seemed to know what the exchange rate was. At last, Aunt Bessie and Miss Woodruff returned to the station in time for yet another baggage inspection, and the train to the border departed.

The Fellowship finally arrived at the border station three hours later—likely today's Lo Wu Station (羅湖站), a major crossing point on the other side of Sham-Chun River (深圳河) in New Territories annexed to Kowloon. But there was another inspection at the border-crossing after they got off the train. This time their pockets were emptied too, and as luck would have it, Miss Pittman had forgotten that she'd hidden $200 in one of her coat pockets. The border patrol officer, a woman, considered whether it was theft, and shouted at Miss Pittman with a Cantonese accent, "American money—no!" Mother used her best Chinese to explain that these were allowances from the Methodist Mission to help them travel back to America and that not exchanging those dollars in Canton had been an honest mistake.

A long discussion among the border patrol officers ensued, as the Fellowship of Ten stood by. If Chum and I had been with them, it might have been a disaster. At last, the border officer returned and handed the $200 back to Miss Pittman. She then opened the barricade and waved the last ten Kiukiang missionaries on, as they walked across to the Hong Kong side, exiting Communist China. Aunt Dee wrote, "We exhaled, and as we went across, we breathed the free air."

But uncertainty loomed in Hong Kong too, as Westerners and Chinese were there to flee China. At the same time, Chiang Kai-Shek was plotting to reinvade China, and his nationalist soldiers who had escaped southwest China were regrouping in Hong Kong. Vessels and barges were few and far between, while battleships and aircraft carriers from both the US and Britain were docked near Victoria Harbor, prepared for a Communist invasion.

The Fellowship of Ten had to stay put and just be patient, not knowing when they might find passage out of Hong Kong, or when the Communist armies might cross the border. Learning about this years later, I lamented that I hadn't tried to swim across Deep Bay to Hong Kong that same month. Could I have gotten there in time? Now that I had a better map, I see that I could have even tried to make it on land. But without a passport or exit permit, swimming or hiking on illegal mountain trails would have been my only options, ones that others took—and for which many died. Fate had other plans for me.

Sometime around January 20, my parents were able to board the *SS Anna Maersk* bound for Kobe, Japan. And two days after that, Aunt Dee and Aunt Bessie boarded a freighter called

Tungus. That same day, Miss Woodruff and Miss Pittman were on yet another ship to Japan. And a week later, the Crook family set sail for India.

The six Americans managed to reconnect at Yokohama Harbor before setting sail for San Francisco. My parents finally reached Brooklyn Harbor forty-three days after leaving Kiukiang, on March 4, having transited the Panama Canal. The others arrived in New York Harbor on March 5. This time it was Aunt Dee's twin sister, Henrietta Veenstra, and two nephews (Aunt Hennie's sons, I believe) who were waiting at the harbor for Dee and Bessie. After spending decades together in Kiukiang devotedly helping Chinese farmers and villagers, most remaining Fellowship members went their separate ways. My aunties took the train from Grand Central Station to return to Grand Rapids, Michigan.

For the next month, my parents roamed Hartford, Connecticut, as well as Washington Square and other parts of New York City. Many friends and neighbors from Kiukiang (九江) and Ku-Ling Mountain (廬山牯嶺) lived in the New York area.

Aunt Olga was ill, but she could still entertain my parents when they visited Hartford. Mother read some of my letters to Aunt Olga, while Olga updated Mother on Evelyn and her children, Oakes, Ned, Olivia, and Joanie. Uncle Henry also traveled to New York and met with Day-Day many times. My parents attended Washington Square Methodist Episcopal Church in Greenwich Village, where Day-Day occasionally gave the Sunday sermons. The pastor was Reverend Phillip Watters, who was Aunt Hyla Doc's brother. Aunt Hyla herself had left Wuhu (蕪湖) before the fall of the Republic of China.

On to Tennessee

In a letter dated March 29, 1951, Mother wrote: "Day-Day [just] walked in to tell me that we are leaving for Pittman Center,

SPRING FLOWER: TORN BETWEEN SHIFTING WORLDS

> **Veteran China Missionary Gives Services in Smokies**
>
> Special To The News-Sentinel
> SEVIERVILLE, Dec. 1—A veteran retired China missionary read Violet Woods's "So Sure of Life." Then he decided to return to spend his "retirement" in the Southern mountains as an aid to home missionary, Dr. Robert F. Thomas.
> He is Dr. Edward Carter Perkins, who built a hospital in China and served without pay as its superintendent and chief surgeon for nearly 40 years.
> He comes to Pittman Community Center, Methodist home missions project in the Great Smokies.
> As in China, he serves without salary.
>
> **Built Hospital in China**
> Dr. Perkins, descendant of a leading New England family, is a native of Hartford, Conn. His father was a banker there. The son graduated from Yale in 1898, began study of law at Columbia University, and then on a trip around the world decided to become a medical missionary. In China he selected Kiukiang, far up the Yangtze River, for a hospital. The city was surrounded by hundreds of thousands of poor people scattered in rural villages.
> He later built and equipped the Water of Life Hospital with his own funds. There for nearly four decades he served through famines, plagues and wars.
> Dr. Perkins headed campaigns which saved thousands of lives in cholera, typhoid, and influenza epidemics. His educational program reached other thousands. He taught simple measures of disease prevention. He was at times pastor of churches, principal of a college, and district missionary evangelist.
>
> **Offered His Services**
> Soon after returning, he read the mission study book which is a biography of Dr. Thomas. Then Dr. Perkins visited Pittman Center and offered his services to Dr. Thomas. He spent the summer resting and reviewing for the Tennessee medical examinations.
> Dr. Thomas' own missionary career began in Malaya, but his 25 years of services as a doctor have been spent in the Southern mountains.
> Dr. Perkins' wife, who was with him in the Chinese medical mission from the time of their marriage in 1916, came with her husband to the new post. In China Mrs. Perkins, who had training in hospital administration, directed the business end of the hospital.

Tennessee next week." And in early April, just a month after returning to the States, my parents headed south by train from Penn Station. Mother marveled at the cherry blossoms as they passed through Washington, DC. In Tennessee, they met Reverend Dr. Robert F. Thomas, the superintendent of Pittman Center. Just days after arriving, Day-Day and Mother committed themselves to serve for two years, helping Pastor Thomas, a country doctor. My parents, it seems, never rested from their missionary endeavors.

Pittman Center is in Sevier County, a very rural area in the Great Smoky Mountains. A local paper reporting on Father's arrival wrote that Day-Day had decided to stay after reading *So Sure of Life: A Mountain Doctor's Life*, by Violet Woods, published in 1950. Mother's letter had mentioned Day-Day's reading the book in mid-May 1951, a month after their arrival there. And undoubtedly, Day-Day had learned about Pittman Center much earlier.

Miss Annie M. Pittman, who was one of the Fellowship of Ten that traveled to Hong Kong with Mother and Day-Day, had been a missionary in China for some thirty years, spending most of her time in Kiukiang. She was a pastor, a teacher, a physical therapist, and a leading figure for the Women's Foreign Mission Society.

Miss Pittman's father was the Reverend Dr. Eli Pittman,

At the Ku-Ling (牯嶺, 廬山) Mountain Resort, ca. 1930s: Left to right: Front row: H. Whitmer, Mabel Woodruff, Georgie, Helen Ferris, and M. Seeck. Back row: Bessie, Dee, Annie Pittman, and Elsie

The day Frances Woodruff left China, ca. late 1930s or early 1940s Left to right: Annie (Pittman), Deanetta, Bessie, Mabel, Frances, and Georgie At front: Helen May, Clara, and "Toby"

superintendent of the Elmira District of the Methodists' Central New York Conference and one of the key figures in the history of Pittman Center, Tennessee. The other key Conference figure was the Reverend Dr. John Sevier Burnett, who had come to the

SPRING FLOWER: TORN BETWEEN SHIFTING WORLDS

From left to right: Edward, Annie Pittman, Mabel Woodruff, and Bessie Ploeg ca. 1942, still in Kiukiang (九江) just before we left

isolated mountains of Eastern Tennessee in 1919 with a vision to build a center that would offer medical and educational needs. The area had been called Emert's Cove, honoring Frederick Emert, a Revolutionary War veteran who first settled there. Dr. Burnett named the Center after Dr. Pittman, for Pittman had raised major funds from philanthropists in New York. In 1974, Pittman Center even became the name of the township. Dr. Burnett's middle name, Sevier, was actually the name of the county. So undoubtedly, Day-Day knew about Pittman Center well before reading Violet Woods's book.

People from this isolated region held Dr. Thomas and his wife in the highest regard. They became local celebrities. Dr. Thomas had delivered the fourth child of the Parton family, named Dolly, who later had a song about him, before her worldwide fame. After their initial, brief stay, my parents returned to New York so Day-Day could study to pass the Tennessee State Medical Board

Exam. He was seventy-five at the time.

In late spring of 1951, just after I celebrated my twentieth birthday in Nanking, my parents took a long train ride to Grand Rapids, Michigan, where they finally met the rest of the Ploeg clan. Aunt Dee and Aunt Bessie took them to every sibling's home, and Mr. and Mrs. Ploeg drove them to the family cottages in Gull Lake, Kalamazoo County. The cottages were named after the aunties, and my parents stayed in Bessy-Dee's and Annie's cottages. Before they left Grand Rapids, Day-Day preached at the Open Bible Church, which the Ploeg family had attended for generations. The local railroad tracks ran right along the Ploeg family property on 28th Street SE, and as Mother and Day-Day's train to New York passed, Mrs. Ploeg and all the aunties stood in their back garden and waved.

In the latter half of 1951, my parents shuttled between Washington Square in New York City and Vineyard Haven on

In the backyard of "some house" on 28th Street in Grand Rapids, Michigan, 1951
From left to right: Edward, Georgie, Dee, Mr. Ploeg, Bessie, and Mrs. Ploeg

SPRING FLOWER: TORN BETWEEN SHIFTING WORLDS

An Ames family photo ca. early 1950s
[Courtesy of Olivia Ames Hoblitzelle]: From left to right: Joanie, Evelyn Perkins Ames, Amyas Ames, Olivia, and "Bingle, for the boxer and Frisky, for the whippet" (quoted from Ned Ames's letter). Missing were Ned and Oakes with both away at Harvard and Oakes soon heading to Johns Hopkins University for graduate studies in physics.

Martha's Vineyard, in Massachusetts. They also spent a lot of time with Uncle Henry and Aunt Olga in Hartford, and saw my cousin Harry in New York. In the summer of 1951, my cousin Evelyn took them to Cold Spring Harbor on Long Island, where she and her husband, Amyas, were living. Their sons Oakes and Ned were off at college, and daughters Olivia and Joan were at home. The girls were fourteen and nine. Mother was in awe of how tall the girls were, but it all made sense, since Evelyn was even taller than Day-Day. That was the first of two or three trips they made to Long Island. Here is a short piece my niece Olivia wrote some years later:

JEAN TREN-HWA PERKINS

I do remember Uncle Edward and Aunt Georgie coming to visit us at Linden Hill, my parents' place on Long Island. He must have been well into his 70s by then, and I do remember being very impressed and moved by how he handled his return to the US. There may have been two visits, years apart. I also remember his being a bit bent over with age and having a limp from some accident earlier in his life. I was touched by that—the sense that his calling to help the poor and forgotten totally overrode any concerns for his physical limitations. Age would never stop him from fulfilling that calling.

Because his medical degree had expired, or whatever, I believe he either took refresher courses or certainly returned to medical training of some form, so he could pass the medical boards (in his 70s!) and practice in this country. That commitment and determination certainly impressed me as a young teenager!

I also remember stories about his going to work for a medical practice in rural Tennessee because it was almost like rural China. He sometimes had to ride by horseback into the backcountry, somehow carrying his medical supplies with him.

In the late summer and early fall of 1951, my parents lived in Vineyard Haven so that Day-Day could study for the Tennessee Board Exam. They also found time for fishing. Then one day, the governor of Tennessee, or perhaps someone from the governor's office, called Day-Day to say they would waive the exam. They accepted his sterling credentials—what a relief! So by Thanksgiving 1951, my parents were settled in Tennessee. Mother

SPRING FLOWER: TORN BETWEEN SHIFTING WORLDS

Day-Day on an outcall in Tennessee, ca. 1953

Day-Day's birthday dinner in 1953

compared the Smokies to the Ku-Ling Mountains, and a new phase began for their missionary work helping poor people who desperately needed healthcare, this time in the United States.

Mother's letters that I never received updated me on Day-Day's daily work at the Pittman Center clinic. Most of his patients were "outcalls," some far in the mountains over terrible roads that could be icy in winter. Grace Butgereit, a nurse, often accompanied him, in part because the locals couldn't understand his New York accent and he had trouble understanding theirs. So Grace served as nurse and translator. There was a pneumonia outbreak and there were cases of TB, reminding Mother of their days in Kiukiang. Many of these mountain people were very poor, and Day-Day was often paid in produce and poultry. Interestingly,

JEAN TREN-HWA PERKINS

[Courtesy of Trudy and Mark Van Solkema]: From left to right: Day-Day, Aunties Bessie, Annie, Dee, and Hennie

[Courtesy of Trudy and Mark Van Solkema]: From left to right: Aunties Annie, Bessie, Hennie, and Dee

patients in China were doing that in the 1970s at the hospitals where I worked.

In addition to helping Dr. Thomas with medical work, Day-Day also preached. Mother taught Sunday School, and on other days she typed letters for Dr. and Mrs. Thomas, mostly replies to thank-you notes. By the 1950s, Pittman Center had become a well-known model for home mission and rural healthcare. Mother and Day-Day stayed in a dormitory that they shared with like-minded folks who had committed their time and energy to help the less-privileged.

In early 1953, Mr. and Mrs. Harry Ploeg and their son John, the Aunties' younger brother, stopped at Pittman Center on their way back to Michigan from their Florida winter home. And on April 1, 1953, Aunt Dee and Aunt Bessie, along with Aunties Annie and Hennie (Aunt Dee's twin sister), visited Mother and Day-Day in Tennessee. The four sisters drove from Michigan to Pittman Center.

Reuniting with familiar faces from Kiukiang, ca. 1951

At the end of 1953, my parents completed their two-year stint and rented a place in New Rochelle, northeast of Manhattan in Westchester County, New York. In her letters, Mother meticulously updated me on each of the missionaries who had worked in Kiukiang and told me where they were living around the world after 1951. I believe Mother had two motives in telling me this: to remind me of these self-sacrificing souls, and also to help her come to terms with the loss of their Kiukiang life and fellowship. I could sense that she was sad, and these names were a thread of connection to her past, which she and Day-Day shared for half a century. I learned that Annie Pittman and Professor Helen Ferris, the last American to leave Gin-Ling (南京金陵女子大學) Women's College, had gone to Borneo, while Aunt Hyla Doc was in Africa. And Dr. Mary Stone had settled in San Francisco.

Last days in Eastern Tennessee, ca. 1953

On to Formosa

During their stay in New Rochelle, Mother and Day-Day visited Yonkers frequently. Many people at the Morsemere Methodist Episcopal Church, including my classmates Jill and Marie, asked about me. Marie's mother was quite ill during that time. Mother seemed ready for a peaceful retirement, seeing friends and families, while Day-Day was organizing a book for the Methodist Church to document mission work in China. It was then that the idea of going to Taiwan (Formosa) germinated in their minds.

They began their journey to Taiwan with a cross-country overland trip in the summer of 1954. They visited Hyla Doc at

SPRING FLOWER: TORN BETWEEN SHIFTING WORLDS

The last reunion with the aunties in Lake Mina, near Minneapolis, ca. 1954 Mother and Day-Day were on their way to Taipei.

Mother and Day-Day visiting Hyla Doc (second from the right), ca. 1954

JEAN TREN-HWA PERKINS

Tupper Lake in Upstate New York and then attended missionary conferences in Greencastle, Indiana, and Lake Mina, near Minneapolis, with Aunts Dee and Bessie, finally reaching San Francisco in early September. Before Mother and Day-Day left the Bay Area, they learned that Aunt Olga had passed away on September 11. After that, they set sail for Taiwan.

In the following years, there were fewer letters to me. I don't know whether Mother stopped writing as much, or if some letters were lost in the mail. A letter dated May 10, 1955 (see Appendix Two) was the last I was able to find.

In Taipei, the capital of Taiwan, my parents helped establish a new Water of Life Clinic. Today that is the location of Taipei Wesley Methodist Church. Day-Day's letter dated February 19, 1955 (see Appendix Three) speaks volumes about what he intended to accomplish. My parents likely returned to the States sometime in late 1957.

I'm still not sure why they went to Taiwan at such advanced ages. The two months at sea alone would have taken a huge toll on them. Perhaps they were envious of their younger Kiukiang colleagues who were scattered around the world continuing their missions. Perhaps they thought being in Taiwan would bring them closer to me if they could cross the Strait and come to see me in China. Or perhaps, after spending most of their life in Asia, they too had become foreigners in their own land and felt more at home in China and with Chinese people.

After they got back to the US, Day-Day became too forgetful to function effectively as a physician. He and Uncle Henry were in the same nursing home, which Aunt Dee and Aunt Bessie often visited. Day-Day passed away in 1958 at the age of eighty-three, and Uncle Henry died the following year.

After my father's death, my mother lived alone, and she was suffering from cancer. Sometime in 1961, Aunties Dee, Bessie, and

Louise drove to Hartford and took her with them back to Grand Rapids, where she stayed until the end of her life. Aunt Louise cared for her. Her funeral service was at Zaagman Memorial Chapel in Grand Rapids. Evelyn came to attend, before taking Mother's body back to Hartford to be buried next to Day-Day at Cedar Hill Cemetery. Mother had given Aunt Louise a few boxes of items collected from Kiukiang, along with a metal suitcase containing more than 2,000 photos, and asked Louise to keep them until I returned — if I were still alive. In 1985, Aunt Louise gave these boxes and photos to my son, Richard.

My beloved parents in Taipei, ca. 1956

Mother's Only Letter to Me from Taipei (1955)

#9 GeeHan Road, Section 3, Taipei, Taiwan, May 10, 1955

Precious Jeanie

    Of course Mummie is thinking of her dearie and praying for her and Paul, but every day on April 29th, I was specially praying for the birthday Treniiva ! "Many Happy returns of the day." May God guide and direct you in all that you think and do and say during your new year. I am so thankful that Paul and you have eachother. Do give him my love when you see him, or write to him. It is a satisfaction to think of you both helping your land in good ways. I hope you both have happy church relationships, where you are. As I write this, I hope that you are both in good health. I love to look at your photos of other days, and there is one I like so much, which shows Elsie and you together, when you were a tiny tot. Take care of yourselves, the two of you, and keep well !

    As you read the above address you will see that we are on an island. We came here near Christmas time last year. We are very, very happy here and enjoy our work. DayDay conducts The Water of Life Clinic daily, and goes on outcalls. as you know there are many many folks here who speak the language you use: so when we talk to them they can always figure out what we are trying to say !!

    We attend the Methodist Church here, and the kidlets here enjoy having the Sunday School lesson story told with the aid of the flannelgraph pictures as much as the youngsters in Kiukiang did. They also like to receive a picture card with a pink slip pasted on it, like the enclosed pink slip.

    The home we now live in is a Japanese style house. Instead of riding about in a rickshaw, we ride in a pedicab; we don't have to be sorry for the one who drives the pedicab, as we felt for the rickshaw men, for the pedicab driver is propelling a bicycle, behind which is a comfortable seat for two.

    The folks here are very cordial and kind, and many have called to see us and invited us to their homes for a meal. There are two trained nurses living with us: one is Miss Hsia, and the other Miss Brindenverg. It seems natural does it not, that there are 2 trained nurses with us, but not "the aunties."

    As you probably know, the two aunties work each in a different hospital in their own home town. The two hospitals are for needy people, and they surely do take in some terrible cases !

    You probably know that Marie is married. Her mother is in a very splendid home for the aged. Marie sends her love to you.

    Who do you suppose called on us on "Mothers' Day"? Siao KwohChiang and his wife and pretty daughter. They called because it was "Mother's Day". You may remember that KwohTsiang's father was our cook for some years in Kiukiang. And his wife was our amah. KwohChiang says they are well. SiuMing has children.

    Aunt Adelaide has gone to Heaven. Mrs. Jones who used to work in Kiukiang is in South Africa now. Aunt Hyla works there, too, in the Gants Mission. Laura Schlemen is in Kuala Lumpur; the Argelanders are in AUSTRIA Jenny Lind and Rose Waldron are in Japan. Aunt Maybel Thompson is in a missionary home in California. Mabel and Frances Woodruff live and work in their old home town in Northern N.Y. The Argelanders are in Austria. Mr. Johannaber has a church in Gerber, California where he is the pastor. Miss Clara French is now a superintendent of the work of the Woman's Society of Christian Service, and her headquarters are at the Board of Missions building on Fifth Avenue, New York. So, our "mission family" is now well scattered, isn't it.

    Do you remember the Chinese doctor, Dr. Mary Stone, who long ago used to work at Danforth Hospital, then worked with Bethel Mission? She has now gone to heaven, and her co-worker, Miss Jennie Hughes (who you may remember worked at Knowles School and then with Bethel Mission) has also gone to her heavenly home.

    You would be interested to see the multitudes of tall palm trees that grow here; they are very handsome. "The aunties" sent me a package of dwarf marigold seeds, like those my Mother used to have in her Yonkers garden; she loved these little yellow flowers. The seeds have been planted and are growing nicely, and I am looking forward to seeing the yellow flowers !

    DayDay sends his love to you and Paul. As I write this, he is working at the clinic, which is in our house.

    Keep on with your good work; blessings on you. Loads of love from

P.S. Auntie Edna Goodele stays with a lady, as companion and helper. Edna has kept a room or two at 80 Highland Avenue. You may remember "Uncle" who had su

1955 Letter from Dr. Edward C. Perkins from Taipei

No. 9 Tsinan Road, Sect.3 TAIPEI
FORMOSA
February 19, 1955

Dear Friends and partners,

You have been so kind as to be interested in this shift of our field of labor back to the Far East, and we want to report to you impressions and something of the experiences of these past days.

The journey to Formosa began in the Pennsylvania Railroad Station in New York: and the car which we boarded, went flying along without change, all the way across our wonderful country (the precious gift of God to our people) until we could look out on the sparkling waters of San Francisco Bay. After three or four days in the bustling city of San Francisco, we boarded a freighter of the Maersk Line named the "Jeppesen Maersk." This ship left San Francisco in the evening, and the first experiences we had were of looking out toward the surrounding shores of San Francisco Bay, sparkling with lights. Leaving America by this route, one goes under the bridge that spans the Golden Gate, and which in the evening, shows a beautiful succession of twinkling lights, beyond which one starts on the long stretch of the Pacific Ocean, where, for days, one may not see signs of human life, but where one is habitually charmed by the beautiful blue color of the water. Our voyage was made especially delightful because of the

JEAN TREN-HWA PERKINS

eleven passengers on board; nine were missionaries. Each Sunday morning that we were at sea, we enjoyed a helpful morning service conducted by one of the groups. During the voyage, we learned a good deal about the island to which we were going, because it was well known to some of the missionaries on board who had worked there. There is much of beauty in the Philippine Islands, where we first saw land, and the mountains of Formosa, rising out of the blue Pacific, give it always the attractiveness, which in the first place gave it its name FORMOSA (signifying "beautiful.")

The hubbub and confusion of disembarking and landing, after the comparative serenity of a trans-oceanic voyage, is a little like being suddenly aroused from peaceful dreams, to face the realities of life. Landing at Keelung the port of Taipei, which is the capital of Formosa, is made as little of a distraction as can be, by the orderly arrangements, and courteous attitude of the authorities who control the disembarkations.

When we were free to move onward, we went to the hospitable home of the Rev. and Mrs. E. K. Knettler in Taipei, by their kind invitation, to spend some time with them, upon first landing in Formosa.

Years ago in China, we had a similar experience, and were able to become a little acquainted with the country and the people, while living in the home of the Rev. and Mrs. Wilbur F. Wilson, in Nanking. Such an introduction to a new country and new civilization, is exceedingly helpful, as well as being a great pleasure to newcomers.

We knew that Mr. Knettler was the pastor of a Chinese-speaking church in Formosa but were quite unprepared to find so well developed an institution, as his church is. Our first Sunday on shore was spent, in good part, in attending the functions of this Methodist Church in Taipei. The first service, which was at

SPRING FLOWER: TORN BETWEEN SHIFTING WORLDS

eight thirty in the morning, was a service in English, which is a service largely attended by English speaking people, and many Chinese students, who both understand and speak English very well. Then came a well-attended Sunday School session, and at the same time, the morning service in Chinese, all well attended.

Mrs. Perkins, as she did for a long time in China, talked to a division of the Sunday School, telling the lesson of the day with the aid of flannelgraph Pictures.

Early on Sunday afternoon, there was a wedding ceremony in the church. This also was a well-attended service, and it was so conducted that one felt it was a sacrament. One of the very noticeable features of this church, is a well-trained choir, which sings beautifully, under the direction of a very able choir master. During the wedding ceremony, this choir sang twice. In the early evening, came the young People's meeting (the Methodist Youth Fellowship), and following that, as a last service of the day, there was an evening evangelistic service, at which one of the laymen of the church spoke. The sermon at this service was very undramatic but the Presentation of the Gospel was so clear and direct, that three men present signified their wish to become Christians.

After the benediction, the pastor gathered a little group of the congregation, (including the three men who had just come out for the Lord,) together in a little company in a corner of the church, and there held a conference with them. One of the Points of emphasis of this church, is the care used in preparing the prospective members for church membership. Emphasis is also laid on the "follow-up" work in the case of people, who have just made a decision to become Christians. Needless to say, that these two features in the treatment of new members, make a stronger and more intelligent body of church members.

Two weeks after this first Sunday in the Tai Pei Methodist

Church, sixteen adults were baptized and taken into the church; twenty-three more adults were received by transfer. Two very small children were baptized, and two others were "dedicated." It seems only right to add that the financial situation of the church, owing to real loyalty and enthusiasm on the part of the members, is as flourishing as the membership itself. The Official Board reports enough money already in the bank, to meet the budget for the coming year, which the Board has drawn up.

With regard to medical work, the medical authorities here have been most cordial and a license for me to practice medicine here, has already been received.

At the time the land was bought for the church, a larger piece was purchased than was required for the immediate needs of the church, with the result that there is room for quite a little development of the property. For one thing, there is room for an adequate playground for the children, and also room for a parsonage, should it seem desirable to build one near the church. There has been a little discussion, too, about locating the dispensary, which we hope to open on the church property, and this may perhaps be done.

At all events, we are blessed with sufficient room for all the services, which we are glad to report, are well attended. As one of the first items of the Sunday Program the church has an early morning Sunday School, composed largely of the children of the church members, and this is quite an orderly school; but a little later, there is assembled a more or less random group, and this is quite different.

In Kiukiang, Mrs. Perkins conducted the Junior Church at the Chinese Church on the main street, which we attended. This group was large and tended to be tumultuous; nevertheless, Mrs. Perkins had considerable success in holding the attention of the crowd and getting a Bible story to them. Possibly, I told you

SPRING FLOWER: TORN BETWEEN SHIFTING WORLDS

in some Previous message that on our last Sunday in Kiukiang, in December nineteen-fifty, the Junior Church numbered four hundred boys and girls.

Mrs. Perkins has been in the habit of adding a feature to her children's meetings, which is most acceptable to the youngsters. She has given to each boy or girl who attends the meeting, a Picture card, on the back of which is Pasted a Bible text in Chinese. Friends at home have been very kind and helpful in sending old Christmas cards, greeting cards, and picture post cards, which fill the recipients with joy of heart. The average Chinese home is rather lacking in decoration, and the cards with their pretty colors, have been received with enthusiastic appreciation by the boys and girls, and also by older members of the family. This puts a bit of brightness into the meetings, and afterwards, into many homes. Quite a good many people in the USA do not know what to do with their old Christmas and greeting cards; they don't like to throw them away, but do not want to just let them accumulate. My wife would be more than grateful for any cards which friends at home might send.

There is no lack of opportunity here to lend a helping hand in a variety of ways. The president of the Soochow University, recently established here, told of his being called upon one Sunday afternoon, by some members of the Formosa government. They are appreciative of the help that missionaries bring but suggested two more ways in which the foreign workers might add to their avenues of helpfulness. There are multitudes of refugees in Formosa; many of these are educated people, and people who have a means of livelihood; but there are also a good many who never had any educational advantages, and who cannot read or write. The authorities feel that such an element in the population is of doubtful value; they would welcome it if the missionaries would start something of an educational campaign for these most needy folks. I understand that such an educational effort would include an opportunity of giving some Christian instruction. The other proposition which the authorities suggested was that it might be very helpful if another nurses' training school was started. As you probably know, the care of the sick at present is hampered all the world over, by the lack of nurses; and adding more trained nurses would be of distinct benefit. Such an enterprise is within the range of possibility, for there is hospital work going on now, and there are a number of doctors on the island. I heard quite recently that at present, there are at Taipei a number of Chinese trained nurses, who were trained at a first-class foreign hospital in the Province of Shantung, China, by a very accomplished American nurse. Some years ago, I worked with this nurse for a number of months, and any nurses trained by her, would be sure to be good. These matters are to be given more consideration.

Quite a good deal of time has had to be used in trying to find a suitable house in which to live. There are a good many small houses in Taipei, which are for rent or for sale, but one has to be influenced by location, as well as by the size and arrangement of the rooms, and especially, by the price asked. The little place which we have secured seems rather suitable in all ways; among other things, it is so small that we hope to be able to keep it warm in the cold weather, with a very small heater. The climate of Formosa in winter is comparable with that of Florida, for oranges also grow here, sweet, and juicy and so abundant as to be quite inexpensive. Formosan pineapples are delicious, and the fruit of the papaya trees is abundant and good. Plants of all kinds grow beautifully here, indeed, the island is well known for its fertility. There are many nice things about Formosa.

The house hunting, which we have been doing for ourselves in an effort to find a little house, in which we can live, is at an end,

SPRING FLOWER: TORN BETWEEN SHIFTING WORLDS

and a partial payment has been made on a little building, which seems to be convenient and suitable, and which is located close to the Methodist Church which we attend. We are now trying to find one or two rooms, which will also be convenient and suitable for the clinic, which we are planning to open in connection with our missionary work here. A very small personnel should be adequate to handle this enterprise. We are now trying to find a trained nurse for this work.

A superficial, but very real difference between conditions here and those on the mainland of China, is in the matter of transportation. In China, we continually used the little carriages called "rickshaws", which are pulled by a man who runs between the shafts. The longer I lived in China, the more reluctant I became about using these little vehicles because they put too heavy a physical strain on the runner who pulls them. I have seen cases of physical damage because of the use of rickshaws. Here, they have another kind of a machine, called a "pedicab," and in these vehicles, the man who supplies the motive power sits on a seat like a bicycle seat and works two pedals with his feet; in fact, this machine is a kind of tricycle. The result is that the work for the man who is propelling the machine, is much less severe, than where a runner pulls a rickshaw, running between the shafts of the little carriage. The man who makes the pedicab go, gets much less winded, than the rickshaw puller.

Our medical effort has gotten so far as to possess a pedicab, and to have in our employ a very nice young man, who makes it go. We seem to be succeeding in securing an evangelistic worker, who has had four years of Bible training, and who has already been in evangelistic work. Please join us in praying that we may have a really Christian, and really efficient, little staff for our clinic.

Like the Clinic conducted in the Tennessee Mountains, we

plan not only to see outpatients in our clinic rooms but also visit those who are sick in their own homes. In Tennessee our outcalls were quite numerous, and quite a feature of the work of the clinic.

In telling about the place and the work here, another factor should not be omitted, namely, "Wesley Grove." A couple of years ago five acres were acquired on the slope of a large and handsome mountain, a dozen miles or so from this Center. Two or three buildings make this a usable place for holding summer conferences. It is high enough up to be decidedly cooler than the level country below. It has a beautiful wood of shade trees and offers attractive views of the distant countryside. The trees include 400 orange trees.

It has been my privilege to visit a leprosarium, which is a part of the work of the Formosa Presbyterian Mission. This is a truly remarkable place: in the first place, its situation is beautiful, on the breezy slopes of some high hills, with lovely views of the surrounding country. The main division of the institution numbers over seven hundred patients who have leprosy, who are cared for in this well-equipped hospital for lepers. It is distinctly Christian institution, and the devoted care, which is given to the patients, by the loyal staff members, is very obvious. Another division of the institution is given over to the care of very small children, who were separated from their leprous parents so early that they did not take any infection from them, and thus have been saved from leprosy.

Another nicely planned home for children, has also in it small boys and girls, who were early separated from their leprous family, but who had not been taken away soon enough, to make it certain that they were not infected. This division is an isolation hospital, where the boys and girls are under constant observation.

SPRING FLOWER: TORN BETWEEN SHIFTING WORLDS

Still another branch of the institution, is for boys who for one reason or another, have had a poor start in life. These boys are not taken in with any thought of leprosy; this department is really a school, where the students are under devoted, Christian supervision. The most outstanding feature of this part of the work is the atmosphere of joy and happiness, which pervades the school.

As is now well known, this is a new day and a day of hope for people with leprosy, and in this well-run institution, they can look forward hopefully to be being freed someday, to return to normal life, though, of course, where the disease has resulted in the loss of fingers or toes, these cannot be restored, but the patient can be rendered so that he or she is not a danger to others, when they enter again into normal social life. In such an institution, one seems almost to trace the steps of the Master.

Another feature of what one sees in Formosa is the great number of beautiful poinsettias which grow freely in the Island: there are beautiful hedges of them. Oranges as already said are to be seen in great quantities everywhere, and the multitudes of bananas on sale in the countless fruit shops, have a new and delightful flavor.

Most important of all, is the advanced and advancing civilization, which includes religious liberty, and encourages a spirit of optimism. Do keep on praying for us, and for this Island of promise. With all best wishes from us both, we are, with appreciation for your help,

Yours faithfully,
In His service,
Edward C. Perkins, MD

Epilogue

By Richard Perkins Hsung, Editor
A Tribute to My Mother, Dr. Jean Tren-Hwa Perkins
(裴瓊華醫生)

I vividly recall that moment on a warm day in 1980 when we first arrived in New York. Sitting next to my mother on a wooden pier above the sparkling Hudson River at sunset, somewhere near today's 72nd or 79th Street Pier. I was deeply exhausted from our long journey and shell-shocked by leaving the only home I'd ever known, along with the overstimulation of the New World. It was there that I saw my mother, the pillar of my life, the adult I'd spent nearly every moment of my life with, crying uncontrollably like a little girl. I was confused and frightened of the unknown that lay ahead.

That was only the second time I saw my mother cry. The other was on the train in Japan when she was almost just as sad. And I was equally puzzled at the time, but now I have an idea why she was crying then. During the next thirty-four years, until she died in 2014 at the age of eighty-three, I saw tears in my mother's eyes only twice more. The first was when she saw me off to college. And the other was when it took her almost two minutes to recognize who I was. And for the first time in two decades, she called me "Edward," a name I'd long forgotten.

That afternoon on the pier, I hoped my mother was simply missing my father and sister. It took me many years to grasp the meaning of her river of tears. Her life had gone through drastically different phases that expressed a basic law of physics:

SPRING FLOWER: TORN BETWEEN SHIFTING WORLDS

For every action, there will be an equally powerful reaction—in the opposite direction! Using Chinese idioms (成語), I could say that her life was one of "blessings within disasters, and disasters within blessings (禍中有福-福中有禍)." Or "a negative experience for every positive one, and vice versa (有得必有失-有一利必有一弊)." She lived about "thirty years *east* of the river (suggesting 'poor or troublesome' in Chinese, 三十年河東), and thirty years *west* (implying 'rich and unburdened,' 三十年河西)." While we cannot live by "what-ifs," we might be still haunted by them.

In tribute to Dr. Jean Tren-Hwa Perkins, my mother, the following is a summary of her life in America, along with my own thoughts about the politics of war and peace and how they can be expressed through the life of an individual. I'll also share my own journey in America and how, after many years, I came to compile and edit my mother's writings along with other primary and secondary sources to bring you this book.

———∽∾∽———

From the moment we arrived in America, my mother struggled with a narrow-minded, distrustful, and (in my opinion) incompetent US Immigration and Naturalization Service (INS). In her mind, she had been legally adopted by her parents, who were American citizens, at the US Court for China in Shanghai in 1941, and was then admitted into the US at Ellis Island, New York City, the following year—directly within view of the Statue of Liberty—on the basis of that legal adoption. So she expected to qualify for repatriation and thought she wouldn't even need to reapply for citizenship. Yet she didn't have the documents with her when she arrived in New York in 1980, and it took another eighteen years before she was finally granted citizenship, in 1998.

Getting her citizenship squared away was my mother's

first priority. So after she and I arrived in Boston, we'd pack peanut butter and jelly sandwiches day after day and head to the Immigration and Naturalization Service office in the John F. Kennedy Federal Building at Government Center on Cambridge Street, and we'd sit there patiently under flickering fluorescent lights waiting for our number to be called. The INS at that time was so underfunded, or so it seemed, that they didn't even have the money for new light bulbs, not to mention intelligent, efficient, or even kind staffers. There would be *hundreds* of people ahead of us each time, no matter how early we arrived, and when my mother's number was finally called, each time she'd be told this or that form was missing, or these or those boxes could not be left blank, followed by the dreadful refrain: "*Next!*" I thought only officials in Communist China screamed like that! But I witnessed firsthand that it happens in America, too. Standing next to my mother and seeing her grave disappointment, I felt saddened at how disrespected, if not actually discarded, she was by the land she'd idealized and even worshipped as *home,* and I felt guilt-ridden that I couldn't help.

One day, she finally just lost it. She asked the umpteenth INS officer, "Ma'am, please, we've waited all day since before dawn. Why didn't you tell me I was missing these forms the last time I was here?"

"I wasn't the one who examined your case," the agent replied. "The forms are over there, Lady [behind another long line]. Fill it out and come back again. *Next!*"

We'd waited more than half a day in a room with what seemed like a hundred equally depressed and frightened souls, and this particular interaction lasted less than two minutes, including the time the agent flipped through my mother's application and supporting documents. So, Mother took it to the next level: "Please, *look!* I passed through Ellis Island in 1942 with my

SPRING FLOWER: TORN BETWEEN SHIFTING WORLDS

American parents, which should at least be a starting point for citizenship."

"How would *I* know, Lady? And how would I begin to believe what you just told me?"

"It's all in my application, ma'am. How else would I have acquired the ability to speak excellent English? America is my home, ma'am, please."

"Your parents are dead, so they can't help you. *Next!*" She flipped through my mother's papers one more time, as uninterested as she and all the other INS officers had been when they refused to actually review what the documents said.

At that point, Dr. Perkins went berserk and began to scream at the agent. I grabbed her arm to keep her from crossing the invisible neutral zone of the counter. And I saw in the corner of my eye security guards moving toward us. We left in shame amid startled and sad glares. An African American female guard by the door was more sympathetic and said, "Ma'am, if you leave now, you can always come back and try again." I'll never forget that day. While speaking perfect English had paved the way for us to leave China, it did not seem to help her at all with the INS in Boston.

The expectation of a quick repatriation process turned out to be, from a legal standpoint, sheer fantasy. And it got us off on the wrong foot. On August 25, 1942, my mother had been formally admitted into the US through Ellis Island under a (humanitarian) parole status—a non-immigration classification—because there was a war, and she was a minor assessed on her entry papers as being in the Under-Sixteen category. So my mother's assumptions were *not* consistent with the law, however reasonable her claims were. After all, she had been lawfully adopted by American citizens, and although she was thirty years late declaring her citizenship intent, it occurred during a time when she couldn't possibly have done so. But through these harsh encounters with the INS, my mother had to learn that her so-called *home* did not actually recognize either her status or her right to stay, and it was not about to extend a welcoming hand to her, no matter how reasonable a case she might have. And so her idealization of America that had anchored her through three decades of hell in China was shattered.

Forty years after her first journey to America with her American parents, she was now only one among millions of faces trying to gain entry and take away valuable resources from those already here. From those dreadful days at the INS offices in Boston, I swore to remember that I will forever be an outsider in the United States, and I continue to feel that way today, years after I was granted citizenship.

By the late 1980s, exhausted from her struggles to be recognized as an American, Jean Perkins's hope and dream of bringing her husband and daughter over and having her daughter attend college in America were dashed, even with the help of competent lawyers and a few sympathetic elected officials. She even tried applying for political asylum, based on the atrocities she'd experienced in China as the wife of a political prisoner and someone who could have been jailed or killed because of her American connections. All that history made the denial of her application for seeking political asylum painfully ironic. The decision was that China and the US were now allies, so her claim about political persecution was deemed unreasonable now. That straw nearly broke her faith entirely.

Then came the 1989 Tian-An-Men (also called T'ien-An-Men) Square Incident (天安門事變, or "The Gate of Heavenly Peace"), when hundreds and eventually thousands of Chinese young people took to Beijing's streets, as the generation before them had in 1966. But unlike 1966, this was for a good cause and done in full view of the world. My mother hoped America would finally acknowledge what had taken place in China for three decades behind closed doors, but she soon discovered the relativism of America's commitment to human rights and became even more deeply disappointed in the hypocrisy of her parents' country. She saw that whenever it's convenient, for business or geopolitics, America supports international movements for freedom and democracy. And when it's not, America aligns itself with whatever power structures help keep its own upper echelons comfortable.

As a US citizen now, I'm fully aware of the privileges I have in expressing my thoughts without fear of retribution—an opportunity that billions of people worldwide don't have. But when the US criticizes other countries about democracy or human rights, its own checkered history, both domestically and abroad, cannot be overlooked. Not long ago, slavery was legal in America, and not long before *that*, settlers received bounties for massacring Native Americans. Even today, we're far from creating equal opportunities around gender, race, class, religion, and many other categories. I shudder at phrases like *making ourselves great again*, because, as a species, humans have never *been* great, in my view. And making one's country great again was actually a slogan that the Red Guards (紅衛兵) shouted during Mao's Cultural Revolution. Although every political system has its share of persecution and injustice, and America has more freedom and equality than some and deserves to be recognized for this, it too is grossly imperfect, as my mother sadly discovered. The makeshift Statue of Democracy erected by the students in Tian-An-Men Square in 1989 was a symbol of hope and freedom for millions around the world, but it began to have a different meaning for her during those dreadful days in Boston. And she fell into a deep depression.

JEAN TREN-HWA PERKINS

During the thirty years when my mother was isolated and locked behind a closed border, along with millions of other Chinese, she maintained her stability and even her sanity by idealizing her home along the Hudson, as though everyone in America were as good as her parents, aunts, classmates, and the many others who had served China as missionaries and doctors. She had no way of knowing that during those same thirty years, her idealized home country had gone through its own culture wars that tore at the fabric of the community, which perhaps *needed* to be torn, since so many Americans had been (and still are) excluded from the Dream.

However cuddly a teddy bear America had appeared to be for my mother and much of the world, by the 1970s the goodwill following World War II and the Eisenhower-Kennedy years had evaporated. And clinging to her idealized image of America set her up for despair and disappointment when she came face-to-face with what America had become, and actually already *was*. So when she returned to New York and then Massachusetts, despite the beauty, elegance, and cultural creativity that continued almost unfettered beneath America's spacious skies, it was not the Utopia she'd held in her mind's eye and close to her heart. Her expectations were met with bureaucratic impertinence, and she struggled to make sense of it all.

Those days, when she was trying to find her place in the land that denied her the citizenship she believed she already had, were the low points of my mother's homecoming. Many high points came along, as well. First, she was finally reunited with her extended family, the descendants of her Uncle Henry and Aunt Olga. All her relatives were astonished by the turn of events. The Perkins family's generosity helped her resettle and

SPRING FLOWER: TORN BETWEEN SHIFTING WORLDS

got me a first-rate preparatory education at the famed Milton Academy. At weekends on Martha's Vineyard and rummaging through fairs for hidden gems through the Charles Street of the 1970s, their unconditional love and support helped us transition as well as we possibly could.

The much-anticipated reunion with her Yonkers classmates — Jill, Betty, and Marie — in the days right after we arrived in New York was the first time I saw my mother behaving like a kid at Christmas. I recall four grown women shouting and dancing in the penthouse of the Empire Hotel, with my mother occasionally looking over to tell me not to push or pull anything (including the fire alarm button). On the day she crashed Jill's car into a dune while learning to drive, I heard rare, carefree laughter from her. Jill was trying to teach her, while Betty, Marie, and I sat, frozen with fear, in the back. And in the winter of 1981, my mother and I traveled to Grand Rapids, Michigan, and saw the Ploeg family. "Joy and tears would know no bounds," as my mother often remarked. My mother, her fellow-adopted sister Chum, and Aunt Dee stayed up all night talking, reminiscing, and crying. By then, Aunt Bessie had passed away. My mother also met Katie Louise Ploeg, the youngest sister of Aunt Dee and Aunt Bessie, who took care of my grandmother Georgina Perkins in 1961 during her last days.

At other times, my mother worked as a Research Fellow at the Massachusetts Eye and Ear Infirmary in Boston, an affiliate of the Harvard Medical School. Those were her happiest years professionally. She would jog to and from work, to prevent another heart attack. She was a member of the research team developing Yttrium-Aluminum Garnet (YAG) laser treatment for glaucoma in the Laboratories of Dueker, Grant, and Epstein, which was in part, responsible for today's widespread beneficial use of laser treatment in ophthalmology. Despite her humble persona and her deferential description of her professional life, my mother had published important articles while struggling to raise my sister, Gina, in the early 1960s, and she submitted abstracts and clinical synopses up until the Red Guards came to her apartment. She resumed her research and passion for glaucoma in 1976, soon after the Cultural Revolution ended. She even published the clinical observations she'd made during her arduous *Rustication-Reeducation* periods in the countryside — which I consider another triumph of the human spirit. Including research projects left behind in China and work at Harvard, her publication career did not end until the late 1980s.

While working in America, she received letters from China retroactively granting her the academic title of Professor of Ophthalmology, in honor of the many people she'd taught for nearly two decades, while also formally acknowledging her service and contributions as Acting Chief of the Ophthalmology Division in Hangchow Municipal Hospital dating back to 1965–1966, before all hell broke loose there. In 1983, my mother helped with a TV program called *Eyes Over China*, produced by *NOVA: Adventures in Science* and sponsored by WGBH-TV, Boston. In 1985, she successfully published a single-authored digest, titled *Glaucoma in China* in the journal *International Ophthalmology*, summarizing a lifelong collection of clinical cases. She dedicated it to me and implored me to work hard and become equally successful, if not perhaps more so! Also, sometime in the mid-1980s, China offered my mother boundless resources for research and power and status if she would choose to return. "Over my dead body," she told me laconically.

During part of that time, she lived in a basement on the "poor side" of Beacon Hill. In her later years, she was tucked away — lonely, malnourished, cold, and jobless — in a second-floor studio on a dingy street in Boston's Chinatown, still waiting

SPRING FLOWER: TORN BETWEEN SHIFTING WORLDS

for her Green Card approval from the INS. She survived on Social Security and a paltry pension. But she never lost hope, at least not completely. She persevered in pursuing her rightful American citizenship, with the help of compassionate colleagues at Mass General—in particular, Dr. Thomas Richardson, and also Maureen O'Sullivan, a highly skilled attorney who took on her unusual case. And with the designation "INS Case Pending," a thin veil that separated her from being an actual undocumented alien, she was able to work at many different jobs, including as a nanny while she wrote this extensive memoir. And she battled depression well into the 1990s. Then one day in 1999, while jogging along the Charles River, she forgot her way home, and thus began a fifteen-year bout with dementia. She died in a nursing home on Park Street in Brookline, Massachusetts, in 2014.

———∞———

During that same period, life in China took a dramatic upturn economically, practically beginning the day my mother and I boarded the Japan Airlines flight to Narita. After we left, China rose from the ashes of its own making and gained much respect and legitimacy in the world. During this remarkable transformation, the other half of our nuclear family—Paul and Gina—moved from the moldy, cement-floored apartment we'd shared to a modern, air-conditioned high-rise in Hangzhou's city center, surrounded by steel spires and glass towers. And they exchanged their worn-out bicycles for a car, and later had a personal driver, as well. My father's sudden fame as a world leader in rice agriculture brought him belated yet well-earned recognition, as well as wealth, power, and privilege.

"We can eat chicken every day now," Gina told our mother one day while chatting on the phone. My mother was happy for their improved life but felt saddened by their dwindling desire to be united as a family in America. At the same time, she wasn't the least bit envious that we were missing out on the ride to prosperity in China. Scars from those horrible decades, and especially the Great Cultural Revolution, were hard to heal and impossible for her to forget or forgive. She swore she would never go back, and she forbade me from going back on my own, as well.

Neither turned out to be the case. Fifteen years later, almost to the day when we left Shanghai, she went back and saw the miraculous changes with her own eyes. Later, she agreed to let me visit China, and even encouraged me to follow her American parents' footsteps and help the Chinese people in whatever capacity I could muster.

Arriving "home" to America was not the end, but the beginning of another set of struggles—for which my mother was ill-prepared. What price is one willing to pay for freedom? If she'd had any idea what a long, humiliating process that obtaining citizenship would be, would she do it again? I honestly don't know.

In reviewing my mother's life history, I have come to realize that whatever hurdles and challenges blocked her path, she always managed to live with hope, passion, conviction, and focus. And when her inner resources wore thin, there were always people—perhaps they were angels?—who came into her life exactly when the need was the greatest. The essential goodness of humankind always seemed to prevail around her. People like our working-class neighbors, her Amah, the *Shu-Chi* at her hospital, and the provincial governor and his wife would carry the ball the extra mile so she could survive, even thrive.

My mother was always smarter, quicker, and braver than she realized. Her tears that flowed into the Hudson River that day in

SPRING FLOWER: TORN BETWEEN SHIFTING WORLDS

1980 as I sat with her watching the sun setting in the west were tears not only of sadness but also of courage. And when the day came for her soul to be emancipated from its physical limitations, with her body resting peacefully at Cedar Hill Cemetery in Hartford, Connecticut, lying at last between her parents, the idea of a beautiful and free America that had carried her through hell realm after hell realm, remained emblazoned on her heart. She was guided by an ideal, and she did her best day after day to realize it — to help the people of China and, eventually, to help all humankind. In the end, my mother's life was exemplary and, to me and many others, extraordinary.

My Own American Journey

You've read about my life through my mother's eyes and pen. But at the same time, of course, there was another dimension — my own inner life and views of people, places, and events. And throughout it all, I always had the sense there was something for me to fulfill in this lifetime — while I was watching railroad cars after school, sitting alongside a lake, pulling a fire alarm in a posh New York hotel, or looking up at the blue sky seeking guidance from a greater force. Even when I sank into depression, which has not been infrequent for me, I've always felt called and miraculously pulled back from the brink, sometimes Jimmy Stewart-style, to *something*.

At the tender age of fifteen, I arrived in America and struggled to adapt to support my mother and adjust to a new culture, a new language, and a new world. I may have been the only teenager who migrated from the People's Republic of China to the US between the late 1970s and the early 1980s, a transitional period shortly after China reopened to the West. I've yet to meet another. People have encouraged me to write my own stories as the last volume in this series. While I appreciate the sentiment, my life hasn't been remotely as book-worthy as my mother's. I would say my life has been a mirror image of my mother's—the "non-superimposable" kind. In chemistry, non-superimposable mirror images are two (chiral) entities that are completely identical and, at the same time, distinct and different. The example most often given is that they are like our left and right hands.

As my mother's mirror, I've discovered that my life's purpose has always been to complete her memoir. She created a rough manuscript, and I've taken it the rest of the way, using archives, memories, interviews, and some imaginative mortar to connect the bricks. No matter what was happening on the surface, while I was with her and since, I've been drawn to this task. Although everything in my life seems to have been a preparation for this, it took me a long time to realize it. And fulfilling this task has taken its toll on me, emotionally, physically, and mentally. Whenever I've tried to skirt this responsibility, I've been drawn back—to the point where I made the difficult decision to end my professional career and focus on compiling, editing, and to some extent writing *Spring Flower*, Books One and Two. And in the end, I accept the discomfort brought about by this unrequested burden as my fate and perhaps also as an exercise that can be redemptive and even demon-exorcising.

Now you have it—more than 1,300 pages of my mother's memoir, which in my opinion is a spiritual and cultural history of twentieth-century China through the lens of one woman's life. And perhaps even a meta-history of humankind as we all struggle with the winds of fate and the hands we've been dealt.

As mirror images, just as my mother vanished from Yonkers Junior High School at the end of World War II, I was yanked out of a classroom in Hangzhou, China, on a spring day in 1980 and disappeared from my junior high. Mother never wanted to leave America, and leaving China was not my choice either. When my mother returned to China in 1946, she was fifteen, the age I was when I pulled the fire alarm in midtown Manhattan. The difference is that she had her beloved parents with her at that time, while I had only her, and we were never that close. My father was correct when he reached into my duffel bag and pulled out the Chinese classics and poetry books I'd packed for our journey to America and declared, "You won't be reading these, nor will you need them anymore (你不會再讀這些書啦)." Like my mother, I had to abandon my dream of becoming a writer. The bewilderment of it all—being called the son of an *Anti-Revolutionist* (反革命的兒子) in the early 1970s, to journeying halfway around the world to a place with a language that I knew next to nothing about—left an indelible imprint on my nervous system *and* my life.

Before relocating to Boston, we lived for a few weeks in Brooklyn, then in upper Manhattan near the Columbia University Hospital. I don't remember whether Dr. Fisher or my Aunt Evvie and Uncle Amyas made those arrangements. But my mother was still waiting for confirmation from MEEI-Massachusetts General Hospital, so instead of heading to Boston right away, she thought she might go elsewhere, like to Columbia University's hospital in New York City. And there was also a chance we'd be heading to Baltimore or even Washington, DC.

Apart from my resenting that I had to lug our suitcases around, I actually enjoyed those weeks and felt strangely at peace in New York. I had found postwar Tokyo overwhelming, but the glitter of New York, one of the world's most chaotic cities, was incredible. I was even okay with the smell of urine on the #1-Train, as the stench took me back to our slum compound on Sun-Zhong-Shan Road or Sun-Yat-Sen Road (孫中山路).

JEAN TREN-HWA PERKINS

And while walking around Morningside Heights before the neighborhood's gentrification, I was reminded of beggars and even lepers in China. With memories of Tokyo still fresh, I could grasp why the year before we left China, my mother pleaded with the ticket scalper so that my sister and I could see the movie *Proof of Man* (人證), about a young Amerasian Black man who grew up in Harlem and went to Tokyo looking for his Japanese biological mother. It all felt strangely familiar, to me and, I believe, to my mother.

Yet it wasn't the poverty or the stenches that made me feel at home in New York. I basked in the beauty of the George Washington Bridge, the serenity of the Hudson River, and the peace of Fort Tryon Park. Like my mother before me, I fell in love with New York, which I often call my first American home. And most memorably, our stay in New York was the one period when my mother was willing to explain the new world to me in Chinese. The day we left New York, I stopped speaking Chinese.

After settling in Boston, my mother worked relentlessly to rid me of my accent and become an all-American teen, just as she had strong-armed Gina into learning to walk, speak, and write. I'm not ungrateful, but this approach to pedagogy is exhausting, if not scarring. Night after night, we hardly slept, as my mother shouted English syllables at the top of her lungs, then followed up with "Eddy—sorry, Richard!—enunciate slowly and clearly, don't mumble or stutter! Look at my tongue. Push the tip of your tongue against the back of your upper teeth." One time, our upstairs neighbor, either Mike or Philip, knocked on our door, fearing domestic violence.

On nights she wasn't teaching me pronunciation, she would stay up and translate my textbooks and reading assignments like *Animal Farm*, *1984*, *A Tale of Two Cities*, *The Great Gatsby*, and *Huckleberry Finn* into Chinese. She'd scribble the Chinese

SPRING FLOWER: TORN BETWEEN SHIFTING WORLDS

characters between the lines of English, and I'd get up at 4 a.m. to do my homework before an hourlong MTA commute to Milton. On Sunday afternoons, she would pack a lunch, and after church, we'd sit by the Charles River near the Longfellow Bridge, and she'd coach me through all my readings until the sun disappeared behind the flashing landmark Citgo sign. She desperately wanted me to succeed in the language she was forced to stop speaking for nearly three decades. I was, once again, tasked with continuing her dream.

Unfortunately, I don't share my mother's natural ability with languages. In my defense, I was fifteen and hadn't spoken much English before that. She was a toddler when she learned from her parents. Sitting in my fourth-grade English reading class as a fifteen-year-old in a roomful of kids half my size added to my humiliation. It reminded me of my experience attending first grade in Hangzhou ten years earlier. In the end, it was too little too late. I had barely mastered seventh-grade English when I graduated from Milton Academy, despite hours of tutoring by dedicated teachers. Even today, I remember every one of them, amazing men and women I bonded with during those early years in America.

And I'm deeply grateful for my mother's efforts. I know it was her way of expressing love, even if it didn't always feel that way. Overall, though, my time in Boston was miserable. I mourned the loss of my native-language ability. I'd emigrated at an awkward age, old enough to feel and understand everything and yet young enough to know next to nothing. And at that vulnerable age, I was drowning in personal crises, grieving the loss of my homeland, my father, my sister, *and my very identity*. My mother barely noticed or expressed empathy. Perhaps I hid it too well, and perhaps she was mired in her struggles, so not acknowledging my grief was her way of pushing me to realize her lost dream.

It wasn't all depressing or suffocating, of course. I cherished our long weekends on Cape Cod at Martha's Vineyard with Aunt Evvie and Uncle Amyas, picking blueberries with my cousin Oakes, or playing with Joanie's children. Having dinners with Cousin Olivia and her family made for a great diversion on weekends in Cambridge. We enjoyed beautiful Thanksgiving dinners with Dr. Arthur Grove and Lois, his wife. Traveling on Interstate 95 to Maine by Greyhound Bus and spending July 4th's and Christmases with Dr. Loring Pratt and his large, extended family were highlights of the year. These Americans had been to China and were drawn to my mother's stories. Annual trips to Yonkers to see my mother's high school classmates always seemed to renew her, and the experience also deepened my affection for Yonkers, the town she loved most of all. Serene Lake George, Silver Bay, and the Adirondacks in Upstate New York were always restorative for me as they were for her in the 1940s. And spending a week every summer with Dr. Hyla Watters at her Tupper Lake cottage brought my attention to the richness of my mother's distant past. Dr. Watters had been a missionary in China who helped thousands of Chinese around the same time as my grandparents. And her father was primarily responsible for saving my grandfather, spiritually.

But as I say, my mother and I were never close, which accords with the mirror-image metaphor, as one can never *touch* the image in the mirror. Whatever closeness we did have was the result of our being two victims against the world, a psychodynamic that went back to the streets of Hangzhou when she would shout English sentences to me as we commuted together to school and work. Mostly, I feared her, and her beating me severely when I was nine probably contributed to the distance I always maintained from her.

SPRING FLOWER: TORN BETWEEN SHIFTING WORLDS

At the same time, I know that my mother was a beautiful human being to many others—her patients, her colleagues, her neighbors—as well as a devoted Christian. But her unconditional kindness and care for people in China and America never seemed to include *me*, so I had to settle for feeling her loving kindness *through* these people. Her hesitancy to share her warmth with me seemed irrational and only heightened my loneliness. Even in rare moments of tenderness, she would use a stern tone to explain what Hawkeye and B.J. were saying on *M*A*S*H*, her all-time-favorite TV show, and why it was so funny. She'd fall into a kind of trance watching *M*A*S*H*, and at the time, I wondered why. Now I think I know. She may well have seen her own father in the characters of Hawkeye and B.J., portrayed by Alan Alda and Mike Farrell, and was perhaps mourning the day she lost her parents so suddenly.

Yet I must also mention that she saved my life more than once. Unbeknownst to her, her rare and unexpected gestures of love— such as delivering a chocolate cake to my college dorm, out of the blue—diverted my suicidal ideations, starting with my plan to jump into an icy river on a January night. I was nineteen, her age when her parents left China in 1951. As we left Hangzhou, my father said I had to be "both son and husband to your mother from here on." I took that as my charge, starting with learning to cook. My mother's culinary capacities were nonexistent, and the food she prepared was inedible, if not dangerous. So I quickly learned to make simple meals. My first cooking teachers were nursing students who lived in the apartment complex we resided in on Commonwealth Avenue. We shared a kitchen, and when one of them saw me holding a raw egg above a gas burner to hard-boil it, she patiently explained boiling. Later, when my father's eldest sister (Ruth in the book) lived briefly in Boston, I washed and made food for these two grown women. Both

JEAN TREN-HWA PERKINS

were too busy working at Mass General, and neither even knew how to turn on a burner. And I hand-washed all our clothes and bedding.

I did survive, and then some. I watched an insane amount of *Bugs Bunny* and *Tom and Jerry* before moving on to *The Andy Griffith Show*, *The Brady Bunch*, *Star Trek*, *Dr. Who*, and *Different Strokes* (I fell madly in love with Kimberly, both the character *and* the actress). Their dialogues were straightforward and easy to understand, and they met my need for distraction, educated me about my new country, and offered a friendly environment for learning English. I learned to play pickup basketball and shoot behind the arc. I worshiped Larry Bird but was terrified every time Dr. J stepped onto the court. I could pronounce "Beat L.A.!" better than native-speaking kids. I hated the Yankees — my mother's team — like every Boston kid must, and I feverishly checked Jim Rice's and Dewey Evans's daily stats like my mother did in 1943 when she was enthralled with the Yankees. I cried with the Red Sox Nation after Game Six of the 1986 World Series. I could feel the pain Billy Buckner unfairly endured; by then, I, too, had muffed many groundballs on a softball field *and* in real life. Sport is an international language, and I adapted well to that culture.

I managed to attend Calvin College, now Calvin University, a private evangelical school in Grand Rapids, Michigan, and aspired to master writing at a high school level. I learned about American history and culture from Aunt Katie Louise Ploeg, whom I regard as my second mother, or perhaps even the loving mother I never had. She took my cooking skills to another level, including the "better than sex" cake recipe. And she instilled in me the joys and the pains of gardening and owning a house. More important, Aunt Katie Louise improved my English vocabulary by challenging me to come up with words using letters on license plates whenever we were stalled in traffic. She also forced me to play Scrabble with her every Saturday until she accused me of cheating when she could no longer beat me consistently.

The Ploeg family of Grand Rapids all pitched in to "raise me." Uncles Ken, John, and Morton, Katie Louise's brothers, took turns to be my roadside AAA or car insurance agent. They were highly skilled career mechanics, and with their tutoring, I quickly mastered the skills needed for auto maintenance. Those were the days when you could still see through to the ground when popping the hood of any car. Aunt Dee, the "Big Ploeg (浦大)" of Kiukiang, was still living and going strong, and she cooked soy sauce-soaked rice and potatoes and turnips every Friday night. The food was insufferable, but her stories of faraway Kiukiang became immensely meaningful to me. Thus began Stage One of this book project. On Sundays, after attending church and visiting Aunt Annie at the nursing home, we would devour Aunt Henrietta's delicious pies, which more than made up for the soy-sauce dinners. I felt I was part of a family for the first time in my life. And I got to experience my mother's sister Chum's life in Michigan during the wartime in the 1940s.

When I left to live on campus in 1985, Aunt Katie Louise bequeathed to me the well-traveled suitcase that contained over 2,000 photographs my grandmother had taken in China. She said, "Now that I've given this Perkins family heirloom to Georgie's grandson, my job is done. Take excellent care of these photos, kid; they may be useful to you someday. Your grandmother was quite the amateur photographer, especially during an era when even owning a camera was rare, let alone operating one skillfully." This sped me to Stage Two of this book project.

At Calvin College, with the patience and understanding of a host of English and literature professors as well as help from college friends and tireless roommates, I could finally write a coherent, thousand-word essay on white-out-laden pages. The day finally came when I received a C+, my highest writing grade ever on an essay, and my professor told me, "Richard, you've earned every bit of that grade. You now write better than some of these kids who were born and raised here." As appreciative as I was, it mostly saddened me to think of what I had lost. I had *two* languages—but really none. I had lost my native Chinese language skills, and I could never become proficient in English. And I knew C+ was far below my mother's expectations.

Miraculously, I found solace in English poetry and fell in love with Emily Dickinson. Poetry was the only place where fragmented, if not incoherent, English sentences and grammar didn't seem to matter. And Miss Dickinson showed me that a dash or an ellipsis could replace any punctuation. I tried using dashes and ellipses throughout this book, but my editors kept taking them out. Well—whether correct or not, that was my understanding....

Ultimately, tired of struggling with the new language and wanting to keep life simple, I chose to major in science. But organic chemistry became yet another language in which I had no natural ability. I often imagined what my life might have been like if I'd chosen a career path consistent with my interest in computer programming/writing algorithms and art. Even with my broken English, I found a niche writing sound algorithms using BASIC or Pascal languages at Milton Academy and Calvin College in the early 1980s. I guess the logic was not lost on me.

One summer afternoon in the mid-1980s, I got bored watching some dark-brown slurry that I was stirring in a flask for a chemistry project, so I spent the rest of the afternoon writing a program that would help analyze and tabulate photochemical quantum yields. I left the program at Calvin without knowing the meaning of "licensing"—since I had done it for fun. I was surprised to later learn that they were still using my program in the lab in the mid-1990s. But my mother was neither impressed nor approving of my spending hours and hours writing line after line of code just to make a computer draw a square or a twinkling star on its own. She believed I had found a way to waste my life and questioned how any of this would be useful to humankind. She was smug and self-righteous, and unaware that I likely could have worked for and retired early from Google a millionaire (sigh).

I was, however, given latitude to draw and paint. But after my mother had to pay a few entry fees for local exhibits, she asked, "What will you be eating when you become an artist and move to L.A.?" The sarcasm on her face reigned supreme, and I never understood the "L.A." part. But by then I'd gotten used to doing things I was terrible at, so I stayed with organic chemistry, not realizing how awful I was at it, even after flunking my first two midterm exams. Fortunately for me, the faculty at Calvin College let me continue (Were they right? Was I?), and I managed to work hard enough to receive an MS and a PhD in organic chemistry from the University of Chicago. And I had a thirty-year career teaching chemistry, for which I'm indebted to so many people who helped me along the way. Through teaching, I learned and relearned all I had missed in college and graduate school, and I got to work with thousands of wonderful young people in classrooms and labs, as well as to present research papers worldwide. How lucky I've been! In that regard, my career also mirrors my mother's. She became a highly successful professor of clinical ophthalmology after being shoved into the medical profession and struggling her way through college (oh yes; she, too, sucked in organic chemistry!).

Fast forward to 2003—four years after my mother took the oath of loyalty to her new country and finally became a citizen—

JEAN TREN-HWA PERKINS

when the Perkins-Hs(i)ung family was reunited in Back Bay Boston, a quarter of a century after that fateful day at the Hong-Qiao Airport. I take pride in having played a role in making that reunion happen. I'd come a long way from being the celebrity kid who pulled the fire alarm in Manhattan, and the sad kid who just wanted to go home (wherever that was). And now Gina (whose official American name is now Jane) and her son, Edward, are bona fide American citizens. Edward is a graduate of Northeastern University and has been working at Massachusetts General Hospital as a graphic designer. And he's also an amateur novelist and illustrator. Of that, my mother would be extremely proud.

———∞———

Sometime in the mid to late 1990s, my father retired from all his lucrative and powerful posts in China. In his own words, "Yes, I can readily ascend to an even higher stratosphere politically and academically, but I would have to be corrupted. So, I've reached the ceiling to lead without compromising integrities." Given my mother's deteriorating health, he decided to migrate to the US to care for his wife. In one of our few civil conversations, my father urged me to visit China, solely because he was proud of its transformation. For years my mother had prevented me from going back for fear of a déjà vu, that is, being trapped in China for thirty years, as had happened to her. But with her approval, in 2000, I made my first pilgrimage back to China, the first time I left America after twenty years, proudly holding a US passport.

On October 9, 2000, I flew from Minneapolis, where I lived at the time, to New York's JFK airport, following the reverse itinerary of our journey twenty years earlier (Pan Am had sadly gone out of business, so I had to use a different airline). I landed in Tokyo-Narita and spent a week in Japan. While lecturing

SPRING FLOWER: TORN BETWEEN SHIFTING WORLDS

and attending a meeting, I unsuccessfully tried to find where my mother and I had briefly stayed (most likely near Shinjuku Station). On October 17, 2000, I boarded a Japan Airlines flight to Shanghai Hong-Qiao Airport. My heartbeat accelerated as the wheels touched down. I felt extremely nervous as I looked out the window; Hong-Qiao looked eerily familiar but seemed more like an airport now and less a jailhouse.

I scheduled my two-week stay in China tightly, with seminars and time-consuming grad student recruitment at universities in half a dozen cities, including my first trip to Beijing. And I also hoped to find time to retrace my steps in Hangzhou, "a city south of Shanghai," as my mother had taught me to say in 1979. My father told me that both places where we'd lived—the slum compound on Sun-Zhong-Shan Road (孫中山路) and Yan'an New Village (延安新村)—were still there. So I made Hangzhou my second stop. There I saw my sister, Gina, for the first time in twenty years, and met her three-year-old son, Edward (named after his American grandfather, although it was also, for the same reason, my name when I was young and we lived together as a family). That was still a few years before Gina would emigrate to America. She received her baccalaureate degree in library science from Hangchow Community College in 1992 (another triumph of the human spirit!) and worked as a librarian at a food research institute in Hangchow until she was placed on medical leave after being battered by her ex-husband. Who would beat up anyone, let alone a disabled woman! We had a wondrous and tearful reunion although, sadly, we'd lived very different lives and could no longer effectively communicate with one another, and not only because of language barriers.

Gina was still resentful that twenty years earlier, she hadn't been the one to go to America with Mother, which was sad because I'd never wanted to go. She remains bitter about this to this day. While supportive of my assembling and editing this memoir, she has been deeply concerned about what Mother might have written about her, despite my assurances that it was 100 percent positive. While I stayed with our mother the rest of her life, Gina lost her beloved mom the day we left in 1980. She was just nineteen! With our mother's US citizenship application dragging on and on, Gina's hope of pursuing college in America was dashed. She did the best she could in China, but she would almost certainly have fared better in America, given her exceptional intellect and the United States' more-progressive approach to disabilities. Like our mother, my sister, Gina, has lived a life with many what-ifs.

During that trip to China, I saw the luxurious, midtown-style condominium the other half of my family had lived in since the mid-1980s. Intriguingly, one of the rooms was locked, and when my sister opened it, I was speechless. The room was like a museum! My father had preserved the old, worn-out furniture we'd had in the 1970s and even earlier. Sitting on the wooden dresser was the French clock that had belonged to my grandmother, Georgina. It had stopped ticking, of course. Beneath the dresser was an old, deflated basketball (see below). And on the floor not far away sat our old gramophone, covered with cobwebs, with a dozen vinyl records leaning inside a box and Bing Crosby's head poking out from one album cover. And there was a 1980 calendar on the wall showing the month we'd left.

I pulled over a dusty bamboo chair and sat down to try to absorb these haunting memories. The last time I'd sat on that chair, I was trying to comprehend the meaning of *The Dream of Red Mansions* (红楼梦, or *Dream of the Red Chamber*), a Chinese classic novel from the eighteenth century, unaware of events that would soon alter my life. Peeking through the dust-coated glass cover of the dresser, I saw many old books including, to

SPRING FLOWER: TORN BETWEEN SHIFTING WORLDS

my surprise, the books and other items my father had taken out of my duffel bag the day I left China. I felt no desire to open the case and touch those books, but a chill went up my spine as I wondered why he had kept all this in a locked room.

Just before I left for China, my father, who by now lived in America and was both excited and concerned about my first trip back, asked his "connections" to meet me at Hong-Qiao and escort me everywhere. As I passed through customs and entered the arrival area, I was surprised to realize that I couldn't utter a word of Chinese! Like my mother in 1946 and Chum in 1947, when they returned after living in America, I struggled with *oh's* and *ah's*, and nothing came out of my mouth naturally. Instead, what came were broken, stammering, incoherent curt phrases, and when I managed to squeeze out real words, I could hear my American accent and mispronunciations. Trying to communicate with these strangers who were waiting for me at the airport, I simply waved my arms, realizing this would be a long trip.

One afternoon, I decided to go out by myself and walk the streets of Hangzhou in search of my footprints as a child. A security guard in a green uniform was standing in front of a beautiful modern office building, so I asked him for directions, using the best rehearsed Chinese pronunciations my sister had painstakingly taught me the night before. I had bravely repeated these words before her until she was satisfied. My sister was concerned how awful my Chinese had become.

"Sir, sorry for bothering you," I said to the man in the green uniform. "Would you please show me where Yan'an New Village (延安新村) is, if it hasn't been torn down? (先生, 不好意思, 請問您, 延安新村還在, 在哪裏?)" I was really nervous. I had butchered my words while trying to order a cup of coffee on my way there.

The guard looked at me with an amiable smile and said, "Young man, Sir, you are not from here, are you? Are you

Chinese (年轻人, 先生, 您不是這裏的人吧, 你是中國人嗎)?" Then he personally took me to the low-rise compound where I'd lived before leaving for America. While standing in front of the dilapidated building still in use, I felt drowned by a wave of emotions. China had evolved, but many people were still living in poverty. After seeing Yan'an New Village, I lost the courage or energy to look for the slum compound on Sun-Zhong-Shan Road (孫中山路) where we'd lived for eleven years before moving to this rundown but relatively modern place.

I too, it was clear, had become a foreigner in my own country, much like my mother fifty years earlier. I understood then why my father had asked his men to escort me; he knew how difficult it would be to return to China after being away for so long. And he was worried about my safety, because I looked Chinese but couldn't speak or behave like one. Just as he had protected my mother in the 1950s, Professor Paul Hsiung was protecting me half a century later. I understood how my mother must have felt after returning to China in 1946—another example of how my life has been a mirror image of hers.

My relationship with my father, Professor Paul Hsiung, was complex. His unexpected show of love in arranging help during my China trip both touched and surprised me. Perhaps he was flaunting his prowess or his academic and administrative status as he gathered these protective elements for my trip—a jeep ride here, a grand dinner there, a tour escort someplace else. But none of it overshadowed the fact that he and I had been estranged for most of my life, both before and again after 2000.

I cannot confirm or disprove that he is my biological father. During the formative years of my young life, he wasn't there, thanks to Great Leader Chairman Mao Ze-Dong and his

SPRING FLOWER: TORN BETWEEN SHIFTING WORLDS

unprecedentedly brutal purge. Professor Hsiung was in a chain gang shoveling cow pies, living in a *Cowshed* (牛棚) with other talented and educated people, some awaiting execution. Then, in my mid-teens when we finally had a chance to connect, he unselfishly set my mother and me free to go to America, leaving me with just two indelible memories. The first is of him chasing me as I struggled to learn to ride his bike on late nights following my lessons from an elderly, silver-haired Chinese literary poet and artist, who lived with his wife in a dimly lit, dusty attic the size of a twin bed. He and my father had bunkered in the same *Cowshed* in the late 1960s, and the silver-haired man had been brutally persecuted.

My other memory is of my father waving at me while holding a deflated basketball and drunkenly saying he'd teach me how to make a jump shot like the NBA players from the 1950s and bragging that no one in China had been better at it when he was "in his prime." I was ten when I studied with the old couple and had quietly begun to show interest in pencil sketches, water painting, and reading Chinese classics and poetry. And I was thirteen when my father offered to show me how to make a jump shot, which he never did. According to my mother, he had been a basketball star in college, athletic and tall by any standards (unlike me).

After I left China, I rarely called him "Papa" or "Dad" when we spoke on the phone or corresponded. Instead, I called him "sir" or "Professor Hsiung," and we were frequently caught up in resentment and antagonism. Whenever we got into shouting matches, he spoke Chinese and I spoke English, so neither of us could fully understand what the other was saying. Still, I generally got the message, because "Professor Paul Hsiung" would circle back to the same point in almost all of our verbal sparring, the point being money. Among many variations on this topic, the most egregious involved a false claim that originated with my mother. With all of her struggles trying to stay in the US, by the late 1980s my mother had spent down most of her savings. Sadly, using me as a kind of human shield, she lied to Paul and said that all her money had gone toward my Calvin College tuition. Professor Hsiung then demanded that I return it to *him* in full, plus interest.

If what my mother told Professor Hsiung had been true, I would have attended the more prestigious (and expensive) Boston University. Then again, had I stayed in Boston, I wouldn't have gotten to know Aunt Katie Louise, and there may not have been this book! In fact, my mother told me sternly that her precious savings were reserved for her daughter's college education in the US, and also for her husband, once he had immigrated. When Aunt Katie Louise learned I would have to pay my own way through college, she suggested that I attend the far more affordable Calvin College, right in "her backyard" in Grand Rapids, Michigan. I agreed, then stayed with her for a time before living on my own, and worked to cover the costs of my tuition and other expenses. My mother never told Paul the truth about this.

But money was never the real issue that divided Professor Paul Hsiung and me. He was frustrated that the cultural divide between us was wider than the Pacific, and I was too. He and I hardly had a father-and-son relationship. We never even had a real chance, as there were always alternative explanations and extenuating factors.

Not the least of which is that I still don't know whether Paul Hsiung was my biological father.

What and who was my mother looking for that day in Japan? And why was she so heartbroken as we took the train back to Tokyo? When did she learn to speak fluent Japanese? More

SPRING FLOWER: TORN BETWEEN SHIFTING WORLDS

intriguingly, why did my father's mother, Eve, my presumed fraternal grandmother, despise me so? Does a three-year-old, the son of her favorite son, need to learn life's hard lessons from a grandparent? Despite her education at Northwestern University outside of Chicago, she was not beyond the bondage of traditional Chinese values—far from it—and she would be the first to admit that.

For an assortment of what I view as irrational "reasons," sons and grandsons are immensely overvalued in China, except I wasn't. Most damagingly, why would my alleged grandmother, and sometimes even my mother, tell me that the only reason I was "allowed to be born was to take care of my physically challenged sister"? And whenever my birth was spoken of in the presence of my father, he'd remain silent or would joke that I was picked up from the street and they'd adopted me. One winter night when I was eleven, I ran away from home to search for my "real" birth parents. When my bewildered mother found me in the railroad yard, my father promised he would never make that joke again. I will never forget my father's expression when he made that promise, as if there was something else he had wanted to tell me.

There may be reasonable answers to all these questions, but I have none, even though I've spent decades pondering these mysteries. Perhaps it was all part of Chinese values, traditions, and culture that I no longer understood or shared. Perhaps something that happened in the mid-1960s caused my father's mother never to want me to be born. Or, at minimum, perhaps she was suspicious of my conception, given that my actual father was hardly in Shanghai during that period. In 2001, I came very close to asking my presumed grandmother Eve for the truth while she was still alive, living in Los Angeles, but I didn't. Perhaps the answer is "none of the above."

After my mother passed away, my father decided to take a

long vacation in China with one of his beloved woman friends. A few months before that, in late 2014, he and I met up in Shanghai and declared a truce for the umpteenth time. To help me complete this book, his wife's memoir, he gave me a tour of Shanghai's historical Xu-Jia-Hui (徐家匯), particularly the Dong-Ping Road (東平路), where my mother had spent ten years of her life, where my sister was born, and where I was conceived. He had just told me tear-soaked stories of the 1950s and 1960s as we bar-hopped on Heng-Shan Road (衡山路) and Dong-Ping Road (東平路). At a bar named "I'll Keep on Drinking Even After I Die (死了也得喝)" near Huai-Hai Middle Road (淮海中路), he finally passed out.

That turned out to be my last chance to ask him about my parentage. Weeks before Chinese New Year in 2015, my father fell and broke his hip while traveling through Hangzhou. And post-surgery, he suffered a blood clot in his lung. When I got the call, I was in Japan, traveling between Hokkaido and Aomori on a research journey regarding my other father-candidate, Taka, and his extended family. I cut the trip short and rushed to Hangzhou to be with him, and those turned out to be the last two weeks of Professor Paul Hsiung's life. He seemed shocked to see me arrive. After he'd disowned me ten or more times in the preceding twenty-five years, I was the first of his "blood relatives" to be present during his waning moments of consciousness. I sat quietly at his bedside, and in those moments together in his hospital room, we were finally at peace.

Between watching his numbers on the monitors, listening to the prognoses of physicians and nurses, and spending brief moments with those who came to pay respects to their beloved teacher, mentor, and colleague—including people from the Ministries of Education (校閱部) and Agriculture (農業部), and even the Governor of Zhejiang Province—I had time to reflect on events of the past. Doing so, I became profoundly depressed and at the same time enraged, especially after learning his blood type. There were so many questions I still wanted to ask him, and here he was being completely irresponsible by trying to die on me before I could ask. Or so I felt. He drifted in and out, and ultimately, he was intubated, no longer able to breathe on his own.

I desperately needed to raise the alcohol level in my O-type blood. Early on a Sunday afternoon when his woman-friend came to relieve my duty, I found an Irish pub not far from the hospital. It appeared to be family-owned, and the couple kindly invited me to have lunch with them, but I declined. I knew I was too unstable to engage in civil conversation. So, I sat in the corner sipping Murphy's Irish Stout and watching UK soccer (the real football!) on a small TV screen that was on mute. Impulsively, I asked the couple where Sun-Zhong-Shan Road (孫中山路) was. Learning it was a twenty-minute walk away, I asked if they'd draw me a map; and after chugging the rest of the ale, I rushed out to look for the compound on Sun-Zhong-Shan Road (孫中山路), where we'd all lived, the place my mother always called a slum.

It was late February, my first Chinese New Year in thirty-five years. The smell of Hangzhou's renowned plum blossoms (梅花) wafted through the air, and after passing a few plum trees I thought about walking to West Lake (西湖), where I knew hundreds of plum trees would be in bloom along the shores. But I decided to find the compound before the sun went down. The city had been vastly built up, and nothing was easily recognizable.

I did manage to find Sun-Zhong-Shan Road (孫中山路) and tried to superimpose my image of 1976 onto what I was seeing as I walked up and down the street a dozen times. It was getting dark, and the neon signs began flashing. I thought of giving up and perhaps trying the next day. And I regretted I hadn't even attempted to find the compound fifteen years earlier when the area was still as I remembered it. I found a wooden bench and sat down to rest my feet, and when I looked up, I instantly recognized the remains of the slum compound. The front entrance was partly hidden behind two rows of large red lanterns, and ironically, it had a sign noting that it was a protected historic site.

A wave of memories swept over me from present to past, and my mind paused when I reached the eleven turbulent years we'd lived here. Faces young and old flashed before me as if I were seeing them on the Times Square Megascreen under neon lights, an image quite like my first night in New York. Their smiles and tears, joys and agonies, took me back to unforgettable moments in my life as well as in global history.

I silently asked myself, "In what period of human history has there *not* been oppression, injustice, war, famine, and massacre — human-made atrocities? And if the answer is none," I thought, "that means there has never been an era of peace. And if that's the case, what motivates us to endure as a species, and what might my mother's memoir offer?" As I looked at all these faces in my mind's eye, an answer began to take form. Our neighbors, my mother's medical colleagues, my teachers, tutors, principals, and thousands more like them — they all were pillars of their communities and the salt of the earth. They saved my mother's life, and they saved mine, too!

And at that moment, another layer of meaning was added to this project. I realized that the focus of this book would not be the atrocities that devastated my family and a nation, but these fundamentally kind, compassionate people who had lovingly, if not divinely, intervened in our lives, and especially in the life of my mother, time after time. Yes, I thought, the book must be dedicated to them: the essence of humanity, the angels next door.

SPRING FLOWER: TORN BETWEEN SHIFTING WORLDS

I stood and breathed in the cool February air. I had to smile, feeling that life's ironies know no bounds. Thirty-five years after fleeing China, I was able to feel to the core of my being that I was at last returning to my *roots*, my Chinese ancestors, and the depths of all humankind. We had just buried my mother, and now the man she married who fearlessly protected her and helped her survive China's atrocities was dying a mile away from where we'd all lived together, the theater of my childhood.

Embracing the damp, chilly air, I walked back to the hospital, where I found the attending physician and signed the "morphine paper" that had been waiting for me. A few days earlier, when he came to for a few fleeting seconds, my father pleaded with me, calling me by the English name I no longer remembered, *"Eddy, please don't let them torture me."* The man who had endured four long years of his own torture in a labor camp refused to live another day in pain. Those were his last words to me. In his final hours, I bent down and whispered to him, "It doesn't matter if you are my father or not. I promise you I'll finish this book, just as I promised your wife. Today, I realized that it's also about you. You made sure my mother could live through it all so someday she could tell her stories of many kind souls, including you! Thank you. You've done all you could in this world. Go and find her somewhere up there. I can take it from here."

———∽∾———

The work of compiling and editing my mother's memoir began *in earnest* the day my father, Professor Paul Hsiung, died. But counting from the day Aunt Katie Louise gave me my grandmother's photos, it has actually been a thirty-year adventure. And during those three decades, I've gone through oceans of self-pity and self-absorption, struggling to adapt to ever-changing circumstances, to become a person who could understand and accept his simple mission in life. The book became my ark to build to ensure my survival from the flood of history. Although it has been an enormous burden to shoulder, it has also been the vehicle for me to begin to process and express all that has transpired in my own life as well.

My American Dream ended in the mid-1990s. I was a postdoctoral associate in New York, and my then-spouse was a chaplain-in-training at the New York Methodist Hospital in Brooklyn—across the street from where my mother and I had stayed fifteen years earlier. We took a memorable trip trying to follow my mother's footsteps from 1942 to 1944. We visited 6 Arthur Place in Yonkers, where my mother and her parents had lived, spent a day on Ellis Island searching for her name on the American Immigrant Wall of Honor, and walked along the Hudson as I shared with my wife my first memories of America. Ironically, she was more into the story than I was. But sadly, shortly after that, our lives began to drift apart.

I had been deeply in love with her family, who came from the Indiana cornfields and were the warmest group of human beings I'd ever met, although not that different from our neighbors in the slum compound on Sun-Zhong-Shan Road. Somewhere between losing a possible pre-born infant to moving out of our beautiful house in the Seward neighborhood of Minneapolis, bordered by the natural beauty of the Mississippi River, where I'd run or bike to work every day, our relationship was by then beyond repair. I was devastated.

I rented a tiny room on the seventeenth floor of Riverside Plaza, a Minneapolis urban-renewal, melting-pot complex called by some the "Ghetto in the Sky," across the I-35 interstate from the old Metrodome (where the US Bank Stadium now stands). For three years, I was surrounded by Somalians, Ethiopians, and other struggling immigrants trying to realize the American

SPRING FLOWER: TORN BETWEEN SHIFTING WORLDS

Dream. Many nights, I'd catch the last call at a local watering hole down the street, filled with depressed but dignified faces where, somehow, I finally felt at home.

That was the about-face I needed in order to move forward with my mother's memoir. I befriended a woman from Southeast Asia who'd had a similar life's journey, and our brief connection reawakened the Chinese in me. For most of my first twenty years in America, I was focused on surviving—and striving to become an American—yet somewhere along the line I forgot who I was. Then for the next twenty years, I did what I could to reconnect with the parts of myself I had buried. I needed to reacquaint myself with China, which had become a foreign land to me. I needed to know its people, culture, language, and history. During several opportunities I had to travel within China, I stayed briefly at places where my mother had lived, and as a result, many stories in this book were compiled, edited, and finished where they occurred.

In closing, I want to come back to the mirror-image metaphor. While in this book I have not dwelled on our similarities and differences, I share with you now that much of my mother's image lives in me, and much of my life has echoed hers. So it has felt natural for me to compile my mother's memoir—even writing some passages in her voice. Given the turbulence of my early life, I've always gravitated toward predictability, keeping changes and ambiguity to a minimum whenever I've had a choice. My mother would also have chosen simplicity and continuity in life, if she could have. But she was unwittingly swept through extremes, starting with her birth during the Great Yangtze River flood to a family that had no use for daughters, being adopted by the kindest American missionaries, living in America, surviving Mao's revolutions, and returning to the land she called home, where, at best, it only worked out partway. These inescapable extremes made her life rich, and although they may be more dramatic than the extremes that most of us live through, I believe her life represents the lives of all who pass through this earth.

Until I grasped the reins of this project, I spent virtually every waking moment trying to escape—or shall I say, run like hell?—from every storm and adversity, and there were many along the way. But that all changed when I stopped resisting compiling my mother's memoir. This book has been a rite of passage for me, a transformational journey to learn who I am. I wish I could have done it better—I can hear my mother scolding me now—but I've done my best, and it's the bravest and most significant thing I've accomplished to date.

Richard Perkins Hsung, PhD
Madison, Wisconsin
January 2022

Richard and his cousin Olivia at her daughter's school fair, ca. 1981

Appendices

APPENDIX ONE: STYLE SHEET

TAKEN DIRECTLY FROM CHINESE

Terms or Phrases	Chinese	Approximate Translation
Frequently Used		
A-I	阿姨	Aunt, a middle-aged woman
Lao-Shih	老師	Secondary school teachers, or professors
Shu-Chi	書記	*See the book*
Less Frequently Used		
Ai-Jen	愛人	Lovers or couples
Hsiao	小	Small or little, or referring to someone who is younger when used in conjunction with a last name
Keng-Tzu Year	庚子年	The year of catastrophic disasters
Ku-Niang	姑娘	Young lady or Miss
Kuo-Min-Tang	國民黨	Republic Nationalist Party
Lao	老	Old, older, or an equivalent of Mr. when used in conjunction with someone's last name
Ma-Ma	媽媽	Mother
Nai-Nai	奶奶	Grandma

Nien-Ch'u-Erh	年初二	Day two of the new year
Nien-Ch'u-Pa	年初八	Day eight of the new year
Pa-Pa	爸爸	Dad
Pai-Nien	拜年	Visiting during the New Year period
Shu-Shu	叔叔	Uncle, a middle-aged man
Ta-Chieh	大姐	A big sister
Ta-Ko	大哥	A big brother
Ta-Ma	大媽	A woman a bit younger than a grandma
Ta-Po	大伯	A man a bit younger than a grandpa
Ta-Sao	大嫂	A woman younger than grandma
Ta-Yeh	大爺	Grandpa

Food and Drink

Chien-Ping-Kuo-Tzu	煎餅果子	A special crêpe from Tientsin
Fu-Li-Chi	符离集烧鸡	A special roasted chicken in Anhwei
Gao-Liang	高粱	A cheap, moonshine-like grain liquor
Hei-Tou-Sha	黑豆沙	A red bean paste
Lung-Ching-Cha	龍井茶	Tea from a "dragon's well"
Pai-Chiu	白酒	A hard rice liquor
Shao-Chiu	燒酒	A hard rice liquor
Shi-Ku-Men	石庫門	Shanghai's yellow rice wine
Wo-Wo-T'ou	窩窩頭	A coarse cornbread

SPRING FLOWER: TORN BETWEEN SHIFTING WORLDS

CITIES <LISTEDALPHABETICALLY>

Postal Romanization Pre-1959	Chinese	Modern Pinyin Post-1958
Canton	廣州	Guangzhou
Ch'angch'un	長春	Changchun
Ch'angsha	長沙	Changsha
Ch'engtu	成都	Chengdu
Chiahsing	嘉興	Jiaxing
Chungking	重慶	Chongqing
Foochow	福州	Fuzhou
Haich'eng	海城	Haicheng
Hangchow	杭州	Hangzhou
Hankow	漢口	Hankou (modern-day 武漢, Wuhan)
Harbin	哈爾濱	Haerbin
Hsiamen or Amoy	廈門	Xiamen
Huangmei (Huangmei County)	黃梅 (黃梅縣)	Huangmei
Kinhwa	金華	Jinhua
Kiukiang	九江	Jiujiang
K'unming	昆明	Kunming
Nanchang	南昌	Nanchang
Nanking	南京	Nanjing
Ningpo	寧波	Ningbo
Peking	北京	Beijing
Sangyüan	桑園	Sangyuan
Shanghai	上海	Shanghai
Shenyang	瀋陽	Shenyang
Sian	西安	Xi'an
Soochow	蘇州	Suzhou
Talien	大連	Dalian
T'angshan	唐山	Tangshan

Tehchow	德州	Dezhou
Tientsin	天津	Tianjin
Tsinan	濟南	Jinan
Weihai	威海	Weihai
Wuhu	蕪湖	Wuhu
Yenan	延安	Yan'an
Yühang	餘杭	Yuhang

PROVINCES <LISTED ALPHABETICALLY>

Postal Romanization Pre-1949	Chinese	Modern Pinyin Post-1958
Anhwei	安徽	Anhui
Chekiang	浙江	Zhejiang
Fukien or Hokkien	福建	Fujian
Heilungkiang	黑龍江	Heilongjiang
Honan	河南	Henan
Hunan	湖南	Hunan
Hupeh	湖北	Hubei
Kansu	甘肅	Gansu
Kiangsi	江西	Jiangxi
Kiangsu	江蘇	Jiangsu
Kirin	吉林	Jilin
Kwangtung or Canton	廣東	Guangdong
Liaoning	遼寧	Liaoning
Shantung	山東	Shandong
Sinkiang	新疆	Xinjiang
Szechwan	四川	Sichuan
Tibet	西藏	Xizang
Tsinghai	青海	Qinghai
Yunnan	雲南	Yunnan

SPRING FLOWER: TORN BETWEEN SHIFTING WORLDS

STREETS AND LOCATIONS <BY CITY>

Pre-1949 Style	Chinese	Modern Pinyin
Harbin: 1954–1955		
Street	街	Jie
Chung-Yang Street	中央街	Zhong-Yang Jie or Center Street
Shanghai: 1955–1965		
Road	路	Lu
Chao-Chia-Pang Road	肇嘉浜路	Zhao-Jia-Bang Lu
Fen-Yang Road	汾陽路	Fen-Yang Lu
Fu-Hsing Road	復興路	Fu-Xing Lu
Heng-Shan Road	衡山路	Heng-Shan Lu
Huai-Hai Road	淮海路	Huai-Hai Lu
Huai-Hai Middle Road	淮海中路	Huai-Hai Zhong Lu
Lin-Sen Road	林森路	Lin-Sen Lu
T'ao-Chiang Road	桃江路	Tao-Jiang Lu
Tung-Ping Road	東平路	Dong-Ping Lu
Yüeh-Yang Road	岳陽路	Yue-Yang Lu

Hope Hotel	好望角賓館	Hao-Wang-Jie
Hsü-Chia-Hui District	徐家匯	Xu-Jia-Hui
Hung-Ch'iao Airport	虹橋機場	Hong-Qiao Ji-Chang
Shanghai Train Station	上海火車站	Shanghai Huo-Che Zhan

JEAN TREN-HWA PERKINS

Hangchow: 1952–1955 and 1965–1980

Chieh-Fang or Liberation Street	解放街	Jie-Fang Jie
Hsiao-Nü Road	孝女路	Xiao-Nü Lu
Hsüeh-Shih Road	學士路	Xue-Shi Lu
Kung-Jen or Workers Road	工人路	Gong-Ren Lu
Lake Shore Road	湖濱路	Hu-Bin Lu
Sun-Yat-Sen Road	孫中山路	Sun-Zhong-Shan Lu

———∽∽———

Hangchow Train Station	杭州火車站	Hangzhou Huo-Che Zhan
Municipal Police Department	公安局	Gong-An-Jü
Shan-Hu-Sha Village	珊瑚沙村	Shan-Hu-Sha
Shih-Ch'ing-Fang	世青坊	Shi-Qing-Fang
T'ien-Ch'iao-Yüan	天橋院	Tian-Qiao-Yuan
Yenan New Village	延安新村	Yan'an New Village

RIVERS, LAKES, MOUNTAINS, AND OTHER LANDMARKS
<BY CITY>

Nanking: 1950–1952

Hsiuan-Wu Lake	玄武湖
Chung-Shan Cemetery	中山陵

Harbin: 1954–1955

St. Nicholas Orthodox Cathedral 聖尼古拉教堂

Shanghai: 1955–1965

Huang-P'u River	黃浦江
The Bund	外灘

Soochow Creek	蘇州河
Wusung River	吳淞江
K'un-Shan	崑山

Hangchow: 1952–1955 and 1965–1980
Ch'ien-T'ang River	錢塘江
Grand Canal	大運河
West Lake	西湖
Liu-Ho Pagoda	六和塔
Hangchow Bay	杭州湾
Su-T'i	蘇踢
Pai-T'i	白踢

Other Cities

Peking
T'ien-An-Men Square	天安門廣場
The Temple of Heaven	天壇
Forbidden City	紫禁城

Tientsin
| Hai River | 海河 |

Soochow
| T'ai Lake | 太湖 |

Ch'engtu
Huang-Lung	黃龍
Chiu-Chai-Kou	九寨溝
Mount Le	樂山
Mount E-Mei	峨眉山
Chin-Sha River	金沙江
Min River	岷江
Tsinghai-Tibet Plateau	青藏高原

Yunnan
    Li-Kiang   麗江
    Shangri-La   香格里拉
Kiukiang
    Ku-Ling Mountain   牯嶺
    Mount Lu   廬山
Canton
    Sham-Chun River   深圳河

SCHOOLS AND HOSPITALS <BY CITY>
Nanking: 1950–1952
Chung-Shan Medical College (中山醫學院)
  – A part of the Fourth Sun-Yat-Sen University in Nanking (南京第四中山大學)
East China Military Medical College (華東軍醫學院)
  – Later renamed the Fourth Military Medical University (第四軍醫大學)
Nanking Gin-Ling Women's College (南京金陵女子大學), also called Gin-Ling Women's College or Gin-Ling College (金陵大學)
  – A sister campus of Smith College in Hampton, Mass. Pinyin: Jin-ling (金陵)
Nanking Teacher's College (南京師範學院)
  – Later called Nanking Normal University (南京師範大學)
Nanking University Medical School (南京大學醫學院)

Nanking Agricultural College (南京農學院)
Nanking University School of Agriculture (南京大學農學院)
National Gin-Ling University (公立或國立金陵大學)
Private University of Nanking or Gin-Ling Men's College (金陵男子大學)

SPRING FLOWER: TORN BETWEEN SHIFTING WORLDS

Harbin: 1954-1955
　　Harbin Medical University (哈醫大, 哈爾濱醫科大學)
　　Harbin Medical University Hospital (哈醫大附屬醫院)

Shanghai: 1955-1965
　　Fudan University (復旦大學)
　　Shanghai Eye and ENT Infirmary (上海五官科醫院)
　　Shanghai Jiao-Tong University (上海交通大學)
　　Shanghai Municipal Hospital (上海市醫院)

Hangchow: 1952-1955 and 1965-1980
　　Chekiang College of Agricultural Sciences (浙江農業科學院)
　　Chekiang Medical College (浙江醫學院)
　　　– Today's Chekiang Medical University (浙江醫科大學)
　　Chekiang Provincial Hospital (浙江省醫院)
　　Chinese Rice Research Institute (中國水稻研究所)
　　Hangchow Municipal Hospital (杭州市醫院)
　　National Chekiang University Medical School
　　　(國立浙江大學醫學院)
　　Research Institute of Agriculture in Hangchow (杭州農科所)

Other Cities
　　Kiukiang Water of Life Hospital (九江生命活水醫院)
　　Peking Union Medical College (北京協和醫学院)
　　Peking Union Medical College Hospital (北京協和醫院)
　　Rulison Girls' High in Kiukiang (九江儒励女子中學)
　　Talien Medical College (大連醫學院)
　　　– Today's Talien Medical University (大連醫科大學)
　　Tientsin Medical College (天津醫學院)
　　West China Hospital in Ch'engtu
　　　(成都華西協和醫院–四川大學)
　　West China School of Pharmacy, Szechwan University

JEAN TREN-HWA PERKINS

(華西藥學院-四川大學)
William Nast Academy in Kiukiang (九江同文中學)
Wuhu General Hospital (蕪湖總醫院)

NEWSPAPERS, BOOKS, AND MOVIES
Newspapers

	Chinese
Reference News (Ts'an-K'ao-Hsiao-Hsi)	參考消息 (Pinyin:*Can-Kao-Xiao-Xi*) The official international newspaper
People's Daily (Jen-Min-Jih-Pao)	人民日報 (Pinyin: *Ren-Min-Ri-Bao*) The official national newspaper

Books

The Dream of Red Mansions or *Dream of the Red Chamber*	紅樓夢
Journey to the West	西遊記
Poems of Pai Chü-I	白居易诗
Precious Red Book or *The Little Red Book*	紅寶書
Quotations from Chairman Mao	毛主席語錄
Romance of the Three Kingdoms	三國演義
Spring and Autumn Annals	春秋
Sun Tzu's The Art of War	孫子兵法
Three Hundred Tang Poems	唐诗三百首

Movies

Myriad of Lights or *Lights of Ten Thousand Homes*	萬家燈火

SPRING FLOWER: TORN BETWEEN SHIFTING WORLDS

Proof of Man 人證
The White-Haired Girl 白毛女

NAMES NOT IN GLOSSARY <LAST NAME–FIRST NAME>

Pre-1949 Style	Chinese	Modern Pinyin
Chang Chung-Ch'iao	張春橋	Zhang Chun-Qiao
Chiang Ch'ing	江青	Jiang Qing
Chiang Kai-Shek	蔣介石	Jiang Jie-Shi
Chou En-Lai	周恩來	Zhou En-Lai
Chu Teh	朱德	Zhu De
Hua Kuo-Feng	華國鋒	Hua Guo-Feng
Kang Sheng	康生	Kang Sheng
Lin Piao	林彪	Lin Biao
Liu Shao-Ch'i	劉少奇	Liu Shao-Qi
Mao Tse-Tung	毛澤東	Mao Ze-Dong
Soong Chi'ing-Ling	宋慶齡	Song Qing-Ling
Soong Mei-Ling	宋美齡	Song Mei-Ling
Sun Yat-Sen	孫中山	Sun Zhong-Shan
Teng Hsiao-Ping	鄧小平	Deng Xiao-Ping
Wang Hung-Wen	王洪文	Wang Hong-Wen
Wu I-Fang	吳貽芳	Wu Yi-Fang
Wu Lien-Teh	伍连德	Wu Lian-De
Yao Wen-Yüan	姚文元	Yao Wen-Yuan

JEAN TREN-HWA PERKINS

KEY MOVEMENTS AND RELATED TERMS
<LISTED CHRONOLOGICALLY>

1951–1952
    Three-Anti and Five-Anti Campaigns (Chinese: 三反-五反運動)

    Ideological Remolding
        or *Thought Reform Movement*   思想改造運動
    Collectivism   集體主義-集體化
    People's Communes   人民公社

1956–1957
    Hundred Flowers Campaign (Chinese: 百花齊放)
    Hundred Schools of Thought (Chinese: 百家争鸣)

1958–1960
    Great Leap Forward (Chinese: 大躍進)
    Three Red Banners 三面紅旗
    (1) Long Live the Great Leap Forward 大躍進萬歲
    (2) Long Live the *People's Communes* 人民公社萬歲
    (3) Long Live *General Line* 總路線萬歲
    Three-Year Natural Disasters 三年自然災害
    Three-Year Great Famine 三年大饑荒

1966–1976
    Great Proletariat Cultural Revolution 無產階級文化大革命
        or Great Cultural Revolution 文化大革命
        or Cultural Revolution 文革
    Red Guards 紅衛兵

SPRING FLOWER: TORN BETWEEN SHIFTING WORLDS

Related Terms from the Revolution	Chinese
Four Olds	四旧
Old Society	旧社會
Capitalist Values and Ideology	資本主義思想
Five Black Categories	黑五類
Five Red Categories	紅五類
Pillaging–Burning–Looting	打砸搶
Stinking Number Nine	臭老九
Extreme Rightist	極右派
Anti-Revolutionist	反革命分子
Cowsheds	牛棚
Neighborhood Management Center	居民區管理中心
Workers' Declaration Team or WDT	工宣隊 (Pinyin: Gong-Xuan-Dui)
Revolution's Bright and Shining Broadway	革命的光明大道
I-K'u-Szu-T'ien	憶苦思甜
Rustication–Reeducation for hospital personnel:	巡回醫疗-上山下鄉
Young people:	知青 (Chih-Ch'ing)
Workers:	拉鍊 (La-Lien)
Workers-Farmers-Soldiers College	工農兵大學
Proletariat Class	無產階級
Barefoot Doctors	赤腳醫生
The Gang of Four	四人幫

OTHERS

Chinese Measuring Units
Mǔ (畝): Chinese acre unit of land measurement:
   1.0 *Mǔ* = 1/6 of an American acre (~800 square yards)
Jin (斤): Chinese *pound* unit for weight:
   1.0 *Jin* = ~1.1 American pound
Mǔ-Chan (畝產): Chinese production unit: *Jin* per *Mǔ*
RMB (人民幣): From Pinyin, *Ren-Min-Bi*. Chinese dollar unit or *Yüan* (元)

Hospital Titles
Hospital Superintendent (院長)
Chief or Chief Attending Physician (主任醫生)
Full Attending Physician (正主治醫生)
Associate Attending Physician (副主治醫生)
Resident (住院醫生)
Intern (實習醫生)

Miscellaneous
Ch'ing Dynasty, Ch'ing Court, or Manchu Dynasty: 1644–1911 (清朝)
Southern Sung Dynasty: 1127–1279 (南宋)
Chinese idiom (成语)
The Eight-Nation Alliance (八國聯軍)
Emperor Ch'in (秦始皇)

APPENDIX TWO: GLOSSARY OF NAMES

College Years: 1950–1955

Freshman Year at Nanking Gin-Ling Women's College (南京金陵女子大學): 1950–1951

The six kids from Rulison Girls High to attend Gin-Ling in 1950: Mollie, Tsai, Yen, Chen, Phoebe, and me

My Roommates at Gin-Ling:
- Yen (尹) – from Rulison High
- Chen (陈) – from Rulison High

New Friend(s): Shou (寿) – from Shanghai

Teacher: President and Biology Professor Dr. Wu Yi-Fang (吳貽芳校长)

Nanking University of Medical School (南京大學醫學院): 1951–1952

Friends and Roommates:
- Chen (陈) – from Rulison High, who died young
- Shou (寿) – from Shanghai
- Hu (瑚) – Shou's high school classmate from Shanghai

Chekiang Medical College (浙江醫學院): 1952–1955

Friends and Roommates:
- Shou (寿) – from Shanghai
- Hu (瑚) – Shou's high school classmate from Shanghai
- Tung (腾)
- Bao (包) – a friend during the Kinhwa (金華) Summer

JEAN TREN-HWA PERKINS

Internship
Chair of the Ophthalmology Department:
> Professor Wu (吴)

Anatomy Professor at the College:
> Assistant Professor Ma (馬)

Harbin Medical University (哈醫大) Hospital (哈醫大附屬醫院): 1954-1955

Chief Attending Surgeon:	Dr. Zhou (周)
A Russian Cataract Specialist:	Dr. Demyanov

In Shanghai: 1955-1965
Characters of Shanghai Eye and ENT Infirmary (上海五官科醫院):

Friends and Colleagues:
> Shou (寿): Briefly left for Canton
> Her husband: Liu
> Sen Gui 森贵 (もりたか) or later known as Taka Mori
> Lian (莲): Left in 1960 for Szechwan
> Peng (蓬)

Other Key Characters of Shanghai Eye and ENT Infirmary:
> Chief Attending Ophthalmologists: Professor and Dr. Qian (钱)
> Associate Chief: Dr. Yan (严)
> The Administrator: Zheng *Shu-Chi* (郑)
> Daycare Center at the Infirmary: Aunt Yang (楊) or Yang *A-I* (楊阿姨)

SPRING FLOWER: TORN BETWEEN SHIFTING WORLDS

Two Key Neighbors on Tung-Ping Road (東平路):
- Upstairs, next door: Ms. Cheng, a retired high school teacher: Referred to as Cheng A-I (程阿姨, meaning Aunt Cheng) or Cheng Lao-Shih (程老師, meaning Teacher Cheng)
- Downstairs: Grandma Liu (劉奶奶, Liu Nai-Nai)

Two Key Physicians for Gina's Cerebral Palsy:
- The Primary Care Pediatrician: Dr. Ye (叶)
- Specialist: Dr. Sun (孫)

The Hsiung (熊) Family:
- Father: Russell, Headmaster of William Nast Academy
- Mother: Eve, teacher at Rulison Girls High
- Six Children: Bart, Ruth, Grace, Mary, Paul, and Simon
  (Bart's wife – Jane: A famous concerto pianist)

My Children:
- Gina
- Eddy

Hangchow: 1965–1980

Hangchow Municipal Hospital (杭州市醫院):
- Chief: Dr. Fan (樊)
- Ophthalmologist: Jade (Dr. Wang)
- Nurse: Gong Su-Yun (鞏素云) or Sue – later the Head of Nursing
- Her husband – Train Conductor Hsie (谢)
- My nurse: Hsiao Hu (小胡)

New Residents: Dr. He (河) and Dr. Chen (陈)
Pediatric Ward: Dr. Lin (林)
Internist: Dr. Lee (黎)
Nurse: Ms. Feng (冯)
Hospital's Superintendent Post-1976: Dr. Wen (文)
Ophthalmology Division Shu-Chi: Li Shu-Chi (李)
The Pediatrician from a Provincial Hospital: Dr. Gu (顾)

Hangchow Experimental Elemental School (杭州試驗小學)
Principal Teng (鄧)
Chang Lao-Shih (張老師) [Our neighbor at the compound on Sun-Yat-Sen Road]
Wu Lao-Shih (吳老師)

Public High School No. 8 (第八中學)
Principal Guan (關)
Vice Principal Wang (王)
Yuan Lao-Shih (袁老師)
Ma Lao-Shih (馬老師)
Liu Lao-Shih (劉老師)

At Paul's Chekiang College of Agricultural Sciences (浙江農業科學院): 1951-1960
Professor Pan (潘) - Paul's academic mentor

Other Central Characters: 1965-1980
Peng Shu-Chi (彭書記) and Governor Peng (彭省長)
Mr. Wu (吳) or Hsiao Wu (小吳)
The jeep driver in 1980: Shan (善)
Sargent Liu (劉) at Hangchow Municipal Police Department

SPRING FLOWER: TORN BETWEEN SHIFTING WORLDS

From Japan and America
Japan
  Ms. Tiyo Nishiyama (西山ていよ)
  Masako Murakami (村上正子)
From America
  MGH, Boston, Mass: Dr. Arthur Grove
  Maine: Dr. Loring Pratt
  United Methodist Church: Dr. Edwin Fisher

JEAN TREN-HWA PERKINS

NAMES OF THOSE ALREADY IN BOOK ONE

My Nuclear American Family

Mother: Georgina MacDonald Phillip Perkins (裴家纪: Pei Jia-Ji)
Father: Dr. Edward Carter Perkins (裴敬思: Pei Jing-Si)
Me: Jean Tren-Hwa Perkins (胡春花: Hu Tren-Hwa)
Hannah (吴): One of the girls whom Mother and Day-Day supported before I was born. She was a nurse at Water of Life Hospital (WLH) before moving to Hong Kong and was my sole contact to the outside world.

My Extended American Family

Maternal Grandma: Jean Sword Phillip
Maternal Grandpa: William Phillip
Uncle Henry Perkins, my father's older brother:
    Professor of Physics at Trinity College
His wife: Aunt Olga
Their children: Henry Jr. (Harry) and Evelyn
    Children of Evelyn and Amyas Ames:
    Oakes, Edward (Ned), Olivia, and Joans
Aunt: Ms. Deanetta "Dee" Ploeg (浦大: Po-Da): a nurse at WLH
Aunt: Ms. Elizabeth "Bessie" Ploeg (浦二: Po-Er): a nurse at WLH
Their Daughter: Chum, my de facto sister

SPRING FLOWER: TORN BETWEEN SHIFTING WORLDS

My Biological Family: The Hu (胡) Family and Known Siblings

Mother: Mm-Ma
Father: Mr. Hu
Brother-1: Kuo-Hsiang (阔祥): The MIA pilot 14 years my senior
Brother-2: Yan-Feng (延丰): A cook at WLH   8 years my senior

Chinese Staff at Our House

Amahs: Wang-Ma (王妈, and later Wang-Sao <王嫂>) for Chum
           Chang-Ma (常妈) for me
           Lo-Ma (羅妈) for my grandmother
Cook: Chef Tian (田) and his daughter "Sarah"
Doorman–Gardener: Grandpa Shui (水爷爷)
Butler–Laundry Man: Uncle Paddle (大板叔叔)

Yonkers, New York, 1942–1945

Yonkers Public School No. 16
    Teachers: Mrs. Hughes and Ms. Ryan
    Friend-Classmate: Jill, Betty, and Marie
Nathaniel Hawthorne Junior High in South Yonkers
    Teacher: Mrs. Eaton
    Friend-Classmate: Doris C.
Lake George–Silver Bay: Ju-Ju

India, 1945–1946

Friends/Classmates: Phyllis and Joe – from Woodstock School
                          Nancy and Patrick – Nadia

JEAN TREN-HWA PERKINS

Rulison Girls High School in Kiukiang, 1946–1950
Teacher/Principal:　　　　　　Ms. Wu (Grace Wu – 吴懋诚)
Home Room Teacher/Advisor: Miss You (尤)
Friend/Classmate:　　　　　　Mollie

Photo Credits

Title Page (Left)	1972	Alamy* — The Color Archives
Title Page (Right)	1980	Alamy — INTERFOTO / History
Page 29	Feb 1972	Alamy — CSU Archives / Everett Collection
Page 112		Alamy — Alain Le Garsmeur China Archive
Page 165	August 1978	Wikipedia Commons — Museum of Yugoslavia**
Page 175	1980	Alamy — Alain Le Garsmeur China Archive
Page 204	Oct 1984	Wikipedia Commons - Luis Bartolomé Marcos***
Page 212		Alamy — DPA

* License rights purchased from Alamy Stock Images.
** https://commons.wikimedia.org/wiki/File:Poseta_Hua_Kuo_Fenga_Jugoslaviji.jpg
*** https://commons.wikimedia.org/wiki/File:Hangzhou_1978_01.jpg

Acknowledgments

FIRST AND FOREMOST, I thank my cousins Olivia, Joanie, and Ned for their unwavering support throughout this entire process of compiling and editing my mother's memoir, including the initial efforts to set up a website honoring my grandparents, Dr. and Mrs. Edward Carter Perkins (https://www.yangtzeriverbythehudsonbay.site/home-page.html). And, Olivia, thank you in particular for painting the image of people standing on the sidelines cheering as I am coming around the corner on mile 13 of an endless marathon. That image provided me the inspiration I needed these past fifteen months.

I am also indebted to Olivia for introducing me to Arnie Kotler, who generously agreed to work with me on this book and became my editor, consultant, and literary agent. I am grateful for his skillful and knowledgeable editing, his timely encouragement, and his invaluable advice. I've learned so much from him about writing and expressing things in a plain, simple, easy-to-understand manner. Aside from his in-depth linguistic insights, I am amazed by his incredible knowledge of history and geography. And Arnie, thank you for your gentle reminder that this book project was no longer mine or my mother's alone, but one bearing so many people's fingerprints and their efforts and good hearts.

In terms of editing, Doti Browning, mother of Daral and Kip Smalligan, my good friends at Calvin College, edited the book's early chapters. My academic mentor at Milton Academy in Massachusetts, Barclay Feather, had helped my mother with her writing. My mother submitted some chapters as writing assignments for a course she was taking at the Institute of

SPRING FLOWER: TORN BETWEEN SHIFTING WORLDS

Children's Literature (ICL, today's Institute for Writers, in Madison, Connecticut). The names of the ICL instructors I was able to gather with whom she corresponded are Tom Bethancourt, Mimi Bourne, and Pat Murray. Although these collective editing efforts took place more than thirty years ago, I remain appreciative, as I am confident my mother would be if she were still in our lives. My apologies to anyone I've missed.

I extend my heartfelt appreciation to Mark Woodworth for his meticulous copyediting and proofreading. And Mark, during perhaps one of the lowest periods for me in this writing process, your email and the stories you shared brought me to tears and inspired me to march on.

Although much of the Japanese was removed by my editors, I should note that the Japanese in the book was generously edited by Professors しゅう Chou andのり Tanaka. Your passion for my mother's journey was infectious. I am indebted to F. Wei for taking on the daunting task of translating volume one into Chinese, and you did it with such awesome precision and literary skill–thank you. I am also extremely grateful to Dr. C. L. Xu for proofreading the translated book 1 overnight.

Finally, through perhaps angelic intervention, Arnie and I met Graham Earnshaw, founder and publisher of Earnshaw Books. I am eternally grateful for his in-depth experience in publishing as well as his command of the Chinese language, culture, and history. And Graham, thank you for standing your ground with your utmost professionalism when I seemed to crack. But you were wrong about one thing: While playing "midwife" is an important role, you were much more than that on my journey! I am also grateful to Jason Wong for patiently designing all three volumes—the covers and interior layout, including the photos and figures. And thank you, Tash Galasyuk, for your valuable help to date and for working with me to promote my mother's memoir from here on.

I am indebted to Lisa Carta and her amazing ability to track down many valuable, descriptive photos online, and for providing advice on photo layouts and meticulous work on improving the qualities of these photos.

I gratefully acknowledge Helen Zia, the author of *Last Boat Out of Shanghai*, and Margaret Sun, the author of *Betwixt and Between*, for their generous endorsements. These two women's stories and journeys are in the same spirit and equally inspiring and amazing as my mother's. To Eddie Wong, editor of the *East Wind* ezine, I offer my sincere apologies for failing to mention your name at the end of Book 1. Thank you for introducing Helen Zia to us, and, even more gratefully, for unconditionally stepping in and helping us, strangers on the same road.

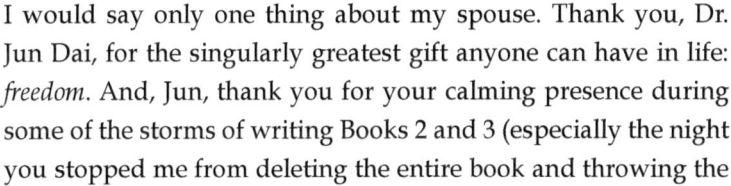

I would say only one thing about my spouse. Thank you, Dr. Jun Dai, for the singularly greatest gift anyone can have in life: *freedom*. And, Jun, thank you for your calming presence during some of the storms of writing Books 2 and 3 (especially the night you stopped me from deleting the entire book and throwing the laptop across the frozen street).

I am grateful to Trudy and Mark Van Solkema, and to Ginny Sinclair, the Ploegs' descendants, for finding and reconnecting me with the family. Thank you for your unbound enthusiasm about my mother's story and for giving me voice memoirs from Aunt Dee and Aunt Bessie, recorded in 1978.

I could not have completed this book without the Rev. Dr. Margaret McCray of Westminster Counseling Center at the Presbyterian Church in Minneapolis. "Putting one foot ahead of another and staying in the moment" became my mantra, as I got up every morning during this long and arduous journey, which is not yet complete. There were times it was the only way I could survive the bitter winters of Madison, Wisconsin. And Margaret, thank you for saving my life, twice.

To Georgio, my barber of sixteen years, your brotherly and even fatherly presence has kept me focused and determined all these years, including while writing this memoir. On a spring day in 2018, after surviving a dangerous vocal cord spasm-induced suffocation, I got on Bus-2 and went to your Madison downtown shop to be spruced up. I had just had a cut from you two weeks earlier, but you were the only person I could think of seeing.

I offer a special shout-out to Dr. G. O'Doherty. I'm sorry there won't be a Book 4, with the title of *A Tale of the Mississippi* or *A Tale of Three Rivers* (meaning from the Mississippi to the Monongahela to the Charles). Thank you for preventing me from destroying myself in the late 1990s. You would be the only one who knew me well, from the time I uttered a few sentences describing my troubled early years as a struggling assistant professor in Minneapolis. You were the very first person who learned of my desire to leave chemistry (before I'd even begun the process) so I could complete my mother's memoir. And you believed in me!

Thank you, Dr. M. Hii, for the copy of Djerassi's book and for your wonderful note, both of which have sat on my office desk throughout this writing journey. In your own words, I believe this has become the bravest thing I've ever done in life. And to you, Dr. P. Chiu, it was when we stood side by side on Stanley Beach in Hong Kong that I realized there's no shame in leaving chemistry, because sometimes a person can take a leap and live for a few months on a container ship sailing the seven seas. And Dr. T. Lu, thank you for your invaluable help in managing my website all these years.

Many other people have offered encouragement and enthusiasm for this book, all of which has been essential for me to persevere. Unfortunately, I won't be able to write a note of thanks to each of you here. If you happen to be reading this, you know who you are! And you might even find yourself or your stories here. I hope you'll understand why I withheld your names. I am incredibly grateful to each of you, from the bottom of my heart.

───∽∾∽───

Over the past seven years, I've sat in many places to compile and edit the three volumes of *Spring Flower*, my mother's memoir (before COVID-19 hit). Coffee shops, cafés, and bars littered along University Avenue and hotel lobbies in Madison were among my frequent stops. One place in particular was the Blue Moon, which I have known the longest in Madison. I drafted many chapters there, and for the past seventeen years, people at the Blue Moon have witnessed my transition from leading a research group of thirty students to sitting by myself in the corner—writing! When I was in transit, the Van Galder USA bus became my office on wheels, and the lobby bar at the O'Hare Hilton became my home away from home, so much so that people at that airport hotel bar came to know me. I could also be found around Coolidge Corner in Brookline, Massachusetts; on Charlee Street by Beacon Hill; Commonwealth Avenue; North Station; and Charlestown Navy Yard. I actually wrote the epilogue in Boston.

I fondly remember the places along Heng-Shan Road (衡山路) and Dong-Ping Road (东平路) in Shanghai, on South Ta-Ling Road in Jiujiang (塔陵南路, 九江), and in the Russo-Japanese town of Dalian (大連), as well as in the Chao-Yang (朝陽) and Hou-Hai (后海) Districts in Beijing, and on the entire Gu-Ling (廬山-牯嶺) mountaintop. While I did much planning and research in Singapore, I drafted many early chapters in Hong Kong, particularly around the Mid-Level Areas, and even at the Peaks where I'd frequently run to up from sea level during my extended stays there in the late 2010s. I worked on the very first word of

SPRING FLOWER: TORN BETWEEN SHIFTING WORLDS

Book 2 in the Central Area. One-third of Book 2 was drafted while I stayed in small towns along the entire Hokōsō Line, in coffee shops and cafés in Wako-Shi and Aomori, and in ever-so-beautiful Yokohama. Last but not least, I will not soon forget the Little White Building District (小白楼), Hai-He Riverside (海河边), the European District, and even the pigeon-invaded, dusty Fifth Northern Village in Tianjin, where I compiled and edited most of Book 1.

I've tried my best to portray the historical elements of the book accurately, relying mostly on Wikipedia and on its Chinese version (维基百科) as well as on the New World Encyclopedia and Encyclopedia Britannica. I also found an excellent website called *A Blog Out of the Wall* (局外人), which contains an insightful summary of the History of Methodist Missions in Kiukiang/Jiujiang (九江), and whose author has in-depth knowledge of the Water of Life Hospital. Some documentation comes from the Yale University Archives, while other information was drawn from the Perkins family's letters. I read and abstracted information from voice transcripts recorded by Deanetta and Elizabeth Ploeg in 1978. These valuable documents were kindly given to me by their nieces and nephews. I also consulted on many occasions with my cousin Ned and his wife, Jane Sokolow, who coauthored *Chronology of Dr. Edward C. Perkins* (unpublished).

Two other books have been useful as resources. The first is *Hyla Doc: Surgeon in China Through War and Revolution 1924–1949*, edited by Elsie H. Landstrom (Fort Bragg, California: QED Press, 1991). Dr. Hyla Watters was a close friend of my grandparents. My maternal grandmother, Georgina, was Dr. Watters's Sunday School teacher. My maternal grandfather, Dr. Edward Perkins, became a missionary because of the direct influence of Dr.

JEAN TREN-HWA PERKINS

Watters's father, the Rev. Philip M. Watters. The phrase "Water of Life" came out of their fellowship. Dr. Watters herself was a surgeon in Wuhu General Hospital (蕪湖總醫院) in the city of Wuhu (蕪湖), downriver from Kiukiang. She and my grandfather always helped each other in times of need.

The editor of the above memoir, Elsie Landstrom, also wrote a manuscript describing Wuhu General Hospital's history. My grandfather and numerous other physicians and nurses who were also missionaries are prominently featured in these writings. The second resource is *My China Years,* by Helen Foster Snow (New York: William Morrow and Company, 1984). Helen Foster was married to the American journalist Edgar P. Snow.

For all three volumes, most photos come from the Perkins or Hsiung family collections. Others are from Wikimedia Commons, Chineseposter.net, or purchased from Alamy. Please see the Photo Credits pages for detail.

Last, although I have been careful in arranging my time and allocating my space to work on this book project, I would like to thank my colleagues from the School of Pharmacy at the University of Wisconsin–Madison for their perennial support and encouragement. I would also like to acknowledge the Kremers Family Foundation and the Vilas Foundation of the University of Wisconsin–Madison. When readers follow this story in its entirety, they will surely agree that this writing project is very much within the spirit and distinction of these academic foundations.

Richard Perkins Hsung, PhD
Editor of *Spring Flower*,
my mother's memoir
Madison, Wisconsin
January 2022

About the Author

Dr. Jean Tren-Hwa Perkins (裴瓊華醫生) attended Nanking Gin-Ling Women's College (南京金陵女子大學), a sister campus of Smith College in Northampton, Massachusetts, and received her MD degree from Chekiang Medical College (浙江醫學院) in Hangchow. After an internship at Harbin Medical University Hospital (哈醫大附屬醫院) in 1955, she became a Resident at the Department of Ophthalmology in the Shanghai Eye and ENT Hospital (上海五官科醫院), which later was an affiliate of Fudan University (復旦大學). She rose through the ranks and was promoted to Attending Ophthalmologist in 1963. Dr. Perkins transferred to Hangchow Municipal Hospital (杭州市醫院) in 1965 and was initially the Acting Chief of the Ophthalmology Department. She remained there until she left for America, and shortly after, she was confirmed as Professor of Ophthalmology. During the late 1970s, she worked as a professional translator, and even translated for China's Communist Party Chairman and Premier Hua Kuo-Feng (華國鋒主席). Although she became widely known for her skills in surgery, as well as her patience in teaching, her passion for clinical research and genetic disorders, particularly in the area of glaucoma, began in the early 1960s. Her last professional stop was, fittingly, the Mass Eye and Ear Infirmary (MEEI), a Harvard Medical School affiliate and part of Massachusetts General Hospital in Boston. She held the title of Research Fellow in several esteemed laboratories and worked on YAG-laser treatment of glaucoma.

About the Editor

Richard Perkins Hsung attended Milton Academy, in Milton, Massachusetts, as did many of the Perkins children. He went to live with his adoptive mother, Kate Louise Ploeg, the youngest sister of Deanetta and Elizabeth Ploeg, while earning his BS in Chemistry and Mathematics from Calvin College in Grand Rapids, Michigan. He studied organic chemistry and obtained his PhD at the University of Chicago. After working as a research associate there and also at Columbia University, he became a faculty member at the University of Minnesota–Twin Cities before moving to the University of Wisconsin–Madison. Richard received a National Science Foundation Career Award and the Camille Dreyfus Teacher-Scholar Award. Before retiring, he was the Laura and Edward Kremers Professor of Natural Products Chemistry and the Vilas Distinguished Achievement Professor at the University of Wisconsin–Madison.

www.ingramcontent.com/pod-product-compliance
Lightning Source LLC
LaVergne TN
LVHW011942060526
838201LV00061B/4189